KEITH HENNING

Crushing The Technical Interview: Data Structures and Algorithms

The study guide for data structures and algorithms interviews (Python Edition)

Spore Press

To my son, Jay.

Contents

1   Introduction   1

  What to Expect   1

  Why I Wrote This Book   2

  Who This Book Is For   3

  Conventions in this Book   4

2   The Interview Process   7

  Overview   7

  Recruiter Phone Interview   8

  Coding Challenge   10

  Coding Project   14

  On-Site Interviews   18

  Data Structures & Algorithms Interviews   22

  System Design Interviews   27

  The Process and Communication Interview   32

  Manager/Team Matching Interviews   35

  Now What Happens   37

3   Big-O Notation   39

  Simplifying Big-O Notation   39

  Constant Time   40

  Logarithmic Time   41

  Linear Time   43

  Super-Linear Time   44

  Polynomial Time   47

  Exponential Time   50

  Factorial Time: Final Boss Fight!   52

4   Software Theory   55

Introduction 55

Single Responsibility Principle (SRP) 56

Open-Closed Principle (OCP) 56

Liskov Substitution Principle (LSP) 57

Interface Segregation Principle (ISP) 59

Dependency Inversion Principle (DIP) 61

Don't Repeat Yourself (DRY) 63

KISS Principle 65

OOP Design Patterns 67

5   Data Structures 74

What Is A Data Structure? 74

Arrays 75

Lists 77

Stacks 79

Queues 84

Linked Lists 90

Graphs 96

Trees 109

Heaps 112

Hash Maps 129

6   Algorithms 138

Bubble Sort 138

Merge Sort 140

Quick Sort 143

Insertion Sort 146

Tree Traversals 148

Breadth First Search (BFS) 154

Depth First Search (DFS) 160

A* Algorithm 167

Dijkstra's Algorithm 183

Two Pointers 193

Sliding Window 200

Backtracking (N-Queens Problem) 206

Trie Data Structure 220

Topological Sort 227

Bucket Sort 233

Quickselect 239

Prefix Sum 249

Monotonic Stack 253

Union Find 258

Prim's Algorithm (Minimum Spanning Trees) 265

Kruskal's Algorithm 270

Binary Manipulation 278

Floyd's Algorithm 287

Median-of-Medians Algorithm 292

Recursion with Memoization 297

Huffman Coding Algorithm 303

Red-Black Tree Algorithm 309

Ford-Fulkerson Algorithm (Edmonds-Karp) 316

Array Mutation 322

7   Practice Coding Problems 326

1. Arrays & Hashing: Character Pattern Matching 326

2. Arrays & Hashing: Product Price Pairing 327

3. Arrays & Hashing: Vocabulary Pattern Clusters 328

4. Heap/Priority Queue: Trending Hashtag Analysis 329

5. Arrays & Hashing: Supply Network Resilience Calculator 330

6. Sliding Window: Optimal Document Segment 331

7. Sliding Window: Extrema Product 332

8. Arrays & Hashing: Longest Palindromic Substring 333

9. Arrays & Hashing: Two Sum 334

10. Trees: Level Order Traversal 334

11. Dynamic Programming: Fibonacci with Memoization 335

12. Graphs: Number of Islands 336

13. Arrays & Hashing: First Non-Repeating Character 337

14. Linked List: Reverse a Linked List 338

15. Heap/Priority Queue: Balanced Network Traffic 338

16. Graphs: Dependency Resolver   339

17. Intelligent Cache System   339

18. Trees: Text Editor Line Tracker   340

19. Sliding Window: Message Rate Limiter   341

21: Arrays & Hashing: Circular Array Rotation Sequence   342

22. Greedy Algorithm: Optimized Task Scheduler   344

23. Greedy Algorithm: Interval Coverage Optimization   345

24. Graphs: Dynamic Maze Flood Fill   345

25. Heap/Priority Queue: Adaptive Resource Scheduler   347

26. Graphs: Distributed Cache Consistency   348

27. Arrays & Hashing: Maximum Subarray With Target Sum   349

28. Sliding Window: K-Nearest Neighbors   349

29. Backtracking: Matrix Circuit   350

30. Dynamic Programming: Artwork Gallery Heist   351

31. Sliding Window: Range Duplicate Finder   352

32. Stack: Temperature Forecast Analysis   353

33. Two Pointers: Scenic Skyline Viewpoints   354

34. Two Pointers: Mountain Valley Rainwater Collection   355

35. Greedy Algorithms: Maximum Property Value Appreciation   356

36. Arrays & Hashing: Frequency Threshold Detection   357

37. Arrays & Hashing: X-Sudoku Validator   358

38. Greedy Algorithms: Vehicle Convoy Formation   359

39. Stack: Maximum Productivity Zone   360

40. Matrix Operations: Layered Security Clearance Search   362

41. Binary Search: Document Processing Throughput   363

42. Binary Search: Encrypted Circular Buffer Search   364

43. Matrix Operations: Parallel Matrix Diagonal Sum   365

44. Binary Search: Version-Based Configuration Store   366

45. Binary Search: Minimum Processing Power   368

46. Trees: Clone Bi1nary Tree with Connection Pointers   369

47. Linked List: Rotate Linked List Around Pivot   370

48. Linked List: Interleave K Linked Lists   370

49. Trees: Path Matching Binary Tree   371

50. Trees: Symmetric Tree Transformation   372

51. Stack: Expression Tree Execution   373

52. Stack: Balanced Bracket Sequence Generator   374

53. Trees: Balanced Tree Reconstruction   375

54. Trees: Optimal Node Removal for Minimum Height   377

55. Tries: Context-Sensitive Search Suggestion System   378

56. Tries: Fuzzy Word Finder   379

57. Binary Search: Minimum Allocation Threshold for Equal Array Groups   380

58. Binary Search: Kth Ancestral Element in Sorted Arrays   381

59. Graphs: Key Collection Sequence   382

60. Arrays & Hashing: Group Anagrams By Frequency   384

61. Dynamic Programming: Maximum Product Path   384

62. Graphs: Island Count with Restrictions   385

63. Binary Search: Find Kth Element in Two Sorted Arrays   386

64. Stack: Evaluate Reverse Polish Notation with Custom Operations   386

65. Matrix Operations: Optimal Kennel Assignment   387

66. Matrix Operations: Wedding Seating Arrangement   388

67. Linked List: Boat Fleet Chain Inspection   389

68. Linked List: Baseball Lineup Rotation   389

69. Two Pointers: Coffee Bean Blend Matcher   390

70. Sliding Window: Holiday Card Joy Maximizer   391

71. Stack: Fashion Display Stack Optimizer   391

72. Heap/Priority Queue: Restaurant Priority Seating System   392

73. Backtracking: Optimal Race Day Strategy   394

74. Graphs: Detective Case Assignment Network   395

75. Dynamic Programming: Seasonal Orange Grove Harvest   396

8   Problem Solutions   398

1. Character Pattern Matching   398

2. Product Price Pairing   399

3. Vocabulary Pattern Clusters   399

4. Trending Hashtag Analysis   400

5. Supply Network Resilience Calculator   400

6. Optimal Document Segment   401

7. Sliding Window Extrema Product   403

8. Longest Palindromic Substring   404

9. Two Sum   405

10. Level Order Traversal   406

11. Fibonacci with Memoization   407

12. Number of Islands   408

13. First Non-Repeating Character   410

14. Reverse a Linked List   410

15. Balanced Network Traffic   412

16. Dependency Resolver   413

17. Intelligent Cache System   414

18. Text Editor Line Tracker   416

19. Message Rate Limiter   421

20. Evidence Processing Queue   422

21: Circular Array Rotation Sequence   423

22. Optimized Task Scheduler   424

23. Interval Coverage Optimization   426

24. Dynamic Maze Flood Fill   427

25. Adaptive Resource Scheduler   428

26. Distributed Cache Consistency   429

27. Maximum Subarray With Target Sum   431

28. K-Nearest Neighbors in Sliding Window   432

29: Matrix Circuit   434

30. Artwork Gallery Heist   435

31. Range Duplicate Finder   436

32. Temperature Forecast Analysis   437

33. Scenic Skyline Viewpoints   437

34. Mountain Valley Rainwater Collection   438

35. Maximum Property Value Appreciation   439

36. Frequency Threshold Detection   439

37. X-Sudoku Validator   440

38. Vehicle Convoy Formation   441

39. Maximum Productivity Zone   442

40. Layered Security Clearance Search   443

41. Document Processing Throughput   443

42. Encrypted Circular Buffer Search   444

43. Parallel Matrix Diagonal Sum   445

44. Version-Based Configuration Store   446

45. Minimum Processing Power   447

46. Clone Binary Tree with Connection Pointers   448

47. Rotate Linked List Around Pivot   449

48. Interleave K Linked Lists   450

49. Path Matching Binary Tree   451

50. Symmetric Tree Transformation   452

51. Expression Tree Execution   454

52. Balanced Bracket Sequence Generator   455

53. Balanced Tree Reconstruction   456

54. Optimal Node Removal for Minimum Height   457

55. Context-Sensitive Search Suggestion System   459

56. Fuzzy Word Finder   461

57. Minimum Allocation Threshold for Equal Array Groups   463

58. Kth Ancestral Element in Sorted Arrays   464

59. Key Collection Sequence   465

60. Group Anagrams By Frequency   467

61. Maximum Product Path   468

62. Island Count with Restrictions   469

63. Find Kth Element in Two Sorted Arrays   470

64. Evaluate Reverse Polish Notation with Custom Operations   471

65. Optimal Kennel Assignment   472

66. Wedding Seating Arrangement   474

67. Boat Fleet Chain Inspection   477

68. Baseball Lineup Rotation   478

69. Coffee Bean Blend Matcher   479

70. Holiday Card Joy Maximizer 480

71. Fashion Display Stack Optimizer 481

72. Restaurant Priority Seating System 483

73. Optimal Race Day Strategy 485

74. Detective Case Assignment Network 487

75. Seasonal Orange Grove Harvest 488

9 Tips for Hiring Managers & Interviewers 491

Take-Home Coding Project Challenges 491

Why Top Tech Companies Don't Use Take-Home Tests 493

A Better Hiring Funnel 493

For Candidates 494

Final Thoughts 494

10 Resources 495

Top Leetcode Problems 495

Recommended Books 500

11 Appendix: Take Home Code Project 502

In-Memory Cache For Online Advertising Agency 502

About the Author 504

1

Introduction

What to Expect

I am passionate about developer advocacy and education. Helping developers thrive has always been a top priority at any company I have worked. Additionally, we have passed on hiring many great developers over the years by simply having poor screening processes. I can't reform the hiring model for thousands of companies, but I can do this.

I have taken a code-first approach to preparing for technical interviews in this book. In the following pages, I will go through four main areas: First, what the hiring process looks like today and how to succeed. Second, how to use Big-O notation to describe an algorithm's computational and space complexity. Next, you need to know the primary data structures and how they work. Lastly, you should concentrate on the primary algorithms and techniques and the steps to perform them well in your interviews. You will also find many sample questions to practice with the answers provided.

All of the code for this book is available at my website:
http://technical-interviews.com

Why I Wrote This Book

A bit about me so that you can be comfortable that the information and guidance I am providing in this book is worth following:

I have been in the software and technology industry for over 30 years. I started my career as a developer at Dell in the mid-1990s. Since then, I have worked chiefly leading technical teams with various titles such as Chief Operating Officer, Vice President of Technology, Director of Software Development, and Chief Architect. I have held these roles in Silicon Valley unicorn startups, mid-sized technology companies, and Fortune 500s, including Walmart, Dell, and Dollar General. IBM acquired a startup where I was the founding technologist and VP of R&D, and Cox Communications acquired a startup where I was the VP of Technology. I have consulted on projects as the lead architect for companies such as AT&T, Bank of America, and Caterpillar. I hold patents in personalizing online advertising and content based on accumulated buyer behavior online. I also write articles on the intersection of Intellectual Property law and innovation. I have a Masters in Computer Science from Georgia Institute of Technology, where I also help teach, and a Juris Doctor from the University of Arkansas. As of the writing of this book, I am Director of Enterprise Architecture for a Fortune 500 company. I hope to give you information you can use to get through an interview when I am on the other side of the table asking the questions.

The one thing I have always disliked about this industry is the non-standard nature of the technical interviews. If you are a UX/UI designer, you bring your portfolio. If you are a mechanical engineer, you bring your portfolio and license. If you are a landscape architect, you bring your portfolio and license. If you are a software developer, it is convoluted and different from company to company. We need a professional licensing structure, not just whatever certifications different companies are handing out.

Also, I hate having to do them (because the impostor syndrome is real). I find technical interviews stress-inducing, doubt-producing, and sometimes heart-wrenching processes where your best self seldom shines, and I will avoid them whenever possible. However, I have only done one technical interview without an offer because I always go prepared. As much as I dislike them, technical interviews are a necessary part of the process because they are the worst form of selecting developers, except for all others. No alternate process produces the desired results with the same accuracy: matching your skill-set with the current and future needs of the role and company interviewing you. This protects you as much as it does the company. Who wants to work in a role for which they are unqualified or unprepared? Certainly not me. The technical interview should set you up for success in your new job.

I also know this process from both sides of the table. Throughout my career, I have conducted many hundreds of technical interviews. I am one of the people who will be interviewing you. In this book, I have attempted to distill the minimum knowledge you need to crush any technical interview and get an offer.

Thank you for purchasing this book.
Sincerely,
Keith Henning

Who This Book Is For

This book is for anyone looking for a software developer role, whether you are just starting out and are looking for your first role or you are a senior trying to level up your career and need a quick refresher. If you think you are not good enough or talented enough, I am here to say you are wrong. Anyone, including you, can master the skills needed to succeed in a technical interview.

And here is a secret nobody else will tell you: Interviewers are looking for a reason to say yes to your application. Except for the largest tech companies, the interviewers don't want to interview dozens of people to fill one position. Your only role in the interview is to give them every reason to say yes. They want to hire you.

You've got this.

Conventions in this Book

This book is centered around coding patterns. The goal is to learn the code patterns and how to solve problems by applying those patterns to similar problems. I will not give step-by-step instructions on problem-solving generally; other books do that better than I ever could. However, if you are a critical thinker and can break down problems into logical and manageable chunks to identify the type of pattern(s) you are encountering and then apply the correct solution pattern to it, this is the book for you. Anyone can use this code pattern matching to problem facts to solve problems.

All code examples will be in the programming language edition you purchased.

I've omitted extensive error checking for brevity, but in production code, you'd want to add Input validation, Bounds checking, Empty array handling, etc. For each data structure and algorithm, I have included a list of the interview questions you can expect. Take some time to understand why the solution pattern would be a good choice for solving that type of problem.

I have added the **includes** and **imports** of libraries where they will better help you understand the code, but I have omitted them for standard libraries. All languages used for this book are Object-Oriented. Many others are popular options for different use cases. I chose these because they cover a more extensive scope of languages used. These are all imperative languages. I will not be covering functional languages such as Scala or Clojure in this book.

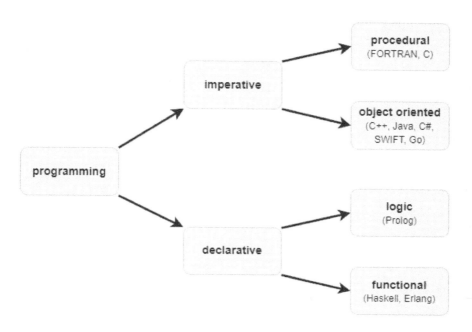

Back-end and front-end development are two very distinct beasts. I have worked as a back-end developer and a full-stack developer. Neither is superior, but they have technology preferences, different cultures, and subcultures. This book is aimed toward general-purpose back-end development.

In this book, you will see each concept or problem followed by Key Tips, which help you understand the problem, and/or Pro Tips, which will help set you apart from other candidates in an interview.

Each concept section may have any or all of the following parts:

- Core Concept
- Python Implementation
- Real-World Application
- Performance Characteristics
- Key Tips
- Pro Tips
- Common Interview Questions

- Typical Follow-up Questions

2

The Interview Process

Overview

Technical interviews are inherently challenging and often anxiety-inducing experiences for developers at all levels, including myself. The process typically begins with a recruiter screen, followed by remote technical interviews as a coding challenge. Depending on the company, it may include additional stages involving a take-home coding project and on-site interviews.

Hiring is also changing rapidly, with **online assessments** becoming a standard part of hiring before you talk to anyone. Some companies email you a link to take an online coding test the moment you apply for a position, and your application will not be looked at until you have successfully passed the assessment. Doing these quickly will put you ahead of others applying for the same role.

Most companies follow a familiar pattern. The recruiter screen introduces the role and company; technical remote/phone screens assess coding abilities; later stages might evaluate system design and cultural fit.

I would be worried if you didn't feel nervous about technical interviews. Everyone gets some amount of interview anxiety. What's important is recognizing that interview performance is a distinct skill from day-to-day engineering work. Like any skill, it improves with practice and preparation. Remember, luck = preparation + opportunity.

I will break down each interview phase and provide concrete strategies for success. Whether this is your first technical interview or you are returning after years of experience, understanding the process will help ease at least some of the anxiety, and you can focus on being prepared.

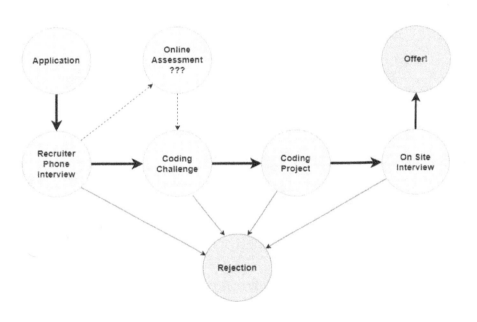

Recruiter Phone Interview

The recruiter phone interview is a critical first step in the technical hiring process.

Before diving into any recruiter call, proper preparation becomes your strongest ally. You should research the company's mission, examine its tech stack, review its GitHub contributions, review engineering blog posts, and understand its core values. Creating a detailed document with this information helps structure your preparation and demonstrates genuine interest in the role. It doesn't have to be fancy; it's just a list of information to help you remember what the company is about in your favorite note-taking tool. Your note-taking tool is also a place to track applications, phone calls, recruiter contact information, application status, and the requirements for each role.

Timing and presence during the call can make or break your impression. Through years of working with distributed teams, I've learned that while different cultures view time differently, interview punctuality is universal. Always join video calls five minutes early, ensuring your audio and video are crystal clear. This will also allow you to resolve any technical difficulties that may arise. Finding a quiet space with good lighting isn't just about professionalism—it's about creating an environment where you can focus entirely on the conversation at hand.

Questions during the interview should demonstrate both technical under-standing and genuine interest. When it comes to questions, this is where you can truly shine. Rather than asking basic queries about office culture, I've found success in demonstrating technical depth through thoughtfully crafted questions. Asking about their micro-services architecture approach or their strategy for balancing technical debt with feature delivery shows you're thinking at a deeper level. These questions often spark engaging technical discussions that help you stand out from other candidates.

The conversation should also explore the human aspects of engineering - you want work/life balance, don't you? Inquiring about team collaboration practices and learning opportunities reveals the company's commitment to developer growth. Understanding these elements helps you evaluate the fit between your career goals and the organization's values. A recruiter call isn't just an evaluation - it's an opportunity to discuss mutual fit.

Before wrapping up, always discuss the next steps so you can set your expectations.

Your recruiter call is your first opportunity to demonstrate your value to their engineering team, so try to approach it with a strategy that showcases both your technical skills and your enthusiasm for the opportunity ahead.

Success in recruiter calls comes from balancing technical knowledge with effective communication.

Through numerous interviews on both sides of the table, I've learned that you find the right fit for you by treating each interaction as a chance to learn and grow while staying true to your technical expertise and professional aspirations. By this, I mean don't fake what you don't know, don't exaggerate on your resume, and don't take credit for work you didn't do. You will be found out in the process. The key is finding that sweet spot between showcasing your technical skills and demonstrating your ability to communicate effectively with various stakeholders.

Coding Challenge

How to Crush Your Coding Challenge

You will move on to a coding challenge if your recruiter phone interview goes well.

Occasionally, this is also the point where you will be asked to log into a website and test your technical knowledge before moving forward. CodeSignal is one of these and offers a General Coding Framework (GCF) scoring system. GCF is a standardized coding exam companies use to evaluate candidates' coding skills. Similar to the SAT or ACT, these automated screeners are becoming more common. The company also offers tests for senior developers called the Industry Coding Framework and tests (i.e., Frameworks) covering Data Analytics, Front End, System Design, Machine Learning, and Quality Assurance.

The coding challenge is typically done in one-hour increments and conducted remotely on a platform like Zoom or Microsoft Teams. You will usually be paired with a developer in the company and asked a coding challenge(s) that you will do in a shared desktop or web-based IDE. It may be a large challenge or several smaller ones. For some companies, the initial problem is not what they are scoring but one of the follow-up questions that comes after you solve the problem. I give examples of these follow-up questions where appropriate. You may also be asked some general technical knowledge questions during the interview.

In this book, I will give you everything you need to know to crush your coding interview. Pure software companies have different requirements for their developers than small, mid-sized, and Fortune 500 companies that may focus on supply chain management or call center routing. There are plenty of online resources where people break down their interviews with FAANG companies - Facebook (Meta), Amazon, Apple, Netflix, and Google - and which problems they were asked to solve, and most other companies typically follow their lead. You are welcome to read these over, but in this book, I am distilling all the methodologies you will need and a handful of specialized algorithms you should memorize to do well. I know from experience that the questions asked at a company like Walmart and those requested at Amazon are nearly identical and focus on the same areas. Of course, there are always differences in technical cultures between companies; Google tends to include Dynamic Programming questions, and Meta tends never to ask Dynamic Programming questions.

What language should you use for your study and coding challenge? The one you are most comfortable with and experienced with. In short, unless you are interviewing for a company that exclusively uses Scala and Scala is also your daily driver language, use a different language for study and your code interviews.

Data Structures and Algorithms

I have limited this book's algorithms and data structures to those you will most likely see in an interview. Any other interview questions you face may be a variation on one of these or one that is entirely novel and needs memorization.

The top algorithms to focus on include sorting algorithms like Merge Sort and Quick Sort, searching algorithms like Binary Search and Quickselect, graph traversal algorithms (BFS, DFS), greedy algorithms, backtracking, and basic data structure operations on arrays, linked lists, and trees. There is a strong emphasis on understanding each algorithm's time and space complexity. Some understanding of dynamic programming is also needed.

Sorting Algorithms:

- Merge Sort: Efficient for large datasets, uses divide and conquer strategy.
- Quick Sort: It also uses divide and conquer and can be faster than Merge Sort in specific scenarios.
- Heap Sort: Good for finding the maximum or minimum element quickly.

Searching Algorithms:

- Binary Search: Efficient for sorted arrays, halves the search space with each iteration.
- Linear Search: Simple search for unsorted arrays.
- Quickselect: When finding the kth smallest/largest element in an unsorted array.

Dynamic Programming:

- Breaks complex problems into smaller sub-problems, often used for optimization problems.
- Examples: Longest Common Subsequence, Knapsack Problem

Graph Algorithms:

- Breadth First Search (BFS): Visits all nodes at the same level before moving to the next
- Depth First Search (DFS): Explores as deep as possible in one branch before backtracking

Greedy Algorithms:

- Makes locally optimal choices at each step to find a global solution

Backtracking:

- Explores all possible solutions by recursively trying different options and backtracking when necessary

Data Structures:

- Arrays: Efficient for random access
- Linked Lists: Flexible for insertions and deletions
- Trees: Hierarchical data structure with various traversal methods
- Heaps: Useful for priority queues
- Hash maps: Fast key-value lookups

If you are short on time, less than three months to prepare, the most common data structures and algorithms that you absolutely must know are stacks, heap, hash map, merge sort, quick sort, linked list, depth-first search (DFS), and breadth-first search (BFS). I have included a table below based on how often and what importance is placed on each, from A-tier algorithms and concepts you must know to lower-tier algorithms you may only encounter occasionally. You will notice that most of the A-Tier items are foundational concepts.

A	B	C	D	F
DFS	Two Pointers	Merge Sort	Quickselect	Binary Manipulation
BFS	Dynamic Programming	Trie	Monotonic Sort	Kruskal's
Binary Search Tree	Sliding Window	Topological Sort	Dijkstra's	String Search Algorithms
Hash Map	Linked List	Prefix Sum	Union Find	Floyd's
Stack	Backtracking	Bucket Sort	Prim's	Bubble Sort
Heap			0/1 Knapsack	
			A*	

The specialized algorithms you need to memorize to master are A*, Dikstra's Algorithm, Kruskal's Algorithm, Topological Sort, Trie, Prefix Sum, Floyd's Algorithm, and Quickselect. These are typically impossible to reason through quickly if you don't understand the optimizations they are doing beforehand.

Coding Project

How to Crush Your Coding Project

I will provide you with everything you need to succeed. In the appendix, I have included an example of an actual take-home coding project.

Take-home coding projects offer a unique opportunity to showcase your development skills in a realistic environment. Unlike the high-pressure atmosphere of live coding interviews, these projects let you demonstrate your thoughtful approach to software development, attention to detail, and technical craftsmanship.

You will sometimes be given a take-home project instead of an on-site technical interview or coding challenge. Some may require all of them. You will be prompted to create a small application or a few in your take-home coding project.

Setting Yourself Up for Success

Understanding project expectations before diving into code is crucial. I've learned through experience to ask clarifying questions about the tech stack requirements. Don't spend hours crafting a solution in C++ when the team is specifically looking for someone with Java expertise. Always confirm key details, such as preferred frameworks, submission format, and evaluation criteria. So be sure to clarify any requirements before you begin.

What's Being Assessed?

Take-home challenges evaluate multiple dimensions of your capabilities. Code quality is paramount - companies want to see if you can write clean, maintainable code that meets their standards. Your decision-making process also comes under scrutiny, as the choices embedded in your code reveal your technical judgment. Adherence to the instructions demonstrates your attention to detail. Additionally, your communication skills shine through in your README and documentation, speaking volumes about your ability to explain technical concepts clearly.

Set Clear Boundaries

Time and scope management is crucial. Rather than trying to implement everything imaginable, allocate a specific time frame for completion. Analyze what's realistic within that window and prioritize quality over quantity. While other candidates scatter their focus across multiple features, your concentrated effort on fewer, well-executed components will stand out. Be realistic about what you can accomplish with the time you have allotted.

Break Down and Plan

Treat this like a small project: divide the challenge into smaller, more manageable chunks. Write out your flow chart and list of components before you start. Solve the problem conceptually before writing a single line of code. You can estimate time requirements for each component so you don't go over your allotment. Being methodological at the beginning ensures you don't miss critical requirements.

Prioritize Testing

Even when not explicitly required, automated tests elevate your submission significantly. Consider using Test-Driven Development if it suits your style, and aim for meaningful test coverage and code coverage that demonstrates you understand what's worth testing and what isn't. Include unit tests at a minimum. Tests signal that you are a professional and care about code quality. Some companies will specify that you need "at least 70% test case coverage" or similar in the design document.

Documentation

Consider your documentation your project's handshake - the first inter-action reviewers have with your work. Your README should guide them through:

- How to setup the application and any dependencies
- Running the application seamlessly
- Understanding your technical decisions
- Navigating the code base efficiently
- Following your thought process

You will typically submit your project as a Zip file or a Github link.

A take-home project isn't just about proving you can code - it's about demonstrating how you approach real-world software development challenges. Your solution should reflect the same care and consideration you'd give to the production code. Here is a template for an exceptional README file:

```
# Project Title

## Quick Start
[Clear setup instructions]

## Problem Understanding
[How you interpreted the requirements]

## Solution Approach
[Your overall strategy]

## Implementation Details
[Key components and how they work together]

## Decisions and Trade-offs
[Explain why you made certain choices]

## Future Improvements
[What you'd enhance with more time]

## Testing Strategy
[How you verified correctness]
```

The "Decisions and Trade-offs" section is particularly valuable. It shows that you can think critically about engineering choices.

Final Steps

Before you send off your code, I want you to do the following:

Remove Code Comments. Once you are done with your code, step away for a while, then come back and read through it, cleaning it up and removing unnecessary comments, such as the many ToDos you have scattered throughout.

Refactor Poor Code. If any areas of your code could perform better, refactor them to optimize them. If you have a nested for-loop, it is time to eliminate it.

Include Your Design Document. Clean up your design document and submit it with your code, even if it is not requested. It will demonstrate how your code is supposed to operate and that you are a detailed developer.

The goal isn't to create a perfect solution but to show how you think, work, and communicate. By approaching take-home coding projects with intention and care, you'll outshine the competition and genuinely improve as an engineer.

Sample Coding Projects

The appendix shows an example of an actual take-home coding project. It is a slightly changed actual project from a real company. Look these over and go through the process of making a design document and estimating the time for each module. This will help you better prepare for a coding project and ensure you have your tool-sets set up to build and deliver an application.

On-Site Interviews

How to Crush Your On-Site Interview

Before COVID-19 (BC), on-site interviews were standard; I will cover it here. However, After COVID-19 (AC), many companies have elected to conduct multiple (5-6 on average) remote interviews with various team members. Do not let the fact that you are not receiving an invitation for an on-site interview make you think you are not a strong candidate. Many teams, such as mine, are primarily remote. Having you come to an office to interview would mean flying you in for several days and many of the people you would interview with. Instead, the market seems split on whether to conduct on-site or not. As of this writing, the trend has been for more on-site interviews again for many prominent tech companies.

The on-site session is often the most stress-inducing part of the hiring process. You will typically arrive at the company office early in the morning, wait until someone gathers you, be issued a visitor badge, and are led to the first of your 4-6 consecutive interviews, each lasting 45-60 minutes. You will usually receive an email with your interview schedule beforehand. Expect several of these to be Data Structures and Algorithms interviews, usually one on Systems Design, Process and Communication (i.e., Behavioral), and Manager/Team Matching.

You may be asked to go to lunch with a team member. Do not let your guard down! Consider the time spent at lunch with team members as also being graded. Be polite and professional, and ask some questions about the company you have prepared as part of your interview preparation. I have witnessed every sort of self-sabotage during the lunch period. Don't let it happen to you.

During your lunch, do not order anything expensive or difficult to eat. People will be asking you questions and also evaluating your table manners (really!). You don't want a mouth full of spaghetti when they ask you a question about your long term goals. And you don't want to be wearing any of that spaghetti sauce the rest of your day. Simple, bit sized, and not messy. Just keep it simple, you can go have a nice dinner later to celebrate.

During your On-site interview, you will spend at least half a day doing difficult mental work while also explaining what you are doing and why you are doing it to an ever-changing cast of complete strangers repeatedly. I couldn't imagine a more nerve-wracking process.

You will also have additional factors adding to your stress: what clothing to wear, how to commute in a new city to a new building, and possibly how to navigate an unfamiliar corporate campus. Please do not spend too much time on this and have it sorted well before you are nearing your interview date.

Decide a week ahead of time which two outfits you could wear depending on the weather: one for cooler weather and one for warmer weather. You will take both with you. And if you are going in cooler weather, please layer. The temperature of the building you will be in may be frigid in most locations but nearly sweltering in the small interview room you are placed in, or vice versa. Ask your recruiter what constitutes suitable attire, which will likely be business casual.

I carry with me charcoal chinos, a navy blue polo, and a light blue Oxford cloth button-down shirt so I can choose on the day. I pair this with a plain brown belt and brown Oxford shoes with gum soles. I carry a suitable jacket or blazer in navy or dark blue if needed. I am set for whatever weather I face the morning of my interview.

> In fact, this is my everyday uniform as well. You will seldom find me not wearing a navy polo or light blue button-down, though I may pair it with jeans when working remotely behind a camera all day. I have essentially removed this decision from my daily schedule, reducing the number of decisions I have to make and lowering my overall daily decision fatigue. Choose your own work uniform.

For women, it's pretty much the same outfit: dark pants in charcoal, black, or navy or a modest skirt in the same colors if that is what you are comfortable with. Pair that with a plain white button-down or black V-neck, and over that, a blazer or jacket in gray or blue. Complete the look with simple black flats or pumps, and you are good.

For men and women, be sure to wear an appropriate undergarment beneath your shirt or top.

Appropriate dress is different from region to region and from industry to industry. If you are interviewing on Wall Street in New York or for a legal consulting firm in D.C., a suit might be required (when they say dress casual, they mean you don't have to wear a tie, and your shirt doesn't have to be white). If you are in Palo Alto, anything above a t-shirt and hoodie might be seen as dressy.

Do not wear too much perfume or cologne. People will have to be sitting in small rooms next to you all day. Deodorant, yes! Perfume, no.

Also, make sure you understand where your hotel and office are located. Your recruiter should be able to help with this, too. The easiest option is to hail a ride-share service, set up the request when you wake up, and schedule it so you arrive 30 minutes early. You can look in Google Maps and Google Street View to become familiar with your route and what the building looks like. When heading to your interview, do not let stress around these details impact your confidence and mental state.

Once you arrive at your interview, the specific lineup will vary by company, but here are the main types of sessions you're likely to encounter (your recruiter should provide details about your particular schedule):

Data Structures & Algorithms Interviews - These assess your problem-solving abilities and coding fundamentals through whiteboard challenges or laptop coding exercises. Expect questions on time/space complexity analysis and optimization techniques relevant to back-end systems. (This book will prepare you for these.)

System Design Interviews - For server-side roles expect questions on databases (SQL vs. NoSQL), API design principles, microservices architecture, caching strategies, and perhaps designing a scalable system component. You might be asked to diagram a solution for handling high traffic or data processing challenges. (There will be a follow on book specific to System Design interviews)

Process & Communication Interviews - These evaluate how you work with others, handle conflicts, and communicate technical concepts to various audiences. Back-end developers must often explain complex system constraints to product managers and front-end teams.

Manager/Team Matching Interviews - Often more conversational, these help determine which team would best fit your skills and working style. This might include discussions about your experience with specific technologies in the company's stack or how you'd approach particular back-end challenges they face.

Problem-Solving Tips

Interviewers often care more about your problem-solving approach than perfect solutions recall. In an interview, you should always:

1. **Clarify the requirements**. Before starting, ask any questions to make sure you understand the assignment.
2. **Work through examples.**
3. **Discuss potential approaches.**
4. **Implement the chosen solution.**
5. **Always include tests**. Test with happy path and edge cases where appropriate.

Data Structures & Algorithms Interviews

Data structures and algorithms interviews can trigger severe anxiety, especially for developers who don't necessarily use red-black trees or implement quicksort in their day-to-day work. I'll dive deep into specific topics on data structures and algorithms in the upcoming chapters. Don't worry if this feels overwhelming - with structured daily practice, you can master these concepts, even if they're brand new.

Sample On-Site Interview Question

Here is an example of a data structures and algorithms question you may be asked during your on-site interview:

Problem: Merge Overlapping Intervals

"You are given an array of intervals where each interval is represented as a pair of integers [start, end]. Merge all overlapping intervals and return the non-overlapping intervals that cover all the intervals in the input."

```
Example:
Input: intervals = [[1,3],[2,6],[8,10],[15,18]]
Output: [[1,6],[8,10],[15,18]]
Explanation: Since intervals [1,3] and [2,6] overlap, they are
merged into [1,6].
```

Breaking Down My Approach

Don't panic, and don't over-complicate things. Sitting quietly while you get your bearings is OK; tell the interviewer, "Please give me a moment," and then center yourself before you start working on the problem. Don't stay silent while you work on the problem, though. You want to demonstrate your thinking aloud to the interviewer.

This problem is particularly useful because it combines sorting with interval manipulation—concepts that appear frequently in back-end system design, too, like handling time-based data or optimizing database queries.

Here's how to approach it:

Clarify the Problem "Let me make sure I understand correctly—we have intervals that may overlap, and we need to merge them to get a minimum set of non-overlapping intervals, right? Does the input array come sorted, or should I sort it first?" Here, we are making sure we understand the pattern.

Work Through Examples, Including Edge Cases "What if the array is empty? Should I return an empty array? What about single-element arrays or negative numbers?" Here, we are ensuring that we account for all examples, including those not given in the problem statement.

Develop a Strategy by Discuss Potential Approaches. "The key here is that if we sort the intervals by start time, we only need to compare adjacent intervals to determine if they overlap." We are mapping this problem onto a similar code pattern, even if they differ. Making a slight change to the code pattern should get us to a solution. By treating this as a sorting problem, we have several code patterns to choose from.

Write Pseudo-code for your Solution Approach:

First, check if the input is empty and return an empty result. If so:

1. Sorts the intervals by their start time
2. Adds the first interval to the result
3. Iterate through the remaining intervals, either:
   — Merging them with the last interval in the result if they overlap
   — Adding them as a new interval if they don't overlap

```
function mergeIntervals(intervals):
    if intervals is empty:
        return empty array

    sort intervals by start time
    initialize result array with first interval

    for each current interval in intervals (starting from second):
        last interval = last interval in result array

        if current interval's start <= last interval's end:
            merge by updating last interval's end to max(last
            interval's end, current interval's end)
        else:
            add current interval to result

    return result
```

Implement the Solution

Python Implementation

```python
def merge(intervals):
    # Handle empty input case
    if not intervals:
        return []

    # Sort intervals by start time
    intervals.sort(key=lambda x: x[0])

    # Initialize result with first interval
    result = [intervals[0]]

    # Iterate through remaining intervals
    for current in intervals[1:]:
        # Get the last interval from result list
        last_merged = result[-1]

        # Check if current interval overlaps
        if current[0] <= last_merged[1]:
            # Merge overlapping intervals
            last_merged[1] = max(last_merged[1],
                                 current[1])
        else:
            # If no overlap, add current interval
            result.append(current)

    return result

def test_merge_python():
    # Test case with intervals
    intervals = [[1,3],[2,6],[8,10],[15,18]]
    result = merge(intervals)
    print("Python Result:", result)
    # Expected output: [[1,6],[8,10],[15,18]]

# Execute the test function
test_merge_python()
```

Analyze Time and Space Complexity. The time complexity is O(n log n) due to the sorting operation, where n is the number of intervals. The space complexity is O(n) in the worst case where no intervals overlap." (More on how to do this in the next chapter)

Test with Examples. I would trace through the example: [[1,3],[2,6],[8,10],[15,18]]

- After sorting: Same (already sorted)
- Initialize result: [[1,3]]
- Process [2,6]: 2 ≤ 3, so merge → [[1,6]]
- Process [8,10]: 8 > 6, so add → [[1,6],[8,10]]
- Process [15,18]: 15 > 10, so add → [[1,6],[8,10],[15,18]]
- Return: [[1,6],[8,10],[15,18]]

What Interviewers Are Really Looking For

What interviewers are evaluating as you go through this process is:

- **Problem-solving approach**: Do you break down problems methodically?
- **Algorithm design**: Can you identify an efficient approach?
- **Code quality**: Is your implementation clean and bug-free?
- **Analytical thinking**: Can you reason about time and space complexity?
- **Communication**: Can you explain your thinking clearly while coding?

The most common mistake I've seen (and made) is diving into coding without a clear strategy.

You will find that talking through problems out loud, even when practicing alone, will dramatically improve your performance. It will feel awkward at first but do it anyway. I usually have an item on my desk that I talk things out with. For decades, my object was a green rubber duck; today, it is a figurine of my favorite superhero. Your item can be anything or anyone. You can talk to your pet or your partner/spouse (they don't have to listen or respond). Doing this will train you to verbalize your thought process, which is not a skill that comes naturally but is precisely what interviewers want to see.

System Design Interviews

If you are a new developer seeking your first role or have been a developer for a while but have never been asked to do system design, do not worry. This is another task to see how you think and solve problems. Please do your best to work through the problem with the information you have. Like Data Structures and Algorithms, System Design is a skill you can learn through mapping design patterns to problem statements. Repetition is key. This will likely be a white-boarding problem. White-boarding is also a skill you can master with practice.

To practice at home, you can use dry erase markers and any window, mirror, or glass door. Get your drawing legible and understand the shorthand of symbols you will use when working problems: a column (two circles connected by two lines) indicates a data store, a diamond indicates a decision process, etc. You don't want the first time you think of such things to be when you are standing in front of someone trying to solve a problem.

Sample On-Site Interview Question

Here is an example of an on-site interview question you may be asked for the system design portion of your on-site interview:

Problem: Design a Rate Limiter Service

"Your company has a popular API that is experiencing performance issues during peak times. Design a rate-limiting service that allows 100 requests per minute for free-tier users and 1000 requests per minute for premium users. How would you implement this system to be scalable across multiple server instances?"

Breaking Down My Approach

The interviewer isn't looking for a perfect answer; they want to see your problem-solving process. Relax, center yourself, then get to work by going through the problem-solving steps:

Clarify Requirements "Before jumping in, can I confirm a few things? Do we need to track usage across distributed servers? Is there a specific latency requirement? Should users receive feedback when they've hit their limit?"

Work through examples:

"Do we expect the growth to continue? Do we need to account for additional tiers, such as an enterprise level, without rate limiting?"

Discuss the approaches:

"We could use a token bucket algorithm, giving each user a bucket of tokens, and then each request consumes one token. However, this type of system will have problems maintaining consistency under heavy load in a distributed system."

"We could use a sliding window counter to track requests within a moving window time by recording the timestamp and count of each request; when checking limits, only count requests within the last minute and gradually expire old request data. This will provide more accurate limits but require more storage and computation.

"We could use a fixed window counter that used fixed time buckets where we divide time into 1-minute windows, Count requests in the current window, and Reset the counter when the window changes. This does not account for traffic spikes at window boundaries and could be gamed by the client."

"I believe using a sliding window counter will work best, but only if we move the storage and computation out of the API service and into a system where we can scale it across multiple servers."

Implement the chosen solution:

"The most important lesson I've learned implementing these systems: start simple, then iterate. My first-rate limiter was a Redis counter with no backups or fallbacks. It wasn't perfect, but it solved our immediate problem while we built something more robust."

Interviewers are looking for practical wisdom alongside technical knowledge when you're in the interview. Be honest about trade-offs - there's no perfect solution here, just the right solution for specific requirements.

What would you prioritize in your approach? Performance under load or absolute accuracy of the limits? These are the kinds of questions interviewers will really engage with.

High-Level Architecture

- Sketch a basic diagram showing:
- API Gateway as the entry point
- Rate Limiter Service (separate micro-service)
- User Service (to determine tier level)
- Distributed cache (Redis) for tracking request counts

Algorithm Selection:

"I'd implement a sliding window counter using Redis for the actual rate limiting. This provides more accurate limiting than fixed windows while being more memory-efficient than a true token bucket. Using Redis as a central source of truth will allow a fast, in-memory data store with atomic operations, Built-in expiration functionality for time windows, and Cluster mode for high availability."

Sketch out the algorithm in micro-service:

```
FUNCTION check_rate_limit(user_id, tier)
  key = "rate_limit:{user_id}:{current_minute}"
  current_count = INCR key

  IF first increment THEN
    EXPIRE key 60  # Set 60-second expiry
END

  limit = tier == "premium" ? 1000 : 100
  RETURN current_count <= limit
  END
```

Failure Handling

- "Should you fail open (allow requests) or fail closed (block requests) when the rate limiter is unavailable?"

User Experience

- "How will users know they're being rate limited?"
- Return 429 Too Many Requests with clear headers.
- Include Retry-After header suggesting when to try again.
- Provide documentation on rate limits and upgrade paths

Always Include Tests:

Here, we just need to discuss expected failure conditions and how to design to avoid them: "The challenge with distributed systems such as this is race conditions. We can solve this by using Redis' atomic operations. For extreme scale, we could shard by user ID. If the rate limiter fails, we should fail to open temporarily rather than blocking all traffic while triggering alerts."

Recap

By the end of this interview, you should have a high-level architectural diagram drawn on the whiteboard that includes the following:

- API Gateway Layer
- Initial request handling
- Authentication & user tier identification
- Route to rate limiter service
- Rate Limiter Service
- Redis cluster as a central data store
- Distributed cache with eventual consistency
- Circuit breakers for resilience
- Response Handling
- 429 status codes for rejected requests
- Clear headers for limited information
- Monitoring & alerting on rejection rates

What Interviewers Are Really Looking For

Having been on both sides of the table, I can tell you what I and other interviewers are evaluating on this question:

- **Systems thinking**: Can you design beyond a single server?
- **Practical knowledge**: Do you understand real-world constraints?
- **Communication skills**: How clearly can you explain complex concepts?
- **Trade-off awareness**: Do you recognize the pros and cons of your approach?

Please don't dive into code; this is **not** a coding question. Discuss the system architecture, the pros and cons of different approaches (you want to present at least two options), and why you would choose one solution over another.

Remember to explain your thinking out loud while drawing your system diagrams. Your existing back-end experience is incredibly valuable here, and you should draw on this experience when discussing your solution.

The Process and Communication Interview

One is the interview I bombed. Their preferred project management style differed too widely from mine. I should have been better prepared for this portion.

This is a **behavioral interview**. When they say that they want you to have a "chat" with one of the senior people about your agile process experience or how you build teamwork, it is the process and communication interview. This is not a casual chat; it is a critical part of the interviewing process that often makes or breaks your chances. Teams will put more weight on the outcome of this interview than any of the others.

During this interview, you'll face questions from hiring managers, senior engineers, scrum masters, or team leads who explicitly evaluate how you'll function within their team ecosystem. They are looking for teammates to help them solve business or user problems daily and want to know if you can get on board. Being a brilliant developer doesn't matter if nobody wants to work with you.

You should focus on your physical presence, how you communicate, and display professional integrity.

Project confidence through posture: Sit up straight and make eye contact consistently. I know it sounds like advice from your mother, but interviewers make unconscious judgments about confidence and competence based on these outward physical cues.

Pause before Answering: DO NOT just start rambling when asked a question. Have a drink of water while you organize your thoughts.

Structure your responses: I use the STAR method (Situation, Task, Action, Result) for most process questions. It keeps me on track and ensures I don't forget the crucial "result" part that demonstrates impact. I have listed two excellent books on the STAR method in the resources chapter. The STAR method stands for:

- **Situation**: Describe the context of your example.
- **Task**: Explain the task you were given or the goal you set.
- **Action**: Describe your steps to complete the task or meet the goal.
- **Result**: Explain the outcome of your actions.

Maintain Professional Integrity (i.e., Never throw anyone under the bus): This is the ultimate red flag in communication interviews. Candidates with stellar technical skills get rejected for speaking negatively about former employers or colleagues. Instead of "My last manager couldn't organize anything well," say, "I developed strategies for working effectively even when priorities shifted frequently." It's the same information but a completely different impression.

Sample On-Site Interview Questions

Here are five Process and Communication interview questions. Consider how you would answer each of these and write down your answer. You never want these to sound rehearsed, but you do want to start thinking about how you would answer questions like these and practice structuring your answer using the STAR method.

"Tell me about a time when you had to make a difficult technical decision with incomplete information."

What they're assessing: Decision-making under uncertainty, risk assessment, and your judgment framework.

Remember to structure your answer to show the constraints you faced, the options you considered, your evaluation criteria, the outcome, and what you learned.

"Describe a situation when you disagreed with a senior engineer or tech lead. How did you handle it?"

What they're assessing: Conflict resolution, communication skills, and whether you'll speak up or silently harbor resentment.

"Tell me about a project where you had to learn a new technology or framework quickly. How did you approach the learning curve?"

What they're assessing: Adaptability, learning strategies, and self-motivation.

This question is one of my favorites because the candidate can talk about what they learned instead of how they learned it. The most substantial answers demonstrate your learning methodology—whether you build small experimental projects, pair with experts, or dive into documentation first.

"Give an example of when you had to balance technical debt against feature delivery. How did you approach that trade-off?"

They're assessing Business awareness, prioritization skills, and technical communication.

This question separates junior engineers from senior ones faster than any algorithm question. When I ask this, I'm looking for candidates who can articulate technical and business perspectives. The strongest responses acknowledge that perfect code isn't always the correct business decision—and demonstrate how you successfully navigate that inherent tension.

"Tell me about a time when you helped a teammate grow or succeed."

They're assessing Collaboration, leadership potential, and whether you'll contribute to team culture.

Don't underestimate this question. Your ability to elevate others often matters more than individual brilliance. When I started my career, this question was a throwaway. Today, I am looking for candidates who demonstrate teamwork and mentorship.

What Interviewers Are Really Looking For

This interview is looking primarily for four things:

Can you resolve conflict constructively? We all know that developer disagreements about architecture or approach are inevitable. I like spirited discussions around these things because everyone is engaged, and the final product will likely improve. But, at the end of the day, what is decided may not be what you want.

Do you communicate technical concepts? Can you explain complex ideas to both technical and non-technical stakeholders? By that, I mean can you get into the technical details enough to hold your own in a technical discussion and generalize it enough for the business team? Being able to explain very complex concepts in an easy-to-understand manner is one of the key skills that has helped my career.

How do you handle ambiguity? Projects rarely come with perfect specs. How do you navigate uncertainty?

Are you adaptable to different workflows? Every team has unique processes. Will you adapt and fit in, or will you fight against the workflow and endlessly complain that they are not doing it right?

Technical skills may get you in the door, but communication skills determine if you'll thrive once you're inside.

Manager/Team Matching Interviews

Many candidates breathe a sigh of relief when they reach the manager interview stage after sweating through algorithm challenges and system design questions. Don't do it! You are nearly there, and this final interview is important. These interviews serve a dual purpose of **evaluating cultural and team fit** and **matching you to the right team**.

I have had terrific candidates come to me as the hiring manager. I wanted to hire them and work with them on a daily basis—just not on my team. The skill set they brought to the table would have been wasted on my team, so I steered them to the team that best fit their skills and interests and brought the most value to the company.

You may interview several managers at some larger companies before finding your home.

Sample On-Site Interview Questions

Expect questions like:

"How do you prefer to receive feedback?"

"Describe your ideal collaboration environment."

"How do you handle tight deadlines or changing requirements?"

I often ask how you would approach joining an established team of engineers who had all been with the company for more than a decade and sometimes two. I am looking for an honest answer that shows they will respect the team's decisions until now while also being able to voice strong opinions about their designs, architecture, or patterns. Being able to thoughtfully respect the work done to date while also suggesting improvements is hard to do.

You should also expect questions that dive deep into your experience. I might pull one project from five years ago and want to discuss it because I am exploring how you would handle similar situations if you were on my team. One good example is migrating from a legacy mainframe to a modern micro-services architecture while maintaining service levels for our clients. If I see you have done this type of project before, I will undoubtedly spend most of our time talking about that project and how you handled it.

You should also expect questions about your career direction - the classic "Where do you want to be in five years?" If you give a generic answer, expect to be pressed further.

Embrace this portion of the interview process. The worst outcome isn't rejection—getting matched with a team where you'll struggle or be unhappy.

This is also a two-way interview. You should use the opportunity to determine if the team or company is the right fit for you. When you hear that this team has had several managers over a handful of years, or the senior member of the team has only been in the role for less than a year, then maybe this isn't a team you want to be a part of. You also get to determine if this is a manager under which you would thrive or stagnate.

Now What Happens

You have a whiskey, go to the gym, nap, or have a slice of pie. The hard work is over, so now you wait. You will either get the job or not, but you should be proud of all you accomplished. In a few days, the recruiter will contact you with an offer or a rejection. If it is a rejection, you take it graciously and email everyone, thanking them for their time and **nothing more**. If it is an offer, your work isn't over. It's time to negotiate.

Congratulations on your offer! You worked hard and earned it. But the offer on the table is just that—an offer. Is it their best and final offer? Probably not.

When I received my first job offer at Dell, I did not negotiate. Nobody ever told me I could negotiate. And frankly, I was so happy to get out of my dead-end town that I probably would have taken any offer. But, as I soon learned after talking with others hired around the same time as me, they would have paid thousands more.

Here is what they did that I didn't: they negotiated. Often, the person negotiating isn't the hiring manager; it's someone in Human Resources (HR), perhaps the recruiter you started with. They have been told that the company has a range for the specific job title between X and Y and that they should bring on new hires somewhere in that range. The hiring manager has let the HR person know what they have budgeted. Depending on the HR person and what the hiring manager has told them, your offer is likely at the bottom or middle of that range. Want to know a neat trick? You can ask the HR person their range for the level you would be coming in at, and sometimes they will tell you. Not always, but often. Be an advocate for yourself and negotiate.

You can also accept the first offer if you are happy with it. Some companies will bring you their best offer first. Just ask the HR person if this is their best offer.

And you don't have to negotiate just on the salary; you can negotiate on anything in the offer, from a sign-on bonus to paid moving expenses. Here is a list of the things open to negotiation:

- Paid time off
- Stock options and equity grants
- Relocation assistance
- Sign-on bonuses
- Performance review timelines
- Annual bonus target
- Annual training and conference budget
- Flexible working hours
- Remote/Flex work

At this point, the company has decided they want you and has invested time and resources into selecting you. Make sure you do all you can during the negotiation portion to ensure you will be happy with the outcome. Ask for what you feel you are worth based on current market rates.

What is the current market rate for your job? You can easily find this information on places like GlassDoor and Salary.com.

Again, congratulations for getting this far. You deserve it.

3

Big-O Notation

We will dive into Big-O notation first because we will use it to describe the computational and space complexity of different concepts throughout the rest of this book. Big-O notation is a tool in computer science for expressing the **worst-case** performance (upper bound) or complexity of an algorithm and the worst-case memory space it uses.

Simplifying Big-O Notation

Ignore Constants: Big-O focuses on the long-term growth rate of functions rather than their exact values. For instance:

- $O(3)$ is simplified to $O(1)$ (constant time).
- $O(2x)$ is simplified to $O(x)$.

Drop Less Significant Terms: Only the term with the highest growth rate matters. For example:

- $O(x2+x)O(x^2 + x)$ simplifies to $O(x^2)$.

This last simplification highlights the dominant factor influencing performance as the input size grows.

Constant Time

Constant time, or **O(1)**, is when an algorithm takes the same amount of time to run, no matter how much input it has.

Think of a simple function that takes no arguments and returns the phrase "Hello World." Since it doesn't rely on any input, its runtime doesn't change—it's always constant. That's what makes it an O(1) algorithm.

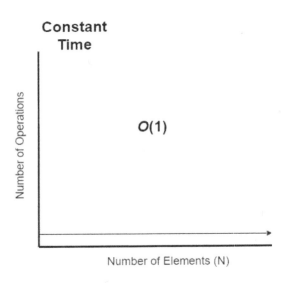

Python Implementation

```
*def* say_hell*O*():
return "Hello World"

print(say_hell*O*())
```

Logarithmic Time

Logarithmic time, or O(log n), describes an algorithm where each step cuts the problem size in half. A great example of this is Binary Search, which you will find below and is discussed in depth later in the book. In Binary Search, every pass through the algorithm halves the amount of data left to process, making it logarithmic in nature.

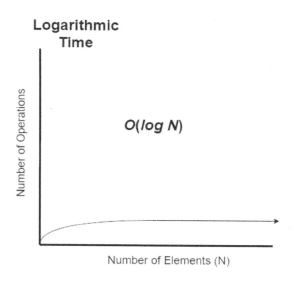

Python Implementation

```python
def binary_search(arr, target):
    """
    Performs binary search on a sorted array.

    Args:
        arr: A sorted list of elements
        target: The element to find
```

```
Returns:
    Index of target if found, otherwise -1
"""
# Initialize pointers for boundaries
left, right = 0, len(arr) - 1

# Search while boundaries haven't crossed
while left <= right:
    # Calculate middle index
    mid = (left + right) // 2

    # Found target
    if arr[mid] == target:
        return mid
    # Target in right half
    elif arr[mid] < target:
        left = mid + 1
    # Target in left half
    else:
        right = mid - 1

# Target not found
return -1

# Example usage
numbers = [1, 2, 3, 4, 5, 6, 7, 8, 9, 10]
target = 7
index = binary_search(numbers, target)

# Display result
if index != -1:
    print(f"Element {target} found at index {index}")
else:
    print(f"Element {target} not found in the list")
```

Linear Time

Linear time, or **O(n)**, refers to an algorithm that takes time proportional to the size of the input. Essentially, as the input gets bigger, the time it takes to process also increases in a straight line.

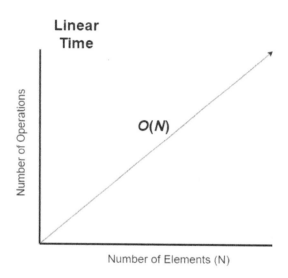

For example, a simple for-loop that goes through each element in an array has a complexity of $O(n)$ time. Let's say you have an array of numbers, and the loop runs once for each number in the array. If there are 10 numbers, it runs 10 times; if there are 100, it runs 100 times. The time grows directly with the number of numbers in the array.

Other common operations, like mapping over an array, filtering it, or cloning it using the spread operator, all follow the same pattern. These actions also take $O(n)$ time, assuming they don't have extra loops nested inside them. So, the larger the array, the more time it takes to process—one element at a time.

Below, I've included a small loop showing Linear Time.

Python Implementation

```python
def find_maximum(arr):
    """
    Finds the maximum value in an array/list.

    Args:
        arr: A list of comparable elements

    Returns:
        The maximum value found in the array

    Raises:
        IndexError: If the input array is empty
    """
    # Initialize max with first element
    max_value = arr[0]

    # Iterate through each element
    for num in arr:
        # If current element is greater
        if num > max_value:
            # Update max_value
            max_value = num

    # Return the maximum value
    return max_value

# Example usage
numbers = [3, 1, 4, 1, 5, 9, 2, 6, 5, 3, 5]
print(find_maximum(numbers))   # Output: 9
```

Super-Linear Time

A super-linear time algorithm is one with a time complexity of **O(n log n)**—it isn't as fast as a linear time algorithm (which runs in O(n)), but it's still way better than an exponential one (like O(2^n), which can get slow, really fast). That's why algorithms like merge sort and heap sort, which fall into this super-linear category, are popular for sorting data. They're not the fastest, but they're a great middle-ground: efficient enough to handle large datasets without a sweat.

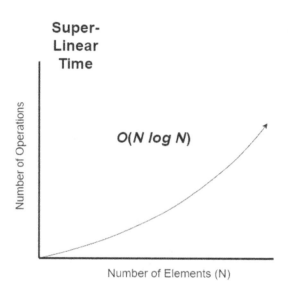

On the other hand, you've got algorithms like Bubble Sort, which runs in $O(n^2)$ time. While Bubble Sort might work fine for tiny datasets, it quickly becomes a nightmare as the data grows. Imagine trying to sort millions of items—Bubble Sort would take forever! That's why, in most real-world scenarios, you'd go with something like Merge Sort or Heap Sort instead. They're not perfect, but they're reliable and efficient enough to finish the job without making you wait ages.

In short, super-linear algorithms are like the "Goldilocks" of the algorithm world—not too slow, not too fast, but just right for many practical problems, such as Merge Sort. We will cover Merge Sort in depth later in the book in the Algorithms chapter, but here is an example of how it works in code. Why is its complexity considered $O(n \log n)$?

Python Implementation

```python
def merge_sort(array):
    """
    Sorts using merge sort algorithm.

    Args:
        array: The list to be sorted

    Returns:
        A new sorted list
    """
    # Base case: already sorted
    if len(array) <= 1:
        return array

    # Divide array into halves
    mid = len(array) // 2

    # Recursively sort halves
    left = merge_sort(array[:mid])
    right = merge_sort(array[mid:])

    # Merge sorted halves
    return merge(left, right)

def merge(left, right):
    """
    Merges two sorted arrays.

    Args:
        left: First sorted array
        right: Second sorted array

    Returns:
        New sorted array with all elements
    """
    result = []
```

```
# Compare and merge elements
while left and right:
    result.append(left.pop(0) if left[0] <= right[0]
                  else right.pop(0))

# Add remaining elements
return result + left + right

# Example usage
array = [23, 16, 6, 59, 3, 11, 37]
sorted_array = merge_sort(array)
print(sorted_array)  # [3, 6, 11, 16, 23, 37, 59]
```

Polynomial Time

Polynomial time complexity refers to the time complexity of an algorithm that can be expressed as a polynomial function of the input size n. In Big-O notation, an algorithm is said to have polynomial time complexity if its time complexity is O(nk), where k is a constant and represents the degree of the polynomial. Algorithms with polynomial time complexity are generally considered efficient, as the running time grows reasonably as the input size increases. Common examples of algorithms with polynomial time complexity include linear time complexity O(n), quadratic time complexity O(n2), and cubic time complexity O(n3).

Here, we will take up the quadratic time complexity example. Quadratic time complexity means an algorithm's runtime grows exponentially with input size – specifically for **O(n²)**, the runtime grows with the square of the input size.

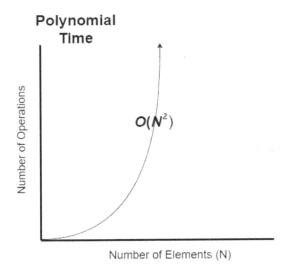

$O(N^2)$

Number of Elements (N)

This quadratic growth occurs because we need to compare each element (n) with every other element (n) in the array, resulting in n * n total comparisons. In these algorithms, the performance is indirectly proportional to the square of the data size. This happens most often when there are two nested for loops, such as in Bubble Sort, which is shown below in a small implementation. We will discuss Bubble Sort in depth later in the book in the Algorithms chapter.

```
def demonstrate_complexity(sizes=[10, 100, 1000]):
    for n in sizes:
        operations = n * n
        print(f"Size {n}: {operations:,} operations")
```

Impact of $O(n^2)$ growth:

- Input size 10: 100 operations
- Input size 100: 10,000 operations
- Input size 1000: 1,000,000 operations

Key characteristic: When input size doubles, processing time quadruples.

Python Implementation

```python
def bubble_sort(arr):
    """Sort list in-place using bubble sort algorithm.

    Time Complexity: O(n²) worst/avg, O(n) best
    Space Complexity: O(1)
    """
    n = len(arr)
    for i in range(n):
        # Track if any swaps occur
        swapped = False

        # Reduce comparisons in each pass
        for j in range(0, n - i - 1):
            # Swap if elements in wrong order
            if arr[j] > arr[j + 1]:
                arr[j], arr[j + 1] = arr[j + 1], arr[j]
                swapped = True

        # Exit if no swaps (array sorted)
        if not swapped:
            break

# Demonstrate bubble sort functionality
if __name__ == "__main__":
    # Test cases
    test_cases = [
        [64, 34, 25, 12, 22, 11, 90],  # Unsorted
        [1, 2, 3, 4, 5],                # Already sorted
        [5, 4, 3, 2, 1]                 # Reverse sorted
    ]
```

```
for case in test_cases:
    orig = case.copy()
    bubble_sort(case)
    print(f"Original: {orig}")
    print(f"Sorted:   {case}\n")
```

Exponential Time

Exponential time complexity $O(2^n)$ means runtime approximately doubles with each additional input element.

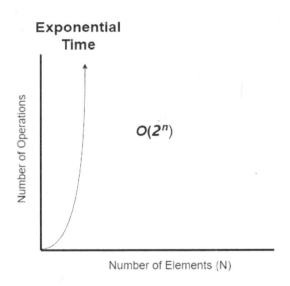

The classic example is the recursive Fibonacci routine:

```
def fibonacci(n):    # O^n(2)
    if n <= 1:
        return n
    return fibonacci(n-1) + fibonacci(n-2)
```

In this code, each call branches into two more calls, creating a binary tree of recursion:

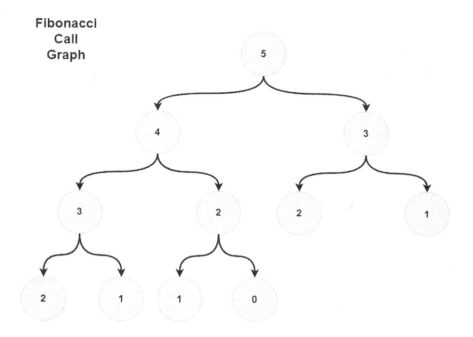

For n=5 this creates this many calls from each node:

- n=10: ~89 operations
- n=20: ~10,946 operations
- n=30: ~1,346,269 operations

This explosive growth makes exponential algorithms impractical for large inputs. This demonstrates why we avoid exponential solutions and look for more efficient polynomial-time alternatives.

Factorial Time: Final Boss Fight!

You and your friends are planning the Ultimate Road Trip™. You have a list of all the cities you want to visit, 20 in total, and you want to find the most efficient route. Simple, right? No, this is where things get decidedly complex. Factorial time, or **O(n!)**, is like the final boss of algorithmic time (computation) and space (memory) complexity. This is the difficulty of the famous Traveling Salesman Problem (TSP), where the calculations quickly explode. With just five cities, you're looking at 120 possible routes (5!). Ten cities? You're now dealing with 3,628,800 possibilities (10!)!

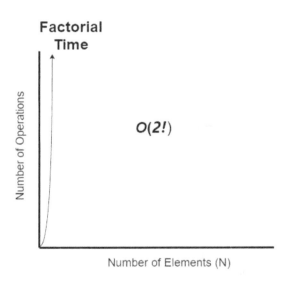

The Traveling Salesman Problem asks: "Given a list of cities and the distances between each pair of cities, what's the shortest possible route that **visits each city exactly once and returns to the starting point?**"

Here's what makes it so challenging:

- For 3 cities: You have 6 possible routes (3!)
- For 4 cities: 24 possible routes (4!)

- For 5 cities: 120 (5!)
- For 10 cities: 3,628,800 (10!)
- For your list of 20 must-see cities? There are more possibilities than atoms in the universe! (20!)

O(n!) algorithms are often called "intractable" because they quickly become impossible to solve through brute force, even with modern computing power. That's why many of the algorithms we are going to look at are based on optimization, approximation, and heuristics to solve them, including two different solutions to the Traveling Salesman Problem.

A common question in interviews that might lead to this type of time and space complexity is finding all possible permutations of a string - a classic example of an exponential time complexity *O(N!)*, which looks like this recursive algorithm in Python:

```python
def get_permutations(string):
    # Base case
    if len(string) <= 1:
        return [string]

    # Recursive case
    perms = []
    for i in range(len(string)):
        char = string[i]
        remaining = string[:i] + string[i+1:]

        for p in get_permutations(remaining):
            perms.append(char + p)

    return perms

# Example usage
result = get_permutations("abc")
print(result)  # ['abc', 'acb', 'bac', 'bca', 'cab', 'cba']
```

Let's break this down so you can recognize the complexity of time and space involved in such a simple method. For a string of length n, here's what's happening at each level:

First Level (n choices):

- We have n choices for the first character.
- We make a recursive call with (n-1) characters for each choice.

Second Level (n-1 choices):

- For each first-level choice, we have (n-1) possibilities.
- Each leads to a recursive call with (n-2) characters.

And so on, until we reach our base case...

The pattern forms a factorial multiplication: n * (n-1) * (n-2) * ... * 2 * 1 = n!

We're not done yet because for each permutation, we're also doing string operations:

- String slicing: $O(n)$ for each recursive call
- String concatenation: $O(n)$ for building each permutation

Therefore, the total time complexity is $O(n * n!)$, where:

- n! comes from the number of permutations
- The extra n factor comes from the string operations at each step

The space complexity is also $O(n * n!)$ because we're <u>storing</u> all permutations, and each permutation has length n. We, of course, drop the least complex operations when describing the complexity and are left with $O(n!)$

Something that seems simple like this in your program: comparing data from a handful of users can quickly explode as the user base increases. It's why this is the Final Boss Fight in complexity.

4

Software Theory

Introduction

There are a few key concepts that you will need to know to get through your interviews, specifically your on-site interviews, where you will be white-boarding. You are likely to be asked questions about any of these concepts. It is best to have a refresher before we continue.

When discussing the design of the software itself, say during a white-board session for your on-site interviews, make sure you are familiar with the following software design principles, starting with the SOLID principles: the Single Responsibility Principle (SRP), the Open-Closed Principle (OCP), the **Liskov Substitution Principle** (LSP), the **Interface Segregation Principle** (ISP), and the **Dependency Inversion Principle** (DIP).

Additionally, I have added **Don't Repeat Yourself** (DRY)and the KISS Principle as key principles for the design of software objects: SOLID, DRY, and KISS are the key guiding guiding ideals for developing functional, maintainable, and extensible software.

I will also provide code examples for the Object-Oriented Programming (OOP) Design Patterns you must know, although familiarity with them is encouraged.

Single Responsibility Principle (SRP)

The single responsibility principle (SRP) is a software design principle that states that "a class or module should have only one reason to change" (Robert C. Martin, "Uncle Bob", 2014). This principle states that a class or module should have a single, well-defined responsibility and should not be responsible for multiple unrelated things.

For example, consider a class that represents a database connection:

```
class DBConnection:
    def __init__(self, connection):
        self.connection = connection

    def execute_query(self, query):
        # Execute the query and return the result set
        pass
```

In this example, the DBConnection class has a single responsibility: managing a database connection. It has no other responsibilities, such as executing queries or parsing result sets. This makes the DBConnection class easier to understand, test, and maintain.

Open-Closed Principle (OCP)

The open-closed principle (OCP) is a software design principle that states that "software entities (classes, modules, functions, etc.) should be open for extension but closed for modification" (Martin, 2014). This principle states that a software system should be designed so that new functionality can be added without modifying existing code, which can help improve maintainability and reduce the risk of introducing bugs.

For example, consider an interface that represents a logger:

```
from abc import ABC, abstractmethod

class Logger(ABC):
    @abstractmethod
    def log(self, message):
        pass
```

In this example, the Logger interface defines a single message logging method. This allows software developers to create multiple implementations of the Logger interface, such as a file logger, a database logger, or a console logger, and to inject the appropriate implementation into a class as needed. This allows new functionality to be added to the system without modifying the Logger interface, which helps to improve maintainability and reduce the risk of introducing bugs.

Liskov Substitution Principle (LSP)

The Liskov Substitution Principle (LSP) is a principle in object-oriented programming that states that objects of a superclass should be replaceable with objects of a subclass without affecting the program's correctness. In other words, any subclass of a class should be able to be used in place of the parent class without causing issues in the program. Violations of the LSP can result in unexpected behavior or errors in the program.

```
class Rectangle:
    def __init__(self):
        self.width = 0
        self.height = 0

    def set_width(self, width):
        self.width = width

    def set_height(self, height):
        self.height = height
```

```
    def get_area(self):
        return self.width * self.height

class Square(Rectangle):
    def set_width(self, width):
        self.width = width
        self.height = width

    def set_height(self, height):
        self.height = height
        self.width = height

def main():
    rectangle = Rectangle()
    rectangle.set_width(5)
    rectangle.set_height(10)
    rectangle_area = rectangle.get_area()
    print(f"Area of rectangle: {rectangle_area}")

    square = Square()
    square.set_width(5)
    square_area = square.get_area()
    print(f"Area of square: {square_area}")

if __name__ == "__main__":
    main()
```

In this example, we have a Rectangle class with a width and height field and methods to set and get their values, as well as a method to calculate the rectangle's area. We also have a Square class that extends Rectangle and overrides the set_width() and set_height() methods to ensure that the width and height fields are always equal (since a square has equal sides).

However, this implementation violates the Liskov Substitution Principle since a Square object cannot always be substituted for a Rectangle object without affecting the program's correctness. If we set the width and height of the Square object separately, the get_area() method will not return the correct area for the Square object since its width and height fields are always equal.

For example, in the code above, we create a Square object and set its width to 5. When we call get_area() on the Square object, we get an area of 25, which is correct for a square with a width of 5. However, if we then set the height of the Square object to 10 (which should not affect the area of a square with a width of 5) and call get_area() again, we get an area of 100, which is incorrect.

To adhere to the Liskov Substitution Principle, we should either remove the Square class altogether or modify it so that it does not extend Rectangle and instead has its own implementation of the get_area() method. This way, clients of the Rectangle class can still use instances of the Square class without affecting the program's correctness.

Interface Segregation Principle (ISP)

The interface segregation principle (ISP) is a software design principle that states that "clients should not be forced to depend on interfaces they do not use" (Robert C. Martin, "Uncle Bob", 2014). This means that a class should not implement interfaces that contain methods it does not use, as this can lead to unnecessary dependencies and make the class more difficult to understand and maintain.

For example, consider an interface that represents a user service:

```python
from abc import ABC, abstractmethod

class UserService(ABC):
    @abstractmethod
    def get_user(self, username):
        pass

    @abstractmethod
    def create_user(self, user):
        pass

    @abstractmethod
    def update_user(self, user):
```

```
        pass

    @abstractmethod
    def delete_user(self, username):
        pass
```

In this example, the UserService interface defines four methods for managing users. However, not all clients of the UserService interface may need to use all four methods. For example, a client that only needs to retrieve users may not need the create_user, update_user, and delete_user methods.

To address this issue, the interface segregation principle should be used to create smaller, more focused interfaces that only contain the methods specific clients need. For example:

```
from abc import ABC, abstractmethod

class UserRetrievalService(ABC):
    @abstractmethod
    def get_user(self, username):
        pass

class UserManagementService(ABC):
    @abstractmethod
    def create_user(self, user):
        pass

    @abstractmethod
    def update_user(self, user):
        pass

    @abstractmethod
    def delete_user(self, username):
        pass
```

In this revised design, the UserRetrievalService interface contains only the get_user, and a different interface has been created for user management.

Dependency Inversion Principle (DIP)

The dependency inversion principle (DIP) is a software design principle that states that "high-level modules should not depend on low-level modules. Both should depend on abstractions" (Robert C. Martin, "Uncle Bob", 2014). This means a class should not depend on concrete implementations of other classes but instead on abstractions (interfaces or abstract classes) that define the required behavior.

For example, consider a class that represents a user service:

```python
class UserService:
    def __init__(self, user_repository):
        self.user_repository = user_repository

    def get_user(self, username):
        return self.user_repository.find_by_username(username)
```

In this example, the UserService class depends on a concrete implementation of the UserRepository class. This makes the UserService class tightly coupled to the UserRepository class and makes it difficult to test or reuse it with other implementations of the UserRepository interface.

To address this issue, software developers can use the dependency inversion principle to create an abstraction that defines the required behavior of the UserRepository class and to depend on the abstraction rather than on the concrete implementation:

```python
from abc import ABC, abstractmethod

class UserService:
    """

    High-level module depending on abstractions.
    """

    def __init__(self, user_repository):
        self.user_repository = user_repository
```

```python
    def get_user(self, username):
        return self.user_repository.find_by_username(username)

    def create_user(self, user):
        if self.user_repository.exists_by_username(
                user.get_username()):
            raise UserAlreadyExistsException()
        self.user_repository.save(user)

class UserRepository(ABC):
    """
    Abstract repository interface.
    """

    @abstractmethod
    def find_by_username(self, username):
        pass

    @abstractmethod
    def save(self, user):
        pass

    @abstractmethod
    def exists_by_username(self, username):
        pass

class MySQLUserRepository(UserRepository):
    """
    MySQL implementation of repository.
    """

    def find_by_username(self, username):
        # Retrieve user from MySQL database
        pass

    def save(self, user):
        # Save user to MySQL database
        pass

    def exists_by_username(self, username):
        # Check if username exists in MySQL database
        pass
```

In this revised example, the UserService class is a high-level module that depends on abstractions (e.g., the UserRepository interface) rather than concrete implementations (e.g., the MySQLUserRepository class). This allows the UserService class to be more flexible and easier to maintain, as it can swap out or replace concrete implementations of the UserRepository interface without modifying the UserService class itself.

The MySQLUserRepository class is a low-level module that implements the UserRepository interface and provides concrete implementation details for interacting with a MySQL database. This allows the UserService class to depend on the abstractions defined in the UserRepository interface rather than on the concrete implementation details of the MySQLUserRepository class.

This separation of high-level and low-level modules allows software developers to design more flexible and easier-to-maintain systems. It allows them to modify or replace low-level modules without affecting the high-level modules that depend on them.

For example, suppose the UserService class needs to switch from using a MySQL database to a PostgreSQL one. In that case, the software developer can create a new PostgreSQLUserRepository class that implements the UserRepository interface and provides concrete implementation details for interacting with a PostgreSQL database. The UserService class does not need to be modified, as it still depends on the abstractions defined in the UserRepository interface rather than on the concrete implementation details of the MySQLUserRepository class.

Don't Repeat Yourself (DRY)

The don't repeat yourself (DRY) principle is a software design principle that states that "every piece of knowledge must have a single, unambiguous, authoritative representation within a system" (Andy Hunt and Dave Thomas, "The Pragmatic Programmer", 1999). Software developers should strive to eliminate duplication and redundancy in their code, as this can lead to maintenance issues and make the codebase more difficult to understand and modify.

For example, consider a class that represents a user service:

```
class UserService:
    """

    Service for user operations.
    """
    def __init__(self, user_repository):
        self.user_repository = user_repository

    def get_user(self, username):
        return self.user_repository.find_by_username(username)

    def create_user(self, user):
        if self.user_repository.exists_by_username(
                user.get_username()):
            raise UserAlreadyExistsException()
        self.user_repository.save(user)
```

In this example, the UserService class contains two methods: get_user and create_user. The create_user method includes a block of code that checks if a user with the given username already exists in the repository and throws an exception if it does. This code block is repeated in several places in the codebase, making the codebase more difficult to understand and maintain.

To address this issue, software developers can use the don't repeat your-self principle to refactor the code to eliminate duplication and redundancy. For example:

```
class UserService:
    """

    Service for user operations.
    """
    def __init__(self, user_repository):
        self.user_repository = user_repository
```

```
def get_user(self, username):
    return self.user_repository.find_by_username(
        username)

def create_user(self, user):
    if self.user_already_exists(user.get_username()):
        raise UserAlreadyExistsException()
    self.user_repository.save(user)

def user_already_exists(self, username):
    return self.user_repository.exists_by_username(
        username)
```

In this revised design, the UserService class has a single, unambiguous representation of the knowledge that a user with a given username already exists in the repository. This makes the codebase easier to understand and maintain and reduces the risk of introducing bugs.

KISS Principle

The KISS (keep it simple, stupid) principle is a software design principle that states that "systems work best if they are kept simple rather than made complicated" (Raymond F. Boyce, 1986). Software developers should strive to design software systems that are as simple as possible while still meeting the system's requirements.

For example, consider a class that represents a user service:

```
class UserService:
    """
    Service for user operations with email notification.
    """
    def __init__(self, user_repository, email_service):
        self.user_repository = user_repository
        self.email_service = email_service

    def get_user(self, username):
```

```
    return self.user_repository.find_by_username(
        username)

def create_user(self, user):
    if self.user_repository.exists_by_username(
            user.get_username()):
        raise UserAlreadyExistsException()
    self.user_repository.save(user)
    self.email_service.send_welcome_email(
        user.get_email())
```

In this example, the UserService class depends on two other classes: the UserRepository and EmailService classes. This adds complexity to the UserService class, as it must manage dependencies on these two classes and ensure they are correctly initialized and used.

To address this issue, software developers can use the KISS principle to design a system that is as simple as possible while still meeting the system's requirements. For example:

```
class UserService:
    """
    Service for user operations.
    """
    def __init__(self, user_repository):
        self.user_repository = user_repository

    def get_user(self, username):
        return self.user_repository.find_by_username(
            username)

    def create_user(self, user):
        if self.user_repository.exists_by_username(
                user.get_username()):
            raise UserAlreadyExistsException()
        self.user_repository.save(user)

class EmailService:
```

```
"""
Service for email operations.
"""
def send_welcome_email(self, email):
    # Send welcome email
    pass
```

In this revised design, the UserService class depends only on the UserRepository class, which reduces its complexity and makes it easier to understand and maintain. The EmailService class is a separate class that can be used by other parts of the system as needed without adding unnecessary complexity to the UserService class.

OOP Design Patterns

You should understand all the object-oriented programming design patterns and when they should be used. The Gang of Four Design Patterns book covers these in-depth (Gamma, Erich, et al. *Design Patterns: Elements of Reusable Object-Oriented Software*. Addison-Wesley, 1985.). The Gang of Four spent nearly 400 pages describing these, so I will not be able to do them justice in a few pages. However, for the primary seven that you will likely discuss in an interview, I have given code examples to demonstrate how they work.

		Purpose		
		Creational	Structural	Behavioral
Scope	Class	Factory Method	Adapter	Interpreter Template Method
	Object	Abstract Factory Builder Prototype Singleton	Adapter Bridge Composite Decorator Facade Proxy	Chain of Responsibility Command Iterator Mediator Memento Flyweight Observer State Strategy Visitor

Below, I provide code examples of the top seven patterns you should know for your interview.

Creational Patterns

These handle the creation of objects.

Singleton

Ensures only one instance of a class exists. I've found this particularly useful for managing shared resources like configuration managers.

```
class ConfigManager:
    _instance = None

    def __new__(cls):
        if cls._instance is None:
            cls._instance = super(ConfigManager,
            cls).__new__(cls)
        return cls._instance
```

```
@classmethod
def get_instance(cls):
    if cls._instance is None:
        cls._instance = ConfigManager()
    return cls._instance
```

Factory Method

We are using Python's ABC module for interface definitions
Creates objects without specifying their exact class:

```
from abc import ABC, abstractmethod

class Document(ABC):
    @abstractmethod
    def open(self):
        pass

class PDFDocument(Document):
    def open(self):
        # PDF specific logic
        pass

class DocumentFactory:
    def create_document(self, doc_type):
        if doc_type == "pdf":
            return PDFDocument()
        # Add other document types
        return None
```

Builder

Useful for constructing complex objects step by step. Useful for when objects have many optional parameters:

```
class Computer:
    def __init__(self, builder):
        # Build computer with specifications
        self.cpu = builder.cpu
        self.ram = builder.ram

class ComputerBuilder:
    def __init__(self):
        self.cpu = None
        self.ram = None

    def set_cpu(self, cpu):
        self.cpu = cpu
        return self

    def set_ram(self, ram):
        self.ram = ram
        return self

    def build(self):
        return Computer(self)
```

Structural Patterns

These deal with the composition of objects and how they behave.

Adapter

Converts one interface to another. This is a go-to when integrating legacy systems:

```
from abc import ABC, abstractmethod

class NewSystem(ABC):
    @abstractmethod
    def process_data(self):
        pass

class OldSystem:
    def process_legacy_data(self):
        # old logic
        pass

class SystemAdapter(NewSystem):
    def __init__(self, old_system):
        self.old_system = old_system

    def process_data(self):
        self.old_system.process_legacy_data()
```

Decorator

Adds behavior to objects dynamically.

```
from abc import ABC, abstractmethod

class Coffee(ABC):
    @abstractmethod
    def get_cost(self):
        pass

class SimpleCoffee(Coffee):
    def get_cost(self):
        return 1.0

class MilkDecorator(Coffee):
    def __init__(self, coffee):
        self.coffee = coffee
```

```
def get_cost(self):
    return self.coffee.get_cost() + 0.5
```

Behavioral Patterns

These define object communication.

Observer

Defines a one-to-many dependency between objects. Useful for event-driven systems:

```
from abc import ABC, abstractmethod

class Observer(ABC):
    @abstractmethod
    def update(self, message):
        pass

class NewsAgency:
    def __init__(self):
        self.observers = []

    def add_observer(self, observer):
        self.observers.append(observer)

    def notify_observers(self, news):
        for observer in self.observers:
            observer.update(news)
```

Strategy

Defines a family of algorithms and makes them interchangeable. This is great for payment processing systems:

```python
from abc import ABC, abstractmethod

class PaymentStrategy(ABC):
    @abstractmethod
    def pay(self, amount):
        pass

class CreditCardStrategy(PaymentStrategy):
    def pay(self, amount):
        # Process credit card payment
        pass
```

123

[1] Gamma, Erich, et al. *Design Patterns: Elements of Reusable Object-Oriented Software.* Addison-Wesley Professional, 1994.

[2] Martin, Robert C. *Clean Code: A Handbook of Agile Software Craftsmanship.* Prentice Hall, 2008.

[3] Hunt, Andy, and Dave Thomas. *The Pragmatic Programmer: Your Journey to Mastery.* 20th Anniversary Edition, Addison-Wesley Professional, 2019.

5

Data Structures

The following two chapters will cover the data structures and algorithms you need to know. After that, a chapter with 75 unique problems follows. You should be able to complete all of them if you learn everything in the following two chapters. Work through all the problems repeatedly to become comfortable with the patterns until you are able to complete each one in under 30 minutes.

What Is A Data Structure?

Definition

A data structure is a specialized format for efficiently organizing, storing, and manipulating data. Each structure provides specific advantages and trade-offs regarding access patterns, memory usage, and performance characteristics.

Implementation Challenges

While many programming languages offer built-in data structures, some languages, such as JavaScript, have limited native options. This can present challenges when preparing for technical interviews, mainly because:

- Many standard data structures must be implemented manually.
- Most educational resources focus on OOP languages like Java, C++, or Python.
- Implementation patterns may differ from traditional computer science approaches.

Key Concepts

The fundamental data structures you should understand:

- Arrays and Lists
- Stacks and Queues
- Trees and Graphs
- Hash Tables
- Heaps

We'll explore these structures in detail, focusing on practical implementations and their time complexity characteristics. Please refer to the resources chapter for some language-specific resources and practice problems.

Arrays

Core Concept

Arrays are one of the most fundamental data structures. Despite their simplicity, they amaze me with their elegance and versatility. In most programming languages, a string is just an array of characters, and the string object is just an abstraction of that array.

Let's explore how arrays work.

Python Implementation

Python's lists (Python's version of arrays):

```
# Creating a list (Python's array)
numbers = [1, 2, 3, 4, 5]
# Dynamic operations
numbers.append(6)    # Adds to end
numbers.insert(0, 0) # Adds at beginning
```

Python's special features:

- Dynamic sizing (grows and shrinks automatically)
- Can store different types in the same list
- Supports negative indexing (numbers[-1] gets the last element)
- Rich built-in methods (append, extend, pop, etc.)

Performance Characteristics

While arrays might look similar across languages, their real-world performance characteristics can vary significantly. While these theoretical complexities are the same, the actual performance can vary considerably based on the language's implementation and overhead, for example:

- C++: Bare-metal performance
- Java: Excellent performance with safety guarantees
- Python: Most convenient but with some performance overhead due to dynamic typing

Time Complexity By Operation:

- Access by index - $O(n)$
- Search for element - *$O(n)$*
- Insert/Delete at end - *$O(1)$*

- Insert/Delete at beginning – *$O(n)$

Amortized time complexity

Space Complexity: O(n)

Key Tips

Almost any project I have worked on in the last decade involved processing massive datasets. Most data engineers these days use Python for its ease of use. Still, eventually, we had to switch some critical sections to Java, C++, Go, Rust, or another language or platform for performance. Most Python libraries are just interfaces into a C library. Apache Spark is an excellent tool in your toolkit for when extensive data has to be modified or interrogated. All of this switching languages for different purposes has taught me an important lesson: understanding how arrays work across languages helps you make better software design decisions.

Lists

Core Concept

Understanding lists is like learning different dialects of the same language – the core concepts remain similar, but each has its unique feel and flavor.

Python Implementation

Let's start with Python lists since they're arguably the most intuitive.:

```
# Creating lists
my_list = [1, "hello", 3.14, True]  # Different types
my_list.append(42)        # Adds to end
my_list.insert(0, "start")  # Adds at position
```

```
popped_value = my_list.pop()   # Removes last element
my_list.extend([5, 6, 7])   # Adds multiple elements
```

What makes Python lists special:

- Dynamic sizing (grows and shrinks automatically)
- Mixed data types (true flexibility!)
- Rich set of built-in methods
- Slicing capabilities (my_list[1:4])

Key features:

- Constant time insertion/deletion at any position
- No random access (you must traverse to reach elements)
- Memory efficiency (only allocates what's needed)
- Bidirectional iteration

Performance Characteristics

Time Complexity:

When you start working on massive datasets, these considerations matter. Here are the performance characteristics of each operation individually.

Operation	Python List	C++ List	Java ArrayList	Java LinkedList
Access	O(1)	O(n)	O(1)	O(n)
Insert Front	O(n)	O(1)	O(n)	O(1)
Insert Back	O(1)*	O(1)	O(1)*	O(1)
Delete	O(n)	O(1)	O(n)	O(1)

* amortized time
  complexity

Space Complexity: $O(n)$

Key Tips

Choose Wisely: I once spent days optimizing a program before realizing I was using ArrayList when LinkedList would have been perfect for my insert-heavy operations.

Memory Matters: In Python, lists might consume more memory due to their flexibility.

Stacks

Stacks are a data structure that is elegant in its simplicity. I visualize stacks as a stack of books beside my desk that I haven't gotten to yet. You can't pull one out from the middle; you can only add or remove it from the top, and this simple constraint is incredibly powerful in programming. However, the downside is that you lose constant-time access to any item in the stack. The further down the stack the item is, the longer it will take to access as we would have to remove each item on top individually, unlike an array that can be accessed directly.

Stack

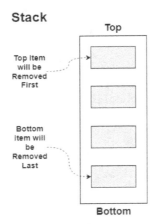

Visualization of a Stack data structure

Core Concept

Think of a stack following the "Last In, First Out" (LIFO) principle. Remember those spring-loaded plate dispensers in cafeterias – the last plate you put in is always the first one you can take out. We use this pattern in programming for everything from managing function calls to parsing expressions.

A stack is perfect for building a browser history feature. Like managing a stack of books on your desk, you can only add or remove from the top.

A stack has three core methods and a few additional helper methods.

Core Operations

push(item) - Adding to Your Stack

```
def push(item):
    stack.append(item)
```

Think of this like adding a new book to the top of your stack. You can see this when using an undo feature in an application - each new action gets pushed onto the history stack.

pop() - Taking from the Top

```
def pop():
    return stack.pop()
```

This removes and returns the top item. It's like picking up the last book you put down.

peek() - Just Looking

```
def peek():
    return stack[-1]  # Returns top item without removing it
```

This lets you check what's on top without actually removing it. It's helpful when you need to decide based on the last item.

Helper Methods

isEmpty() - Stack Status Check

```
def isEmpty():
    return len(stack) == 0
```

This exception check method can save you from null pointer exceptions. Always check if your stack is empty before popping.

get length() - Size Matters

```
def get_length():
    return len(stack)
```

Perfect for when you need to know how many items you're dealing with.

Use this to implement size limits on history stacks.

```
class BrowserHistory:
    def __init__(self):
        self.history = []   # Our stack

    def visit_page(self, url):
        self.history.push(url)

    def go_back(self):
        if not self.history.isEmpty():
            return self.history.pop()
```

When working with stacks: LIFO (Last In, First Out).

Python Implementation

Python doesn't have a built-in stack class, but lists work beautifully as stacks:

```
# Creating lists
my_list = [1, "hello", 3.14, True]  # Different types
my_list.append(42)        # Adds to end
my_list.insert(0, "start")  # Adds at position
popped_value = my_list.pop()  # Removes last element
my_list.extend([5, 6, 7])  # Adds multiple elements
```

Real-World Application

Here's a simple example of checking balanced parentheses that I often use in interviews:

```
def is_balanced(expression):
    stack = []
```

```
pairs = {')': '(', '}': '{', ']': '['}

for char in expression:
    if char in '({[':
        stack.append(char)
    elif char in ')}]':
        if not stack or stack.pop() != pairs[char]:
            return False

return len(stack) == 0
```

Performance Characteristics

Here are the performance characteristics of each operation individually.

Time Complexity By Operation

- Push – $O(1)$
- Pop – $O(1)$
- Peek – $O(1)$

Space Complexity: $O(n)$

Common Interview Questions

- Implementing a min/max stack (keeping track of minimum/maximum elements)
- Converting infix to postfix expressions
- Function call simulation
- Undo/redo functionality

Key Tips

In Python, lists work great but consider collections.deque for better performance.

Common Gotchas:

```
empty_stack = [ ]
try:
    empty_stack.pop()  # Throws IndexError
except IndexError:
    print("Handle empty stack!")
```

Queues

There are many use cases where the "first come, first served" principle is the ideal functional representation– such as a call center on hold list or the order line in a coffee shop.

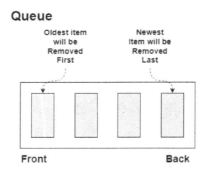

Visualization of a Queue data structure

Core Concept

Think of a queue like a line at your favorite coffee shop. The line follows the "First In, First Out" (FIFO) principle – the first person to join the line is the first one to get to order their coffee. We use this pattern in programming for everything from print job management to handling API requests.

There are three core methods in a queue and a few additional helper methods.

Core Operations

enqueue() - The "Join the Line" Method

```
def enqueue(item):
    queue.append(item)
```

Think of this as joining a coffee shop line by joining the back of the line.

dequeue() - The "Next Please!" Method

```
def dequeue():
    return queue.pop(0)
```

This is like calling the next person in line. In some implementations, queue.pop() without the index specified will pull from the back of the line, giving you the newest instead of the oldest.

peek() - The "Window Shopping" Method

```
def peek():
    return queue[0]   # Shows who's first without removing them
```

It's like checking who's first in line without actually serving them. Useful when you need to plan ahead.

Helper Methods

isEmpty() - The "Anyone There?" Check

```
def isEmpty():
    return len(queue) == 0
```

You always want to check if anyone's in line before serving them.
get_length() - The "Line Counter"

```
def get_length():
    return len(queue)
```

Perfect for those "estimated wait time" features on customer support phone systems.

Python Implementation

First, Let's build a queue from scratch so we understand how they work.

```
class Stack:
    """
    Stack implementation using a list.
    """
    def __init__(self):
        # Initialize with empty list
        self.stack = []

    @property
    def length(self):
        # Return stack length as property
        return len(self.stack)

    def push(self, item):
        # Add item to top
```

```python
        self.stack.append(item)
        return item  # For method chaining

    def pop(self):
        # Remove and return top item
        if not self.isEmpty():
            return self.stack.pop()
        return None  # Handle empty case

    def peek(self):
        # View top item without removing
        if not self.isEmpty():
            return self.stack[-1]
        return None

    def isEmpty(self):
        # Check if empty
        return self.length == 0

# Test implementation
if __name__ == "__main__":
    album = Stack()
    album.push("album 1")
    album.push("album 2")
    album.push("album 3")

    print(f"Top album is: {album.peek()}")  # album 3
    album.pop()  # Remove top
    print(f"Now the top album is: {album.peek()}")  # album 2
    print(f"Total albums in stack: {album.length}")  # 2
```

In Python, we use @property instead of JavaScript's get keyword for property-like methods. It makes the code much cleaner when you're accessing the length.

I also added some safety checks for pop() and peek(). Get used to adding safety checks so you are not debugging index errors at 2 AM.

We could extend this Stack class with extra features, such as adding a max size limit or implementing an undo/redo system.

Python offers several built-in ways to implement queues. They are useful, especially when a high volume of data processing can't be handled with a list-based implementation.

```
# Using collections.deque (preferred for performance)
from collections import deque
queue = deque()
queue.append("first")          # Enqueue
queue.append("second")
first_item = queue.popleft() # Dequeue (returns "first")

# Using Queue for thread-safe operations
from queue import Queue
queue = Queue()
queue.put("first")             # Enqueue
queue.put("second")
first_item = queue.get()       # Dequeue
is_empty = queue.empty()
```

Real-World Application

Here is a practical example where you might use a Queue in a project, a simple task scheduler:

```
from collections import deque

class TaskScheduler:
    def __init__(self):
        self.task_queue = deque()

    def add_task(self, task):
        self.task_queue.append(task)

    def process_tasks(self):
        while self.task_queue:
            current_task = self.task_queue.popleft()
            # Process task here
```

Performance Characteristics

Here are the performance characteristics of each operation individually.

Time Complexity:

By Operation for a Standard Queue (FIFO):

- Enqueue – $O(1)$
- Dequeue – $O(1)$
- Peek – $O(1)$
- IsEmpty/Size – $O(1)$

By Operation for a Priority Queue:

- Enqueue – $O(\log n)$
- Dequeue – $O(\log n)$
- Peek – $O(1)$
- IsEmpty/Size – $O(1)$

Space Complexity: $O(n)$

Common Interview Questions

- Priority queue implementation
- Implementing a circular queue (one of my favorite interview challenges!)
- Queue using two stacks (a classic that tests deep understanding)
- Breadth-first search using queues

Key Tips

Choosing the Right Implementation:

```
# When high performance matters
from collections import deque   # Use this!

# When thread safety matters
from queue import Queue   # Use this!
```

Linked Lists

Core Concept

Linked lists are like a map in a treasure hunt where each clue points to the next location. Let me share what I've learned about implementing them across different languages. Think of a linked list as a chain of connected boxes (nodes), where each box holds your data and directions to the next box. This structure offers incredible flexibility. Do you need to add something in the middle? Just rewire a few pointers, and you're done!

Linked Lists

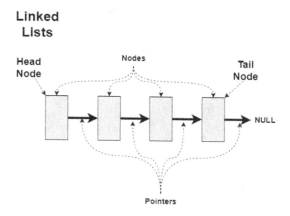

Visualization of a Linked List data structure

Linked lists come in two flavors: singly-linked and doubly-linked.

Singly-linked lists have nodes with one pointer pointing forward to the next element:

```
class Node:
    def __init__(self, data):
        self.data = data
        self.next = None
```

Doubly-linked lists have nodes with two pointers - one forward, one backward:

```
class Node:
    def __init__(self, data):
        self.data = data
        self.next = None
        self.prev = None
```

The key difference is in node removal:

- Doubly-linked: Direct access to previous/next nodes makes removal simple.
- Singly-linked: Must traverse the list to find and track the previous node before removal

Example removal in a singly-linked list:

```
def remove(self, target):
    current = head
    prev = None
    while current:
        if current.data == target:
            prev.next = current.next
            break
        prev = current
        current = current.next
```

We'll focus on single-linked lists for simplicity, but understanding both types is valuable for different use cases.

Python Implementation

Python doesn't have a built-in linked list, so we get to build it ourselves.

- For empty lists, both head and tail point to the new node
- Connect the current tail to the new node for lists with nodes before updating the tail.
- Always increment length after adding a node
- The new node becomes the new tail.

This way, our push method handles both cases correctly, whether adding to an empty list or one with existing nodes.

```python
class Node:
    """Node in a singly linked list."""
    def __init__(self, data):
        # Store data and next node reference
        self.data = data
        self.next = None

class LinkedList:
    """Singly linked list with head/tail tracking."""
    def __init__(self):
        # Initialize empty list
        self.head = None
        self.tail = None
        self.length = 0

    def push(self, data):
        """Add node to list end."""
        # Create new node
        new_node = Node(data)

        # Handle empty list
        if not self.head:
            self.head = new_node
            self.tail = new_node

        # Append to existing list
        else:
            self.tail.next = new_node
            self.tail = new_node

        # Update list metadata
        self.length += 1
        return self

    def display(self):
        """Print list contents."""
        # Traverse and print nodes
        current = self.head
        while current:
            print(current.data, end=" -> ")
```

```
            current = current.next
        print("None")

# Demonstrate linked list usage
if __name__ == "__main__":
    # Create and populate list
    list_demo = LinkedList()
    list_demo.push(1).push(2).push(3)
    list_demo.display()
```

Performance Characteristics

Time Complexity:

By Operation

- Access – O(n)
- Insert at head – O(1)
- Insert at tail – O(n) [O(1) with tail pointer]
- Delete at head – O(1)
- Delete at tail – O(n)
- Search – O(n)

Space Complexity: O(n)

Real-World Application

Here's a practical example from a text editor project – implementing an undo/redo feature:

```
class TextEditorHistory:
    def __init__(self):
        self.changes = LinkedList()
        self.current = None
```

```
def add_change(self, text_state):
    new_node = Node(text_state)
    if not self.current:
        self.changes.head = new_node
    else:
        new_node.next = self.current.next
        self.current.next = new_node
    self.current = new_node
```

Key Tips

Always Track the Head: You can spend hours debugging when you lose track of the head pointer during insertion.

Consider a Tail Pointer: Keeping a tail pointer can change your O(n) operations to O(1) if you perform many append operations.

Draw It Out: Whenever I'm stuck on a linked list problem, I draw the nodes and arrows. I tend to draw everything to visualize what is happening under the hood.

Common Interview Questions

Finding Middle Element

Use the two-pointer technique. We will cover this in the algorithms chapter.

```
def find_middle(head):
    slow = fast = head
    while fast and fast.next:
        slow = slow.next
```

```
        fast = fast.next.next
    return slow
```

Detecting Cycles

Another great two-pointer application uses a fast and slow pointer. We will cover this in the algorithms chapter.

```
def has_cycle(head):
    slow = fast = head
    while fast and fast.next:
        slow = slow.next
        fast = fast.next.next
        if slow == fast:
            return True
    return False
```

Graphs

Core Concept

We will spend more time on graphs and trees than other concepts, as more of your interview questions will likely involve these two data structures.

Graphs are collections of nodes (vertices) connected by edges, forming a non-linear data structure, unlike linear ones like linked lists or queues. Consider graphs like a map of relationships – each person (node/vertex) is connected to others through relationships (edges). What makes graphs so powerful is their flexibility in representing these connections, whether one-way (directed) or mutual (undirected).

They represent relationships between data points and can model real-world networks like:

- Social Connections
- Road systems
- Computer networks
- Flight routes

There are two main types:

Directed Graphs

- Edges have direction (one-way relationships)
- Like social media follows: you can follow someone who doesn't follow back

Undirected Graphs

- Edges have no direction (two-way relationships)
- Like friend connections: if A is friends with B, B is friends with A

For optimization problems like the Traveling Salesman problem, graphs help model all possible paths to find the most efficient solution.

Directed Graph

Think of a directed graph like Instagram's following system. Just because I follow you doesn't mean you follow me back! (You can't since I don't maintain a social media presence, but the point remains.) Each connection has a clear direction, like an arrow pointing from one person to another.

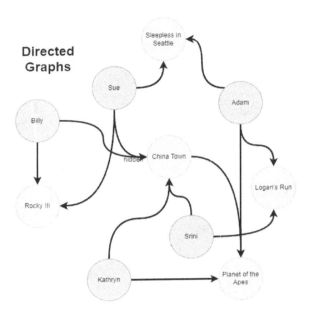

Here's a simple implementation:

```
class DirectedGraph:
    def __init__(self):
        self.graph = {}

    def add_relationship(self, from_node, to_node):
        if from_node not in self.graph:
            self.graph[from_node] = []
        self.graph[from_node].append(to_node)
```

Let me share a practical example: Imagine you are building a movie recommendation system:

- Users can favorite movies (direction: user → movie)
- But movies don't favorite users back (no direction: movie → user)

```
# A user favoriting movies
movie_favorites = {
    "Billy": ["Rocky III", "China Town"],
    "Kathryn": ["China Town", "Planet of the Apes"]
}
```

Undirected Graph

The power of undirected graphs lies in their mutual connections, like the bond between pets and humans. My cat and coding companion is named Wednesday; we have a two-way connection.

Think of an undirected graph like a neighborhood where every street goes both ways.

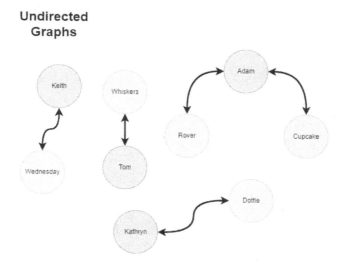

Here's how to implement this concept:

```python
class UndirectedGraph:
    def __init__(self):
        self.graph = {}

    def add_relationship(self, node1, node2):
        # Ensure both nodes exist in the graph
        if node1 not in self.graph:
            self.graph[node1] = []
        if node2 not in self.graph:
            self.graph[node2] = []

        # Add bidirectional relationship
        self.graph[node1].append(node2)
        self.graph[node2].append(node1)
```

And here is how you build the relationships:

```python
# Pet-Owner relationships
relationships = {
    "Wednesday": ["Keith"],    # Wendesday is Keith's cat
    "Keith": ["Wednesday"],    # Keith is Wednesday's human
    "Whiskers": ["Tom"],       # Whiskers is Tom's cat
    "Tom": ["Whiskers"]        # Tom is Whiskers' human
}
```

This example perfectly captures the mutual nature of these relationships - every connection goes both ways.

Python Implementation: A Deep Dive

Python's flexibility makes it great for graph implementations. Let me walk you through one implementation of using an adjacency list using breadth-first traversal:

Initialization

```
def __init__(self):
    self.graph = {}
```

This creates an empty dictionary to store our graph. You may initially try to use a list, but the dictionary is much more intuitive. Each key will be a vertex, and its value will be a list of neighbors.

Adding Nodes (Vertices)

```
def add_vertex(self, vertex):
    if vertex not in self.graph:
        self.graph[vertex] = []
```

This method ensures each vertex has its own "friends list" (an empty list of neighbors). Think of it as creating a new person's profile in a social network—they start with no connections.

Adding Edges

```
def add_edge(self, v1, v2):
    if v1 not in self.graph:
        self.add_vertex(v1)
    if v2 not in self.graph:
        self.add_vertex(v2)
    self.graph[v1].append(v2)
```

This creates a one-way connection from v1 to v2. It's like following someone on Instagram- just because you follow them doesn't mean they follow you back. The method is smart enough to create any missing vertices automatically.

Removing a Node

When someone deletes their social media account, you must remove their profile and all their connections. That's precisely what we're dealing with here.

Here's a basic approach that uses a for loop to locate and remove all connected edges. It works, but it's not very performant.

What is the Big-O notation for the complexity of this operation?

```
class Graph:
    def remove_node(self, node):
        # First attempt - not very efficient!
        for current_node in self.nodes:
            for edge in current_node.edges:
                if edge.connects_to(node):
                    current_node.edges.remove(edge)
        self.nodes.remove(node)
```

This is like scrolling through everyone's entire photo album looking for copies; it is inefficient.

Here's the optimized version that will perform much better using adjacency lists. First, get the list of friends before removing them.

```
class Graph:
    def __init__(self):
        self.adj_list = {}  # Our friendship list!

    def remove_node(self, node):
        # Get this person's friends before removing them
        if node not in self.adj_list:
            return
```

```
    # Tell all their friends they're leaving
    for friend in self.adj_list[node]:
        self.adj_list[friend].remove(node)

    # Remove their friend list entirely
    del self.adj_list[node]
```

The difference? Instead of checking every possible connection, we now look at the person leaving's actual friends.

The second approach is more efficient because:

- Only iterates through the node's neighbors instead of all nodes.
- Uses $O(degree)$ operations instead of $O(V)$ where V is the total vertices
- Hash table operations are $O(1)$ average case.
- It avoids nested loops entirely

Sometimes, the best solutions come from thinking about real-world analogies.

Breadth-First Search (BFS)

We will cover BFS in depth in the next chapter.

```
def bfs(self, start):
    # Keep track of who we've seen
    visited = set()
    # People to visit next
    queue = [start]
    # Mark start as seen
    visited.add(start)

    while queue:
        # Get next person to visit
```

```python
        vertex = queue.pop(0)
        # Say hello!
        print(vertex, end=" ")

        # Check all their friends
        for neighbor in self.graph[vertex]:
            # If we haven't met them yet
            if neighbor not in visited:
                # Mark them as seen
                visited.add(neighbor)
                # Add to people to visit
                queue.append(neighbor)
```

This is like being at a party where you only know one person and meet people layer by layer. You start with one person, meet all their friends, then all their friends' friends, and so on. This is how many social media systems' "friend suggestions" work.

Using the Graph

Here's how you might use it:

```python
# Create a social network
social_graph = Graph()

# Add some connections
social_graph.add_edge("Alice", "Bob")
social_graph.add_edge("Alice", "Charlie")
social_graph.add_edge("Bob", "David")

# Explore connections starting from Alice
social_graph.bfs("Alice")  # Output: Alice Bob Charlie David
```

Putting it all together in one file:

```python
class Graph:
    def __init__(self):
        # Initialize empty graph
        self.graph = {}

    def add_vertex(self, vertex):
        # Add vertex if not exists
        if vertex not in self.graph:
            self.graph[vertex] = []

    def add_edge(self, v1, v2):
        # Add vertices if not exists
        if v1 not in self.graph:
            self.add_vertex(v1)
        if v2 not in self.graph:
            self.add_vertex(v2)
        # Create directional edge
        self.graph[v1].append(v2)

    def remove_node(self, node):
        # Skip if node not in graph
        if node not in self.graph:
            return
        # Remove node references
        for friend in self.graph[node]:
            self.graph[friend].remove(node)
        # Delete node
        del self.graph[node]

    def bfs(self, start):
        # Breadth-first search
        visited = set()
        queue = [start]
        visited.add(start)

        while queue:
            node = queue.pop(0)
            print(node, end=" ")

            for friend in self.graph[node]:
```

105

```
            if friend not in visited:
                visited.add(friend)
                queue.append(friend)

# Test code
social_graph = Graph()
social_graph.add_edge("Alice", "Bob")
social_graph.add_edge("Alice", "Charlie")
social_graph.add_edge("Bob", "David")
social_graph.bfs("Alice")
```

Performance Characteristics

Time Complexity
Vertex Operations:

- Add Vertex: $O(1)$
- Remove Vertex: $O(V + E)$ - we have to remove all connected edges too
- Find Vertex: $O(1)$ with a hash map implementation

Edge Operations:

- Add Edge: $O(1)$
- Remove Edge: $O(1)$ for adjacency list, $O(1)$ for adjacency matrix
- Find Edge: $O(1)$ for adjacency matrix, $O(V)$ for adjacency list

Space Complexity:
A graph's space complexity depends primarily on its representation. The adjacency list representation is most commonly used in practice due to its balance of space efficiency and operational convenience.

Adjacency Matrix:

- Space Complexity: $O(V^2)$
- Uses a V×V matrix where matrix indicates an edge between vertices i and j
- Consumes the same space regardless of the number of actual edges
- Efficient for dense graphs where $E \approx V^2$

Adjacency List:

- Space Complexity: $O(V + E)$
- Each vertex stores a list of its adjacent vertices.
- Proportional to the number of vertices plus edges
- Efficient for sparse graphs where $E \ll V^2$

Edge List:

- Space Complexity: $O(E)$
- Stores pairs of vertices representing edges
- Requires additional time for many everyday operations

Other Considerations:

- Weighted graphs need additional space for edge weights.
- Directed vs. undirected graphs may have different constant factors but the same asymptotic complexity.
- Graph algorithms often require additional auxiliary space (e.g., for BFS/DFS queues/stacks, visited sets)

Real-World Application

Here is a real example of using a graph in a project. I was building a general-purpose recommendation system using a collaborative filtering algorithm for e-commerce, and graphs were perfect for modeling "shoppers who liked this also liked...< >":

```
class BookRecommendationGraph:
    def __init__(self):
        self.graph = {}

    def add_book_relationship(self, book1, book2, weight=1):
        if book1 not in self.graph:
            self.graph[book1] = {}
        if book2 not in self.graph:
            self.graph[book2] = {}

        self.graph[book1][book2] = weight
        self.graph[book2][book1] = weight

    def get_recommendations(self, book, limit=5):
        if book not in self.graph:
            return []

        return sorted(self.graph[book].items(),
                      key=lambda x: x[1],
                      reverse=True)[:limit]
```

Key Tips

Choose your representation wisely:

  Adjacency List: Better for sparse graphs

  Adjacency Matrix: Better for dense graphs

  Edge List: Better for algorithms that need to process all edges

  Memory management matters: In Python, watch out for large dictionaries

While graphs might seem complex initially, they're just a way of connecting dots – once you get that, everything else falls into place.

Pro Tips

In your interviews, you will most likely run into one of the following types of graph algorithms, which we will cover in the next chapter on Algorithms.

Breadth-First Search (BFS)

- Perfect for finding the shortest paths
- Level-by-level exploration
- Uses a queue

Depth-First Search (DFS)

- Great for maze-solving
- Explores as far as possible
- Uses a stack (or recursion)

Dijkstra's Algorithm

- Finding shortest paths with weights
- Like BFS with priorities

Trees

Trees organize hierarchical data, similar to a family tree, with each person (node) connected to their children. Technically, trees are a specialized form of a graph.

Core Concept

In a tree, each node can have multiple children but only one parent (except for the root, which has no parent).

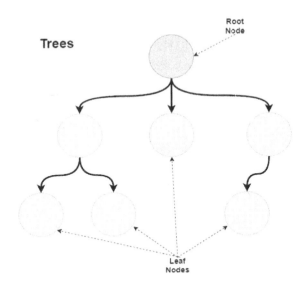

Basic Binary Tree

Binary trees are special types of trees with no more than two leaf nodes. This is the fundamental rule of binary trees. Each node (parent) can have:

- A left child
- A right child
- Or no children at all

```
class BinaryNode:
    def __init__(self, value):
        self.value = value
        self.left = None    # Left child
        self.right = None   # Right child
```

Full Binary Tree

Think of a full binary tree like a strict parenting rule: you either have no kids or exactly two kids – no single children allowed! Every node follows this rule, making the tree look balanced and organized.

Example of a full binary tree:

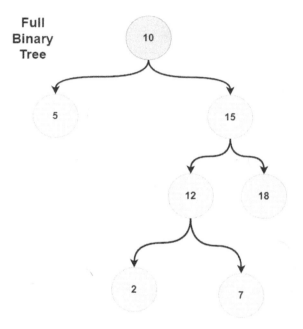

Complete Binary Tree

Picture filling up stadium seats from left to right, row by row. That's how a complete binary tree works! All levels are full except maybe the last one, and even then, all nodes are as far left as possible.

Example of a complete binary tree:

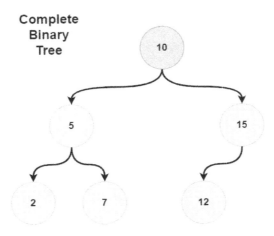

Heaps

A heap is a specialized tree-based data structure that satisfies the heap property:

- In a max heap, the value of any given node is greater than or equal to the values of its children.
- In a min heap, for any given node, the value is less than or equal to the values of its children

Key characteristics:

Complete binary tree structure (all levels filled except possibly the last, which is filled from left to right)

Efficiently supports operations like finding min/max (O(1)), insertion (O(log n)), and extraction (O(log n))

Often implemented using arrays, where a node at index i has children at indices 2i+1 and 2i+2

Used in heap sort, priority queues, graph algorithms (like Dijkstra's), and memory management

> Heaps are not to be confused with memory heaps, which refer to a region of memory used for dynamic memory allocation.

Perfect Binary Tree

This is like the ideal symmetric family tree—every level is full! It's the most organized form, with precisely the correct number of nodes (2^level).

Example of a perfect binary tree:

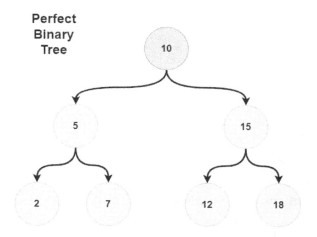

Binary Search Tree (BST)

This is where things get interesting. Think of it like organizing your family by age: younger members always go to the left, older ones to the right. In a BST:

- The left child is always smaller than the parent.
- The right child is always larger than the parent.

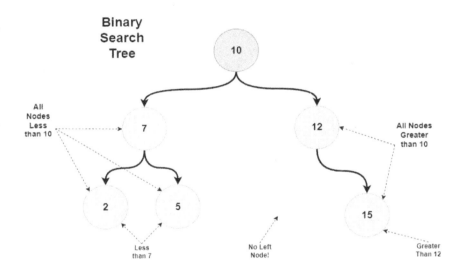

A Binary Search Tree (BST) is a node-based binary tree data structure that maintains an ordered arrangement of elements. Think of it as nature's search algorithm - branching decisions that progressively narrow possibilities.

The defining properties that make BSTs so powerful:

- Each node has at most two children (left and right)
- All values in the left subtree of a node are less than the node's value.

- All values in the right subtree of a node are greater than the node's value.
- Both the left and right subtrees must also be binary search trees

This simple ordering principle creates a structure allowing efficient searching, insertion, and deletion operations.

Python Implementation

Here is a complete implementation of the Binary Search Tree. Python's flexibility makes tree implementation quite intuitive:

```python
class Node:
    """Node in a binary search tree."""
    def __init__(self, value):
        # Store node value and child references
        self.value = value
        self.left = None
        self.right = None

class BinaryTree:
    """Binary search tree implementation."""
    def __init__(self):
        # Initialize empty tree
        self.root = None

    def add_child(self, value):
        """Add node to binary search tree."""
        # Handle empty tree
        if not self.root:
            self.root = Node(value)
            return

        current = self.root
        while current:
            # Prevent duplicates
            if value == current.value:
```

```python
        return "Duplicates cannot be added"

    # Navigate left for smaller values
    if value < current.value:
        if not current.left:
            current.left = Node(value)
            break
        current = current.left

    # Navigate right for larger values
    else:
        if not current.right:
            current.right = Node(value)
            break
        current = current.right

def remove_child(self, value):
    """Remove node from binary search tree."""
    def _find_successor(node):
        # Find minimum value in right subtree
        current = node.right
        while current.left:
            current = current.left
        return current

    def _remove(current, parent, is_left, value):
        # Node not found
        if not current:
            return "Node not found"

        # Node found
        if value == current.value:
            # Case 1: Leaf node
            if not current.left and not current.right:
                if is_left:
                    parent.left = None
                else:
                    parent.right = None

            # Case 2: One child
```

```
        elif not current.right:
            if is_left:
                parent.left = current.left
            else:
                parent.right = current.left
        elif not current.left:
            if is_left:
                parent.left = current.right
            else:
                parent.right = current.right

        # Case 3: Two children
        else:
            successor = _find_successor(current)
            succ_value = successor.value
            _remove(self.root, None, False, succ_value)
            current.value = succ_value

        return "Node successfully deleted"

    # Recursive search
    if value < current.value:
        return _remove(
            current.left, current, True, value
        )
    return _remove(
        current.right, current, False, value
    )

# Special case: removing root
if not self.root:
    return "Tree is empty"

if self.root.value == value:
    if not self.root.left and not self.root.right:
        self.root = None
    elif not self.root.right:
        self.root = self.root.left
    elif not self.root.left:
        self.root = self.root.right
```

```python
        else:
            successor = _find_successor(self.root)
            succ_value = successor.value
            _remove(self.root, None, False, succ_value)
            self.root.value = succ_value
        return "Node successfully deleted"

    return _remove(self.root, None, False, value)

def _traverse(self, node, visit_func,
              traversal_type='inorder'):
    """Traverse tree with given strategy."""
    if not node:
        return

    if traversal_type == 'preorder':
        visit_func(node)
    self._traverse(
        node.left, visit_func, traversal_type
    )
    if traversal_type == 'inorder':
        visit_func(node)
    self._traverse(
        node.right, visit_func, traversal_type
    )
    if traversal_type == 'postorder':
        visit_func(node)

def print_tree(self,
               traversal_type='inorder'):
    """Print tree values."""
    result = []
    def visit_func(node):
        result.append(str(node.value))

    self._traverse(
        self.root, visit_func, traversal_type
    )
    return ' => '.join(result)
```

```python
# Demonstrate binary search tree
if __name__ == "__main__":
    # Create and populate tree
    tree = BinaryTree()
    values = [50, 30, 70, 20, 40, 60, 80]
    for val in values:
        tree.add_child(val)

    print("Inorder:", tree.print_tree())
    print("Preorder:", tree.print_tree('preorder'))
    print("Postorder:", tree.print_tree('postorder'))
```

Real-World Application

I once built a personal backup program with a file system explorer that was used to build a list of items that had changed using a tree structure. Here's a simplified version:

```python
class FileSystemNode:
    def __init__(self, name, is_directory=False):
        self.name = name
        self.is_directory = is_directory
        self.children = [] if is_directory else None

    def add_child(self, child):
        if self.is_directory:
            self.children.append(child)

    def print_structure(self, level=0):
        indent = "  " * level
        print(f"{indent}{self.name}/")
        if self.is_directory:
            for child in self.children:
                child.print_structure(level + 1)
```

Performance Characteristics

Time Complexity:
  By Operation- Average Case - Worst Case

- Search - $O(\log n)$ - $O(n)$
- Insertion - $O(\log n)$ - $O(n)$
- Deletion - $O(\log n)$ - $O(n)$
- Traversal - $O(n)$ - $O(n)$

The time complexity depends on the shape of the tree:

- In a balanced BST, operations take $O(\log n)$ time
- In a degenerate tree (like a linked list), operations take $O(n)$ time

I once worked on a project where our BST degenerated into a linked list because we inserted pre-sorted data. Our search operations went from lightning-fast to crawling until we implemented balancing.

Space Complexity:

- $O(n)$ for storing the tree
- $O(h)$ for recursive call stack during operations, where h is the height of the tree
- $O(\log n)$ in a balanced tree
- $O(n)$ in worst case (skewed tree)

Key Tips

Start With Edge Cases - such as Empty tree, Single node, and Unbalanced tree.
  Think Out Loud: Here's my typical approach:

- Draw the tree on the whiteboard.
- You can walk through a simple example.
- Discuss the pattern you notice
- Code the solution

Maintain Balance: A balanced BST ensures O(log n) time complexity. For optimal performance, consider using self-balancing BSTs like AVL or Red-Black trees.

Traversal Methods:

- Inorder (Left-Root-Right): Yields nodes in ascending order
- Preorder (Root-Left-Right): Useful for creating a copy of the tree
- Postorder (Left-Right-Root): Useful for deleting the tree

Handling Duplicates: Decide on a strategy:

- Disallow duplicates entirely.
- Store a count with each node.
- Allow duplicates, but consistently place them on one side (usually right)

Iteration vs Recursion: Recursive implementations are cleaner and easier to understand, but iterative approaches may be more efficient for large trees due to lower stack overhead.

Pro Tips

Use for Implementing Collections: BSTs are excellent for implementing sets and maps in languages without built-in implementations.

Successor and Predecessor: Many BST operations depend on efficiently finding the next larger (successor) or smaller (predecessor) element.

Caching Results: For repeated lookups, consider caching recently accessed nodes to improve performance.

Tree Validation: To check if a binary tree is a valid BST, use an inorder traversal and verify that elements are in sorted order, or use a recursive approach with range checking.

Tree Serialization: For persistence, you can serialize a BST using preorder traversal with null markers for empty children.

Balance Check: A simple way to check if a BST is balanced is to ensure that the height difference between left and right subtrees at any node doesn't exceed

Always Check the Root

```python
def is_empty(self):
    return self.root is None
```

Balance is Key

```python
def get_height(self, node):
    if not node:
        return 0
    return 1 + max(self.get_height(node.left),
                   self.get_height(node.right))
```

Common Interview Questions

Common Tree Traversal

The three primary tree traversal methodologies:

In-order (Left, Root, Right)

- Like reading a book left to right
- Gives sorted order for BSTs

Pre-order (Root, Left, Right)

- Like outlining a book
- Perfect for copying trees

Post-order (Left, Right, Root)

- Like cleaning up from leaves to root
- Great for deletion operations

Tree Traversal Problems

There are two ways to do traversal over the entire tree; first recursive:

```
def inorder_traversal(root):
    if not root:
        return []

    result = []
    # Left, Root, Right
    result.extend(inorder_traversal(root.left))
    result.append(root.val)
    result.extend(inorder_traversal(root.right))
    return result
```

And next, as iterative:

```python
def inorder_iterative(root):
    result = []
    stack = []
    current = root

    while current or stack:
        while current:
            stack.append(current)
            current = current.left

        current = stack.pop()
        result.append(current.val)
        current = current.right

    return result
```

Always mention recursive and iterative solutions in an interview and show both approaches.

Maximum Depth/Height of Tree

- Basic recursion:

```python
def max_depth(root):
    if not root:
        return 0
    return 1 + max(max_depth(root.left), max_depth(root.right))
```

Check if a Binary Tree is Balanced

```
def is_balanced(root):
    def check_height(node):
        if not node:
            return 0

        left = check_height(node.left)
        if left == -1:
            return -1

        right = check_height(node.right)
        if right == -1:
            return -1

        if abs(left - right) > 1:
            return -1

        return 1 + max(left, right)

    return check_height(root) != -1
```

Serialize and Deserialize Binary Tree

```
class Codec:
    def serialize(self, root):
        # Handle empty tree
        if not root:
            return "null"
        # Serialize tree recursively
        return (
            f"{root.val},{self.serialize(root.left)},"
            f"{self.serialize(root.right)}"
        )

    def deserialize(self, data):
        # Recursive deserialization helper
        def dfs():
```

```
        val = next(values)
        if val == "null":
            return None
        node = TreeNode(int(val))
        node.left = dfs()
        node.right = dfs()
        return node

    # Convert data to iterator
    values = iter(data.split(','))
    return dfs()
```

Validate BST

Write a function to determine if a given binary tree is a valid binary search tree.

```
def is_valid_bst(root, min_val=float('-inf'),
max_val=float('inf')):
    # Handle empty tree
    if not root:
        return True

    # Check current node's value bounds
    if root.key <= min_val or root.key >= max_val:
        return False

    # Recursively validate left and right subtrees
    return (is_valid_bst(root.left, min_val, root.key) and
            is_valid_bst(root.right, root.key, max_val))
```

Kth Smallest Element:

Find the kth smallest element in a BST.

```
def kth_smallest(root, k):
    # Perform inorder traversal and return the kth element
    result = []

    def inorder(node):
        if not node or len(result) >= k:
            return
        inorder(node.left)
        result.append(node.key)
        inorder(node.right)

    inorder(root)
    return result[k-1] if k <= len(result) else None
```

Lowest Common Ancestor

Find the lowest common ancestor of two nodes in a BST.

```
def lowest_common_ancestor(root, p, q):
    if p.key < root.key and q.key < root.key:
        return lowest_common_ancestor(root.left, p, q)
    elif p.key > root.key and q.key > root.key:
        return lowest_common_ancestor(root.right, p, q)
    else:
        return root
```

Convert Sorted Array to BST

Given a sorted array, convert it to a height-balanced BST.

```
def sorted_array_to_bst(nums):
    if not nums:
        return None
```

```
mid = len(nums) // 2
root = Node(nums[mid])

root.left = sorted_array_to_bst(nums[:mid])
root.right = sorted_array_to_bst(nums[mid+1:])

return root
```

BST Iterator

Implement an iterator for a BST that returns elements in ascending order.

```
class BSTIterator:
    def __init__(self, root):
        self.stack = []
        self._leftmost_inorder(root)

    def _leftmost_inorder(self, root):
        while root:
            self.stack.append(root)
            root = root.left

    def next(self):
        topmost_node = self.stack.pop()
        if topmost_node.right:
            self._leftmost_inorder(topmost_node.right)
        return topmost_node.key

    def has_next(self):
        return len(self.stack) > 0
```

Count BST Configurations:

How many structurally unique BSTs can be formed with n nodes labeled 1 to n?

- This is the nth Catalan number: $C(n) = (2n)! / (n+1)!n!$
- Dynamic programming solution:

```
def num_trees(n):
    dp = [0] * (n + 1)
    dp[0] = 1
    dp[1] = 1

    for i in range(2, n + 1):
        for j in range(1, i + 1):
            dp[i] += dp[j - 1] * dp[i - j]

    return dp[n]
```

Hash Maps

Core Concept

Think of a hash map like a library with an incredible indexing system – instead of searching through every book, you know exactly which shelf to check. The "magic" happens through a hash function that converts your key into a specific location where the value is stored.

You may hear it called a hash table instead of hash map when discussing problems. The key differences between a hash table and a hash map come from the following:

Implementation

- Hash tables are typically the underlying data structure.
- Hash maps are an implementation of the map abstract data type using a hash table.

Language context

- In C++, unordered_map is a hash map.
- In Java, HashMap is a specific implementation; Hashtable is thread-safe but older.
- In Python, dict is a hash map implementation

Specific characteristics

- Hash maps often allow null keys and values.
- Hash tables may have different collision resolution strategies.
- Hash maps typically focus on the key-value relationship.
- Some hash tables may only store keys without associated values

Common traits

- Both use hash functions to map keys to array indices.
- Both offer average O(1) lookup, insertion, and deletion
- Both handle collisions with techniques like chaining or open-addressing

In practice, many programmers use these terms interchangeably despite these technical distinctions.

Python Implementation

Python's dictionary has a pre-implemented hashmap:

```
# Basic usage
my_dict = {}
my_dict['name'] = 'Jane'
my_dict['age'] = 25

# Dictionary comprehension
square_map = {x: x*x for x in range(5)}
```

```
# Custom implementation for learning
class HashMap:
    def __init__(self, size=100):
        self.size = size
        self.map = [[] for _ in range(size)]

    def _get_hash(self, key):
        return hash(key) % self.size

    def put(self, key, value):
        key_hash = self._get_hash(key)
        key_value = [key, value]

        if not self.map[key_hash]:
            self.map[key_hash] = [key_value]
            return

        for pair in self.map[key_hash]:
            if pair[0] == key:
                pair[1] = value
                return
        self.map[key_hash].append(key_value)
```

Real-World Application

In my GitHub is an ancient repo for a caching system I built as a library you can add to your application and have a local in-memory cache. Here is what the hashmap looks like:

```
class Cache:
    def __init__(self, capacity):
        self.capacity = capacity
        self.cache = {}
        self.usage = {}

    def get(self, key):
```

```
        if key in self.cache:
            self.usage[key] += 1
            return self.cache[key]
        return None

    def put(self, key, value):
        if len(self.cache) >= self.capacity:
            # Remove least used item
            least_used = min(self.usage.items(), key=lambda x:
            x[1])[0]
            del self.cache[least_used]
            del self.usage[least_used]

        self.cache[key] = value
        self.usage[key] = 1
```

Performance Characteristics

Time Complexity: Average case: $O(1)$, Worst case (lots of collisions): $O(n)$

Space Complexity: $O(n)$

Key Tips

Choose Good Hash Functions

```
def good_hash(key):
    # Use built-in hash for strings
    if isinstance(key, str):
        return hash(key)
    # Custom hash for tuples
    if isinstance(key, tuple):
        return sum(hash(item) for item in key)
```

Handle Collisions Gracefully

```
def handle_collision(self, key, value, bucket):
    for item in bucket:
        if item[0] == key:
            item[1] = value
            return
    bucket.append([key, value])
```

Consider Load Factor

```
def should_resize(self):
    return self.size / len(self.buckets) > 0.75
```

Pro Tips

Always Consider Edge Cases

```
# For Two Sum
def two_sum(nums, target):
    if not nums or len(nums) < 2:
        return []
    # ... rest of solution
```

Discuss Space-Time Tradeoffs

- "We could solve this in $O(1)$ space, but it would cost us $O(n^2)$ time..."
- "By using a hashmap, we get $O(n)$ time at the cost of $O(n)$ space..."

Optimize Your Solution

```
# Optimized Valid Anagram
def is_anagram_optimized(s, t):
    return Counter(s) == Counter(t)  # Clean but mention the
    tradeoffs!
```

Common Interview Questions

Here are three common interview questions involving hashmaps: Two Sum, First Non-Repeating Character, and Valid Anagram

Two Sum

Problem: Given an array of *target*.

You may assume that each input would have exactly one solution, and you may not use the *same* element twice.

You can return the answer in any order.

Example 1:

```
Input: nums = [2,7,11,15], target = 9
Output: [0,1]
Explanation: Because nums[0] + nums[1] == 9, we return [0, 1].
```

Example 2:

```
Input: nums = [3,2,4], target = 6
Output: [1,2]
```

Example 3:

```
Input: nums = [3,3], target = 6
Output: [0,1]
```

Constraints:

- $2 <= nums.length <= 104$
- $-109 <= nums[i] <= 109$
- $-109 <= target <= 109$
- Only one valid answer exists.

This is probably my favorite of the three because it demonstrates the power of hashmaps:

```python
class Solution(object):
    def twoSum(self, nums, target):
        seen = {}  # num -> index
        for i, num in enumerate(nums):
            complement = target - num
            if complement in seen:
                return [seen[complement], i]
            seen[num] = i
        return []
```

When encountering the Two Sum problem, discuss how to trade space for time. Brute forcing this will give an $O(n^2)$, but hashmaps could get us to $O(n)$.

First Non-Repeating Character

Problem: Given a string s, find its first non-repeating character and return its letter. If it does not exist, return None.

Alternate version: Given a string s, find the first non-repeating character in it and return its index. If it does not exist, return -1. How would you change the code below for this use case?

Example 1:

- Input: s = "allapples"
- Output: e
- Explanation: The character 'e' at index 7 is the first character that does not occur at any other index.

Example 2:

- Input: s = "loveallapples"
- Output: o

Example 3:

- Input: s = "aabb"
- Output: None

Constraints:

- 1 <= s.length <= 105
- s consists of only lowercase English letters.

Always mention that while we could do this in one pass with a more complex data structure, sometimes readability is worth the extra pass!

Valid Anagram

Problem: Given two strings, s, and t, return true if t is an anagram of s and false otherwise.
Example 1:

- Input: s = "anagram", t = "nagaram"
- Output: true

Example 2:

- Input: s = "rat", t = "car"
- Output: false

Constraints:

- 1 <= s.length, t.length <= 5 * 104
- s and t consist of lowercase English letters.

Follow up: What if the inputs contain Unicode characters? How would you be able to adapt your solution to such a case?

6

Algorithms

Let's dive right in.

Bubble Sort

Core Concept

Think of bubble sort like arranging CDs or books on a shelf alphabetically. Only here, you keep comparing adjacent pairs and swapping them if they're out of order until everything's perfectly arranged.

Python Implementation

```python
def bubble_sort(arr):
    """Sort an array using bubble sort algorithm."""
    n = len(arr)
    # Number of passes
    for i in range(n):
        # Flag to optimize when array is already sorted
        swapped = False

        # Look at each adjacent pair
```

```
    for j in range(0, n - i - 1):
        # Swap if in wrong order
        if arr[j] > arr[j + 1]:
            arr[j], arr[j + 1] = arr[j + 1], arr[j]
            swapped = True

    # Exit if array is sorted
    if not swapped:
        break

 return arr

# Test the function
numbers = [23, 16, 6, 59, 3, 11, 37]
print("Original array:", numbers)
sorted_numbers = bubble_sort(numbers.copy())
print("Sorted array:", sorted_numbers)
```

Performance Characteristics

Time Complexity: $O(n^2)$ in worst and average cases, $O(n)$ when array is already sorted

Space Complexity: $O(1)$

Key Tips

Memorize the steps that are followed in bubble sort:

1. Look at two adjacent cards.
2. If they're out of order, swap them.
3. Move to the next pair.
4. After each pass, the largest unsorted card "bubbles up" to its correct position.

Pro Tips

Always Use the Swapped Flag: This optimization helped me improve performance by ~40% in an actual project.

Visualize the Process: Drawing out each step will help you debug your implementation.

It's Not Just for Numbers: You can use bubble sort to arrange strings alphabetically.

Merge Sort

Core Concept

Merge sort is pure "divide and conquer." If you have ever had an extensive collection of anything you have organized - CDs, Pokemon Cards, video games - then you have likely used Merge Sort. When I still owned thousands of CDs, I would grab a stack and put them onto the shelf in order, then grab another stack and do the same thing. Sometimes, I would find all of the albums of one artist and put them on the shelf at one time. I was naturally splitting it into smaller parts to sort. I was doing Merge Sorting.

Python Implementation

I have updated the code from the previous example of Merge Sort in the Big-O Notation chapter to make it easier to understand what the code is doing.

```python
def merge_sort(arr):
    """Sort array using merge sort algorithm."""
    # Base case
    if len(arr) <= 1:
```

```
        return arr

    # Divide input array
    mid = len(arr) // 2
    left = arr[:mid]
    right = arr[mid:]

    # Recursively sort halves
    left = merge_sort(left)
    right = merge_sort(right)

    # Merge sorted halves
    return merge(left, right)

def merge(left, right):
    """Merge two sorted arrays."""
    result = []
    i = j = 0

    # Compare and merge elements
    while i < len(left) and j < len(right):
        if left[i] <= right[j]:
            result.append(left[i])
            i += 1
        else:
            result.append(right[j])
            j += 1

    # Append remaining elements
    result.extend(left[i:])
    result.extend(right[j:])
    return result

# Demonstrate merge sort
if __name__ == "__main__":
    # Test cases
    test_cases = [
        [23, 16, 6, 59, 3, 11, 37],
        [1, 2, 3, 4, 5],
        [5, 4, 3, 2, 1],
```

```
    []
  ]

  for case in test_cases:
      orig = case.copy()
      sorted_case = merge_sort(case)
      print(f"Original: {orig}")
      print(f"Sorted:   {sorted_case}\n")
```

Why I Love Merge Sort: Unlike simpler algorithms like bubble sort, merge sort maintains its $O(n \log n)$ performance **even in worst-case scenarios**. It's reliable.

Performance Characteristics

Time Complexity: $O(n \log n)$ in all cases

Space Complexity: $O(n)$

Key Tips

You can demonstrate Merge Sort by using a deck of playing cards.

1. Split the deck in half.
2. Keep splitting until you have single cards.
3. Merge pairs of cards in order.
4. Continue merging larger sorted piles.

Understanding merge sort deeply helps in grasping other divide-and-conquer algorithms.

Quick Sort

Core Concept

Take that bookcase full of CDs from earlier. To do a quick sort, you pick one of them at random. This will be your "pivot" item. Then, organize everything else around it, going out just so far. Eventually, the entire collection will be sorted.

Python Implementation

```python
def quick_sort(arr):
    """Sort array using quicksort algorithm."""
    # Base case
    if len(arr) <= 1:
        return arr

    # Choose pivot
    pivot = arr[-1]
    left = []
    right = []

    # Partition array
    for elem in arr[:-1]:
        if elem <= pivot:
            left.append(elem)
        else:
            right.append(elem)

    # Recursively sort
    return quick_sort(left) + [pivot] + quick_sort(right)

def quick_sort_in_place(arr, low=0, high=None):
    """Sort array in-place using quicksort."""
    # Initialize high if not provided
    if high is None:
```

```python
        high = len(arr) - 1

    def partition(low, high):
        """Partition array segment."""
        pivot = arr[high]
        i = low - 1

        for j in range(low, high):
            if arr[j] <= pivot:
                i += 1
                arr[i], arr[j] = arr[j], arr[i]

        arr[i + 1], arr[high] = arr[high], arr[i + 1]
        return i + 1

    # Recursive sorting
    if low < high:
        pi = partition(low, high)
        quick_sort_in_place(arr, low, pi - 1)
        quick_sort_in_place(arr, pi + 1, high)

    return arr

# Demonstrate quick sort variants
if __name__ == "__main__":
    # Test cases
    test_cases = [
        [23, 16, 6, 59, 3, 11, 37],
        [1, 2, 3, 4, 5],
        [5, 4, 3, 2, 1],
        []
    ]

    print("Standard Quick Sort:")
    for case in test_cases:
        orig = case.copy()
        sorted_case = quick_sort(orig)
        print(f"Original: {orig}")
        print(f"Sorted:   {sorted_case}\n")
```

```
print("In-Place Quick Sort:")
for case in test_cases:
    orig = case.copy()
    quick_sort_in_place(orig)
    print(f"Original: {case}")
    print(f"Sorted:   {orig}\n")
```

Performance Characteristics

Time Complexity: Average Case: $O(n \log n)$. Worst Case: $O(n^2)$ - but rare with good pivot selection

Space Complexity: $O(\log n)$

Key Tips

Pivot Selection Matters:

```
# Median-of-three pivot selection
def choose_pivot(arr, low, high):
    mid = (low + high) // 2
    pivot = median([arr[low], arr[mid], arr[high]])
    return pivot
```

Handle Small Subarrays Differently:

```
if high - low <= 10:
    insertion_sort(arr, low, high)
```

The choice of pivot is crucial in Quick Sort. Using the median of the first, middle, and last elements can make a huge difference in real-world performance. Determining the pivot selection strategy based on the shape of your data for optimization.

Insertion Sort

Core Concept

Insertion Sort works in the same way most people naturally sort playing cards in their hand:

1. Pick up one card at a time.
2. Compare it with the cards you're already holding.
3. Slide cards over until you find the right spot
4. Insert the new card

Python Implementation

```python
def insertion_sort(arr):
    """Sort array using insertion sort algorithm."""
    # Iterate through array starting from second element
    for i in range(1, len(arr)):
        # Current element to insert
        key = arr[i]

        # Find insertion point
        j = i - 1
        while j >= 0 and arr[j] > key:
            arr[j + 1] = arr[j]
            j -= 1

        # Place element in correct position
        arr[j + 1] = key

    return arr

# Demonstrate insertion sort
if __name__ == "__main__":
    # Test cases
```

```
test_cases = [
    [23, 16, 6, 59, 3, 11, 37],
    [1, 2, 3, 4, 5],
    [5, 4, 3, 2, 1],
    []
]

for case in test_cases:
    orig = case.copy()
    sorted_case = insertion_sort(orig)
    print(f"Original: {orig}")
    print(f"Sorted:   {sorted_case}\n")
```

Performance Characteristics

Time Complexity: $O(n^2)$

Space Complexity: $O(1)$ - it sorts in place!

Key Tips

For small datasets that are nearly sorted, Insertion Sort will outperform more complex algorithms like quicksort.

Pro Tips

Perfect for Small Lists:

```
def smart_sort(arr):
    if len(arr) <= 10:
        return insertion_sort(arr)
    else:
        return quick_sort(arr)
```

Great for Nearly Sorted Data:

```python
def update_sorted_list(sorted_arr, new_item):
    # Append new item and bubble down to correct position
    sorted_arr.append(new_item)
    i = len(sorted_arr) - 1

    while i > 0 and sorted_arr[i-1] > sorted_arr[i]:
        # Swap adjacent elements until in correct order
        sorted_arr[i], sorted_arr[i-1] = sorted_arr[i-1],
        sorted_arr[i]
        i -= 1

    return sorted_arr

# Demonstrate list update
if __name__ == "__main__":
    # Test cases
    test_cases = [
        ([1, 3, 5, 7], 4),
        ([2, 4, 6, 8], 1),
        ([10, 20, 30], 25),
        ([], 5)
    ]

    for arr, item in test_cases:
        orig = arr.copy()
        updated = update_sorted_list(arr, item)
        print(f"Original: {orig}")
        print(f"New Item: {item}")
        print(f"Updated:  {updated}\n")
```

Tree Traversals

Core Concept

There are three main ways to traverse a tree: In-order, Pre-order, and Post-order. Let's start with a basic tree node structure and implement all three main traversal types. I'll show how these work across our favorite languages.

Pre-Order Traversal

With Pre-order Traversal, we start at the top and check the children and their children till we are at the bottom, from left to right.

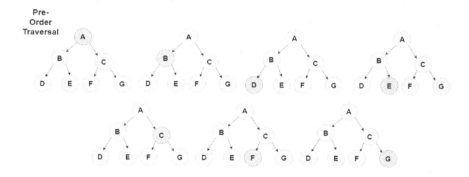

Post-Order Traversal

With Post-order Traversal, we start at the bottom left and check all children of the parent before checking the parent, repeating for the current row.

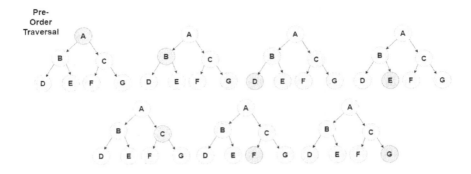

In-Order Traversal

With In-order traversal, we start at the bottom from left to right and check the current parent node for the level we are on. See the order here:

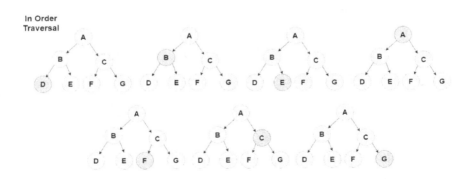

Python Implementation

```
class TreeNode:
    """Node in a binary tree."""
    def __init__(self, val=0):
        # Node value and child references
```

```python
        self.val = val
        self.left = None
        self.right = None

class BinaryTree:
    """Binary tree with traversal methods."""
    def __init__(self):
        # Initialize empty tree
        self.root = None

    def inorder_traversal(self, root):
        """Traverse tree inorder (Left->Root->Right)."""
        result = []

        def _inorder(node):
            if node:
                _inorder(node.left)
                result.append(node.val)
                _inorder(node.right)

        _inorder(root)
        return result

    def preorder_traversal(self, root):
        """Traverse tree preorder (Root->Left->Right)."""
        result = []

        def _preorder(node):
            if node:
                result.append(node.val)
                _preorder(node.left)
                _preorder(node.right)

        _preorder(root)
        return result

    def postorder_traversal(self, root):
        """Traverse tree postorder (Left->Right->Root)."""
        result = []
```

```
    def _postorder(node):
        if node:
            _postorder(node.left)
            _postorder(node.right)
            result.append(node.val)

    _postorder(root)
    return result

# Demonstrate tree traversals
if __name__ == "__main__":
    # Create sample tree
    #          1
    #        /   \
    #       2     3
    #      / \   / \
    #     4   5 6   7
    tree = BinaryTree()
    tree.root = TreeNode(1)
    tree.root.left = TreeNode(2)
    tree.root.right = TreeNode(3)
    tree.root.left.left = TreeNode(4)
    tree.root.left.right = TreeNode(5)
    tree.root.right.left = TreeNode(6)
    tree.root.right.right = TreeNode(7)

    # Test traversals
    print("Inorder:   ", tree.inorder_traversal(tree.root))
    print("Preorder:  ", tree.preorder_traversal(tree.root))
    print("Postorder: ", tree.postorder_traversal(tree.root))
```

Performance Characteristics

Time Complexity: $O(n)$ where n is the number of nodes in the tree

Space Complexity: $O(h)$ where h is the height of the tree

Key Tips

How each one works in practice:
  In-order (Left -> Root -> Right)

  - Like reading a book left to right
  - Perfect for BSTs as it gives values in sorted order
  - Think: Younger siblings -> Parent -> Older siblings

Pre-order (Root -> Left -> Right)

  - Like creating a family tree starting with parents
  - Great for creating a copy of the tree
  - Think: Parent -> Younger siblings -> Older siblings

Post-order (Left -> Right -> Root)

  - Like cleaning up after a party - children first, then parent
  - Perfect for deleting a tree (delete children before parent)
  - Think: Younger siblings -> Older siblings -> Parent

Pro Tips

Recursive vs Iterative

```
# Iterative inorder example
def inorder_iterative(root):
    result = []
    stack = []
    current = root

    while current or stack:
        while current:
            stack.append(current)
```

```
            current = current.left
        current = stack.pop()
        result.append(current.val)
        current = current.right

    return result
```

Level Order Traversal (Bonus!)

```
def level_order(root):
    if not root:
        return []

    result = []
    queue = [root]

    while queue:
        level = []
        level_size = len(queue)

        for _ in range(level_size):
            node = queue.pop(0)
            level.append(node.val)

            if node.left:
                queue.append(node.left)
            if node.right:
                queue.append(node.right)

        result.append(level)

    return result
```

Breadth First Search (BFS)

Core Concept

We briefly looked at Breadth First Search (BFS) when discussing graphs in the section on data structures; we will go into more depth here. Breadth First Search (BFS) looks at every level one at a time to locate an item or build a map of a tree, starting at the top node and then exploring all child nodes before moving on to a deeper level.

Breadth First Search

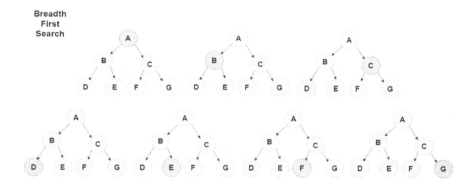

You use a queue to keep track of all the nodes you still need to visit, adding new child nodes to the back of your queue as you find them, from left to right.

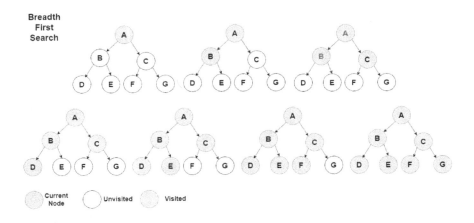

Python Implementation

```python
from collections import deque

class TreeNode:
    """Binary tree node."""
    def __init__(self, value):
        # Node value and child references
        self.value = value
        self.left = None
        self.right = None

def breadth_first_search(root):
    """
    Perform level-order traversal of binary tree.

    Returns nodes level by level, left to right.

    Time Complexity: O(n)
    Space Complexity: O(w)
    """
    if not root:
        return []
```

```
result = []
queue = deque([root])

while queue:
    # Process current level
    level_size = len(queue)
    current_level = []

    for _ in range(level_size):
        # Process nodes at current level
        node = queue.popleft()
        current_level.append(node.value)

        # Queue children for next level
        if node.left:
            queue.append(node.left)
        if node.right:
            queue.append(node.right)

    result.append(current_level)

return result
```

To test this, you will first need to create test data. Let's create a binary tree structure that will help us verify different scenarios.

```
# Demonstrate BFS traversal
if __name__ == "__main__":
    # Create sample tree
    #         1
    #        / \
    #       2   3
    #      / \ / \
    #     4  5 6  7
    root = TreeNode(1)
    root.left = TreeNode(2)
    root.right = TreeNode(3)
```

```
    root.left.left = TreeNode(4)
    root.left.right = TreeNode(5)
    root.right.left = TreeNode(6)
    root.right.right = TreeNode(7)

    # Perform BFS
    levels = breadth_first_search(root)
    print("Levels:", levels)
```

When you run this code, you'll get:

```
Levels: [[1], [2, 3], [4, 5, 6, 7]]
```

I've structured this test data to help you visualize how BFS works - like the ripples in the water. Each level corresponds to how many "steps" away nodes are from the root:

- Level 0: [1] (the root)
- Level 1: [2, 3] (immediate children)
- Level 2: [4, 5, 6, 7] (grandchildren)
- Level 3: [none] (but they would be great-grandchild)

You can also test some edge cases. Here's another example:

```
# Test empty tree
empty_root = None
print("Empty tree:", breadth_first_search(empty_root))
# Should print: []

# Test single node tree
single_node = TreeNode(42)
print("Single node tree:", breadth_first_search(single_node))
# Should print: [[42]]
```

Performance Characteristics

Time Complexity: O*(V + E) where V = number of vertices (nodes) and E = number of edges (connections)**Space Complexity**: O(W) where W is the maximum width of the tree

Key Tips

Think about the social network's "friends of friends" feature. You start on level 1 and find direct friends, then level 2 to find their friends, then level 3, and so on. If you are playing 6 Degrees of Bacon, BFS is the algorithm for you.

Consider this tree:

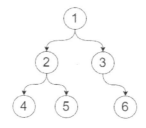

BFS would visit nodes in this order:

1. Level 0: [1]
2. Level 1: [2, 3]
3. Level 2: [4, 5, 6]

Pro Tips

Queue Choice Matters

```
# Bad: Using list as queue
queue = []  # pop(0) is *O*(n)

# Good: Using deque
queue = deque()  # popleft() is *O*(1)
```

Level Tracking

```
def get_tree_depth(root):
    if not root:
        return 0

    depth = 0
    queue = deque([root])

    while queue:
        depth += 1
        for _ in range(len(queue)):
            node = queue.popleft()
            if node.left: queue.append(node.left)
            if node.right: queue.append(node.right)

    return depth
```

Common Interview Questions

- Find the average of each level.
- Find the rightmost node at each level.
- Connect nodes at the same level (like a linked list)

Depth First Search (DFS)

Core Concept

Depth First Search (DFS) uses In-order Traversal to search. Picture being stuck in a maze. To get out, you may follow each path to its end before backtracking and trying the next path. This is precisely how Depth First Search works; each path is explored until it becomes apparent that it is the wrong path. Then, it backtracks to the last starting point and tries the next point until a solution is found.

In DFS, we start on the left branch and travel as far down each branch as possible before moving to the right branch.

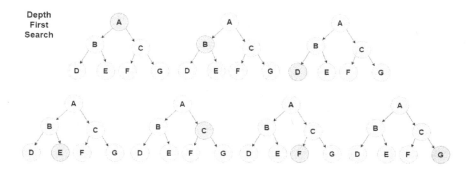

We will use an array to track if a node has been visited.

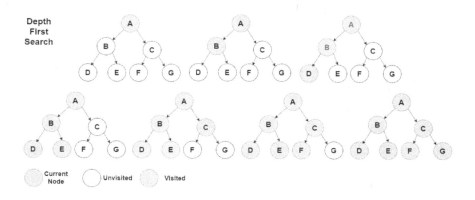

Python Implementation

```python
class TreeNode:
    """Binary tree node."""
    def __init__(self, value):
        self.value = value
        self.left = None
        self.right = None

class DFSTree:
    """Depth-First Search tree traversal."""
    def dfs_recursive(self, root):
        """
        Recursive pre-order DFS traversal.

        Time Complexity: O(n)
        Space Complexity: O(h)
        """
        result = []

        def explore(node):
            if not node:
                return

            # Pre-order: root, left, right
            result.append(node.value)
            explore(node.left)
            explore(node.right)

        explore(root)
        return result

    def dfs_iterative(self, root):
        """
        Iterative pre-order DFS traversal.

        Time Complexity: O(n)
        Space Complexity: O(h)
        """
```

```
    if not root:
        return []

    result = []
    stack = [root]

    while stack:
        node = stack.pop()
        result.append(node.value)

        # Right first, then left (stack order)
        if node.right:
            stack.append(node.right)
        if node.left:
            stack.append(node.left)

    return result

# Demonstrate DFS traversals
if __name__ == "__main__":
    # Create sample tree
    #         1
    #       /   \
    #      2     3
    #     / \   / \
    #    4   5 6   7
    root = TreeNode(1)
    root.left = TreeNode(2)
    root.right = TreeNode(3)
    root.left.left = TreeNode(4)
    root.left.right = TreeNode(5)
    root.right.left = TreeNode(6)
    root.right.right = TreeNode(7)

    # Initialize DFS traversal
    dfs = DFSTree()

    # Test recursive and iterative DFS
    print("Recursive DFS:", dfs.dfs_recursive(root))
    print("Iterative DFS:", dfs.dfs_iterative(root))
```

Next, we will add test data to explore the recursive and iterative DFS approaches. When practicing tree traversals for interviews, it is helpful to create test cases that highlight how DFS works.

```
# Let's create a tree that shows the pre-order traversal
pattern clearly:
#       1
#      / \
#     2   5
#    / \   \
#   3   4   6
#          /
#         7


# Create our test tree
root = TreeNode(1)
root.left = TreeNode(2)
root.right = TreeNode(5)
root.left.left = TreeNode(3)
root.left.right = TreeNode(4)
root.right.right = TreeNode(6)
root.right.right.left = TreeNode(7)

# Initialize our DFS tree traversal object
dfs_tree = DFSTree()

# Test both methods and compare results
recursive_result = dfs_tree.dfs_recursive(root)
iterative_result = dfs_tree.dfs_iterative(root)

print("Recursive DFS:", recursive_result)
# Should print: [1, 2, 3, 4, 5, 6, 7]
print("Iterative DFS:", iterative_result)
# Should print: [1, 2, 3, 4, 5, 6, 7]

# Let's also test some edge cases:
print("\nTesting edge cases:")

# Empty tree
```

```
empty_root = None
print("Empty tree (recursive):",
dfs_tree.dfs_recursive(empty_root))   # Should print: []
print("Empty tree (iterative):",
dfs_tree.dfs_iterative(empty_root))   # Should print: []

# Single node tree
single_node = TreeNode(42)
print("Single node (recursive):",
dfs_tree.dfs_recursive(single_node))
# Should print: [42]
print("Single node (iterative):",
dfs_tree.dfs_iterative(single_node))
# Should print: [42]

# Linear tree (only left children)
linear_root = TreeNode(1)
linear_root.left = TreeNode(2)
linear_root.left.left = TreeNode(3)
print("Linear tree (recursive):",
dfs_tree.dfs_recursive(linear_root))
# Should print: [1, 2, 3]
print("Linear tree (iterative):",
dfs_tree.dfs_iterative(linear_root))
# Should print: [1, 2, 3]
```

I've structured these test cases to help you visualize how DFS works - it always prioritizes going deeper before exploring siblings. The main test tree I created has an interesting shape that helps verify both left and right traversals work correctly.

Verifying that both recursive and iterative implementations give the same results is crucial. While they achieve the same goal, they do it differently under the hood - recursion uses the call stack while the iterative version manually manages its own stack. If they don't match, then your implementation is wrong.

Performance Characteristics

Time Complexity: $O*(V + E)$ where V = number of vertices (nodes) and E = number of edges (connections)

Space Complexity: $O(h)$, where h is the tree's height.

Key Tips

For some use cases, DFS is the ideal solution. For instance, a need to build a list of a file system to list all files in a directory and its sub-directories. The recursive nature of DFS perfectly matched the nested structure of directories.

```python
def explore_directory(path, depth=0):
    if not os.path.isdir(path):
        return

    # Process current directory
    print('  ' * depth + os.path.basename(path))

    # Explore subdirectories (DFS!)
    for item in os.listdir(path):
        full_path = os.path.join(path, item)
        explore_directory(full_path, depth + 1)
```

Pro Tips

Choose Your Ideal Traversal Order:

```python
def dfs_three_ways(node):
    if not node:
```

```
        return

    # Pre-order: Process BEFORE children
    print(node.value)  # Pre-order
    dfs_three_ways(node.left)
    # In-order: Process BETWEEN children
    print(node.value)  # In-order
    dfs_three_ways(node.right)
    # Post-order: Process AFTER children
    print(node.value)  # Post-order
```

Memory Optimization:

```
def dfs_with_yield(node):
    if not node:
        return
    yield node.value
    yield from dfs_with_yield(node.left)
    yield from dfs_with_yield(node.right)
```

A* Algorithm

Core Concept

For pathfinding algorithms, you must understand **Euclidean** distance and **Manhattan** distance. These distance metrics can also significantly improve the performance of Classification, Clustering, and Information Retrieval processes in Machine Learning modeling.

> Euclidean Distance represents the shortest distance between two points.

Euclidean distance measures the shortest path between two points in flat space. The distance equals the square root of the sum of squared differences between corresponding coordinates derived from the Pythagorean theorem.

Manhattan Distance is the sum of absolute differences between points across all the dimensions.

Manhattan distance sums the absolute differences between coordinates, measuring distance along a grid-like path. Also called city block distance or Minkowski's L1 distance represents movement restricted to vertical and horizontal directions, like navigating city streets set up on a grid.

As you see below, the Euclidean distance is 5, and the Manhattan distance is 7

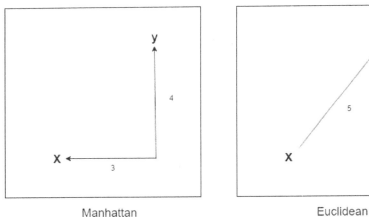

Manhattan   Euclidean

The A* algorithm is a **best-first search algorithm** that finds the shortest path between two points. It uses both:

- The actual cost from the start to the current node (g-score)
- A heuristic estimate of the cost from the current node to the goal (h-score)

Let's walk through all the steps to performing A*

Setup Phase

Create two lists:

- **Open list**: Contains nodes to be evaluated
- **Closed list**: Contains nodes already evaluated.

Define your heuristic function h(n), which estimates the cost from node n to goal.
For each node, track:

- g(n): Cost from start to node n
- h(n): Estimated cost from n to goal
- f(n): Total cost (f(n) = g(n) + h(n))
- Parent node reference

Execution Phase

Add start node to open list with:

- g(start) = 0
- h(start) = calculated using heuristic
- f(start) = h(start)

While the open list is not empty:
Select the node with the lowest f-value from the open list
If the current node is the goal node, reconstruct and return the path
Move the current node from open to closed list
For each neighbor of the current node:

1. If the neighbor is in the closed list, skip it.

2. Calculate tentative g-value: g(current) + distance to neighbor
3. If neighbor not in open list OR tentative g-value < neighbor's g-value:

- Set the neighbor's parent to the current node.
- Update g(neighbor) = tentative g-value
- Calculate h(neighbor) using the heuristic.
- Update f(neighbor) = g(neighbor) + h(neighbor)
- Add neighbor to open list if not already there

If the open list becomes empty without finding the goal, no path exists

Path Reconstruction

- Start from the goal node.
- Follow parent references back to start the node
- Reverse the path

The algorithm's efficiency depends on choosing a good heuristic that never overestimates the actual cost to reach the goal (admissible heuristic). We will use Manhattan distance as our heuristic.

The total estimated cost (f-score) is f = g + h. Let's implement it with a grid-based example:

Python Implementation 1

```python
def astar(grid, start, goal):
    """
    Find the shortest path between start and goal positions
    using the A* pathfinding algorithm.
    """
    # Calculate distance using Manhattan distance heuristic
    def heuristic(a, b):
        return abs(a[0] - b[0]) + abs(a[1] - b[1])
```

```python
# Euclidean distance heuristic
def euclidean_heuristic(a, b):
    return ((a[0] - b[0])**2 +
            (a[1] - b[1])**2)**0.5


# Get valid neighboring cells
def get_neighbors(pos):
    x, y = pos
    # Check right, left, down, up
    neighbors = [
        (x+1, y), (x-1, y),
        (x, y+1), (x, y-1)
    ]
    # Return only valid and walkable neighbors
    return [
        (x, y) for (x, y) in neighbors
        if 0 <= x < len(grid) and
            0 <= y < len(grid[0]) and
            grid[x][y] != 1
    ]


# Initialize sets and tracking
open_set = {start}
closed_set = set()
came_from = {}
g_score = {start: 0}
f_score = {start: heuristic(start, goal)}

while open_set:
    # Find position with lowest f_score
    current = min(
        open_set,
        key=lambda pos: f_score.get(pos, float('inf'))
    )

    if current == goal:
        # Reconstruct the path
        path = []
        while current in came_from:
```

```
            path.append(current)
            current = came_from[current]
        path.append(start)
        return path[::-1]

    open_set.remove(current)
    closed_set.add(current)

    # Check each neighbor
    for neighbor in get_neighbors(current):
        if neighbor in closed_set:
            continue

        # Calculate tentative cost
        tentative_g_score = g_score[current] + 1

        if neighbor not in open_set:
            open_set.add(neighbor)
        elif tentative_g_score >= g_score.get(
            neighbor, float('inf')
        ):
            continue

        # Best path so far
        came_from[neighbor] = current
        g_score[neighbor] = tentative_g_score
        f_score[neighbor] = (
            g_score[neighbor] +
            heuristic(neighbor, goal)
        )

    return []   # No path found

# Visualize path in grid
def print_path(grid, path):
    for i in range(len(grid)):
        for j in range(len(grid[0])):
            if (i, j) == path[0]:
                print('S', end=' ')  # Start
            elif (i, j) == path[-1]:
```

```
            print('G', end=' ')  # Goal
         elif (i, j) in path:
            print('*', end=' ')  # Path
         elif grid[i][j] == 1:
            print█(' ', end=' ')  # Wall
         else:
            print('.', end=' ')  # Empty space
      print()

# Test the algorithm
if __name__ == "__main__":
   grid = [
      [0, 0, 0, 0, 0],
      [1, 1, 0, 1, 0],
      [0, 0, 0, 0, 0],
      [0, 1, 1, 0, 0],
      [0, 0, 0, 0, 0]
   ]

   start = (0, 0)
   goal = (4, 4)

   path = astar(grid, start, goal)
   print("Found path:", path)
   print("\nGrid visualization:")
   print_path(grid, path)
```

When you run this code, it will output something like:

```
Path found: [(0, 0), (0, 1), (0, 2), (1, 2), (2, 2), (2, 3),
(2, 4), (3, 4), (4, 4)]

Grid visualization:
S * * . █
  * █   .
. . * * *
. █     *
. . . █ G
```

In this visualization:

- 'S' is the start position.
- 'G' is the goal position.
- '*' shows the path found.
- '█' represents walls/obstacles.
- '.' represents empty spaces.

The algorithm works by:

1. Maintaining a regular set of nodes to explore (open_set).
2. For each node, calculate its f_score (g_score + heuristic).
3. Always explore the node with the lowest f_score first.
4. Keeping track of visited nodes to avoid cycles.
5. Using a heuristic (Manhattan distance in this case) to guide the search.

The Manhattan distance heuristic is admissible (it never overestimates) for grid movement, guaranteeing that A* will find the optimal path if one exists.

To test different scenarios, you can modify the grid, start, and goal positions. The algorithm will find the shortest path that avoids obstacles or return an empty list if no path exists.

How would you alter this algorithm using a priority queue, better neighbor checking, and more complex data structures such as Tuples? Try it now and check your work against the answer in Python below.

Python Implementation 2

Here is an improved version of the A* algorithm in Python

```python
from heapq import heappush, heappop
from typing import List, Tuple, Dict, Set
```

```python
def manhattan_distance(
    a: Tuple[int, int],
    b: Tuple[int, int]
) -> int:
    """Calculate Manhattan distance between two points."""
    return abs(a[0] - b[0]) + abs(a[1] - b[1])

def get_neighbors(
    pos: Tuple[int, int],
    grid: List[List[int]]
) -> List[Tuple[int, int]]:
    """Get valid neighboring positions."""
    neighbors = []
    for dx, dy in [
        (0, 1), (1, 0), (0, -1), (-1, 0)
    ]:  # right, down, left, up
        new_x, new_y = pos[0] + dx, pos[1] + dy
        if (0 <= new_x < len(grid) and
                0 <= new_y < len(grid[0]) and
                grid[new_x][new_y] != 1):
            neighbors.append((new_x, new_y))
    return neighbors

def a_star(
    grid: List[List[int]],
    start: Tuple[int, int],
    goal: Tuple[int, int]
) -> List[Tuple[int, int]]:
    """
    Implementation of A* pathfinding algorithm.
    Returns the path from start to goal if found,
    empty list otherwise.
    """
    # Priority queue for open nodes
    open_set = []
    heappush(open_set, (0, start))

    # Dictionary to store the best previous node
    came_from: Dict[Tuple[int, int],
```

```python
                    Tuple[int, int]] = {}

# Cost from start to each node
g_score: Dict[Tuple[int, int], float] = {
    start: 0
}

# Estimated total cost from start to goal
f_score: Dict[Tuple[int, int], float] = {
    start: manhattan_distance(start, goal)
}

# Set of visited nodes
closed_set: Set[Tuple[int, int]] = set()

while open_set:
    current = heappop(open_set)[1]

    if current == goal:
        # Reconstruct path
        path = []
        while current in came_from:
            path.append(current)
            current = came_from[current]
        path.append(start)
        return path[::-1]

    closed_set.add(current)

    for neighbor in get_neighbors(current, grid):
        if neighbor in closed_set:
            continue

        # Cost of 1 to move to adjacent square
        tentative_g_score = g_score[current] + 1

        if (neighbor not in g_score or
            tentative_g_score < g_score[neighbor]):
            came_from[neighbor] = current
            g_score[neighbor] = tentative_g_score
```

```
            f_score[neighbor] = (
                g_score[neighbor] +
                manhattan_distance(neighbor, goal)
            )
            heappush(
                open_set,
                (f_score[neighbor], neighbor)
            )

    return []  # No path found

# Example usage with sample data
grid = [
    [0, 0, 0, 0, 1],
    [1, 1, 0, 1, 0],
    [0, 0, 0, 0, 0],
    [0, 1, 1, 1, 0],
    [0, 0, 0, 1, 0]
]

start = (0, 0)
goal = (4, 4)

path = a_star(grid, start, goal)
print(f"Path found: {path}")

# Visualize the path
def visualize_path(grid, path):
    visual = []
    for i in range(len(grid)):
        row = []
        for j in range(len(grid[0])):
            if (i, j) == start:
                row.append('S')
            elif (i, j) == goal:
                row.append('G')
            elif (i, j) in path:
                row.append('*')
            elif grid[i][j] == 1:
                row.append('')
```

```
        else:
            row.append('.')
        visual.append(' '.join(row))
    return '\n'.join(visual)

print("\nGrid visualization:")
print(visualize_path(grid, path))
```

Performance Characteristics

Time Complexity:

- Worst case: $O(b^d)$ where b is the branching factor (number of neighbors) and d is the depth of the solution
- Best case: $O(d)$ when the path is direct and the heuristic is perfect
- Average case: $O(b^d)$ but significantly faster than Dijkstra in practice due to heuristic guidance

Space Complexity: $O(b^d)$ to store nodes in the open and closed sets

Key Performance Factors:

```
def heuristic(a, b):
    # Manhattan distance - fast but may not be optimal for all
    cases
    return abs(a[0] - b[0]) + abs(a[1] - b[1])

    # Euclidean distance - more accurate for diag. but slowewr
    # return ((a[0] - b[0]) ** 2 + (a[1] - b[1]) ** 2) ** 0.5
```

Key Tips

Heuristic Selection

```python
def adaptive_heuristic(a, b, grid_type):
    if grid_type == "manhattan":
        return abs(a[0] - b[0]) + abs(a[1] - b[1])
    elif grid_type == "chebyshev":  # Allows diagonal movement
        return max(abs(a[0] - b[0]), abs(a[1] - b[1]))
```

Memory Optimization

```python
# Use a binary heap instead of sorting open set
from heapq import heappush, heappop

open_set = []
heappush(open_set, (f_score, node))
current = heappop(open_set)[1]
```

Early Termination

```python
def astar_with_max_iterations(grid, start, goal, max_iter=1000):
    iterations = 0
    while open_set and iterations < max_iter:
        # ... normal A* code ...
        iterations += 1
    return None  # Path not found within iteration limit
```

Pro Tips

Bidirectional A*

```python
def bidirectional_astar(grid, start, goal):
    forward_front = {start: 0}
```

```
    backward_front = {goal: 0}

    while forward_front and backward_front:
        # Expand both fronts
        if len(forward_front) < len(backward_front):
            current = expand_front(forward_front)
        else:
            current = expand_front(backward_front)

        # Check for intersection
        if current in forward_front and current in
        backward_front:
            return reconstruct_path(current)
```

Memory-Efficient Version

```
def astar_memory_efficient(grid, start, goal):
    # Store only essential information
    parent = {}
    g_score = {start: 0}

    # Use generator for neighbors
    def neighbor_generator(pos):
        for dx, dy in [(0, 1), (1, 0), (0, -1), (-1, 0)]:
            yield (pos[0] + dx, pos[1] + dy)
```

Jump Point Search (JPS) Optimization

```
def identify_jump_point(node, direction, grid):
    # Skip straight lines until finding a turn
    x, y = node
    dx, dy = direction

    while valid_position(x + dx, y + dy, grid):
        x += dx
        y += dy

        if has_forced_neighbor(x, y, direction, grid):
```

```
        return (x, y)

    return None
```

Dynamic Environment Handling

```
class DynamicAstar:
    def __init__(self, grid):
        self.grid = grid
        self.cached_paths = {}

    def update_grid(self, changes):
        self.grid.update(changes)
        # Invalidate affected cached paths
        self.invalidate_cached_paths(changes)
```

Handling Tie-Breaks

```
def compare_positions(pos1, pos2, goal):
    f1 = f_score[pos1]
    f2 = f_score[pos2]

    if f1 == f2:
        # Prefer positions closer to goal
        h1 = heuristic(pos1, goal)
        h2 = heuristic(pos2, goal)
        return h1 < h2

    return f1 < f2
```

These insights come from implementing A* in various contexts, from game development to robotics navigation. The best implementation often depends on your specific use case - consider factors like grid size, update frequency, and memory constraints when choosing optimizations.

Common Interview Questions

How does A* differ from Dijkstra's algorithm?

```
# Dijkstra - only uses g_score
priority = g_score[current]

# A* - uses f_score (g_score + heuristic)
priority = g_score[current] + heuristic(current, goal)
```

What makes a heuristic admissible?

A heuristic is admissible if it never overestimates the cost. For example: Manhattan distance is admissible for grid movement without diagonals

How would you modify A* for weighted edges?

```
def get_neighbors_weighted(pos, grid):
    neighbors = []
    for dx, dy in [(0, 1), (1, 0), (0, -1), (-1, 0)]:
        new_x, new_y = pos[0] + dx, pos[1] + dy
        if valid_position(new_x, new_y, grid):
            weight = grid[new_x][new_y]  # Weight from grid
            neighbors.append(((new_x, new_y), weight))
    return neighbors
```

How would you handle diagonal movement?

```
DIAGONAL_MOVES = [(1, 1), (1, -1), (-1, 1), (-1, -1)]
STRAIGHT_MOVES = [(0, 1), (1, 0), (0, -1), (-1, 0)]

def get_neighbors_diagonal(pos, grid):
    neighbors = []
    for dx, dy in DIAGONAL_MOVES + STRAIGHT_MOVES:
        new_x, new_y = pos[0] + dx, pos[1] + dy
        # Diagonal cost typically √2 ≈ 1.414
        cost = 1.414 if dx != 0 and dy != 0 else 1
```

```
        if valid_position(new_x, new_y, grid):
            neighbors.append(((new_x, new_y), cost))
    return neighbors
```

Dijkstra's Algorithm

Core Concept

Dijkstra's Algorithm is used to find the fastest route in a graph with weights between each vector in the graph. If you look at an actual map of the cities of Dallas, Chicago, Memphis, Atlanta, Miami, and Boston, you will see the distance between all of these cities. If you want to determine how to visit all of them but want to travel the least miles or the shortest path between Dallas and Boston, then Dijkstra's can give you a solution.

Dijkstra's algorithm is considered without reconsidering previous choices.

Key greedy characteristics:

- It selects the "best" option available at each step (the node with minimum current distance)
- Once a node is marked as visited, that decision is never revisited.
- It doesn't look ahead or consider the global impact of each choice

This greedy approach works for Dijkstra because of the property of the non-negative edge weights. The algorithm relies on the principle that if the shortest path to node X has been found, adding additional edges cannot create a shorter path to X (due to triangle inequality).

Unlike dynamic programming algorithms that might reconsider earlier decisions, Dijkstra commits to its choices permanently, making it a classic example of a successful greedy strategy for shortest-path problems.

Setup Phase

Create two sets:

1. **Unvisited set**: Contains all nodes
2. **Visited set**: Initially empty

For each node, track:

- Distance from the start (initially infinity for all nodes except start = 0)
- Previous node (for path reconstruction)

Execution Phase

Set start node distance to 0

While the unvisited set has nodes:

1. Select the unvisited node with the smallest distance.
2. If the current node distance is infinite, the remaining nodes are unreachable.
3. If the current node is the target node, the algorithm is complete.
4. Move the current node from the unvisited to visited set.
5. For each unvisited neighbor of the current node:

- Calculate the current node distance + edge weight to the neighbor.
- If calculated distance < neighbor's current distance:
- *Update neighbor's distance.*
- *Set the neighbor's previous node to the current node*

Path Reconstruction

1. Start from target node.
2. Follow previous node references back to start.
3. Reverse the path

Unlike A*, Dijkstra's algorithm doesn't use a heuristic and guarantees the shortest path to all nodes from the start. However, it explores more nodes than A* typically would.

Python Implementation

```python
from collections import defaultdict
import heapq

class Graph:
    """
    A graph implementation with Dijkstra's shortest
    path algorithm.

    Represents a weighted directed graph using an
    adjacency list with Dijkstra's algorithm for
    finding shortest paths.
    """

    def __init__(self):
        """Initialize an empty graph."""
        self.graph = defaultdict(list)

    def add_edge(self, from_node, to_node, weight):
        """
        Add a weighted edge to the graph.

        Args:
            from_node: The source node
            to_node: The destination node
```

```python
        weight (numeric): The edge weight/distance

    Raises:
        ValueError: If weight is negative
    """
    if weight < 0:
        raise ValueError(
            "Negative weights are not allowed"
        )

    self.graph[from_node].append(
        (to_node, weight)
    )

    # Ensure to_node exists in the graph
    if to_node not in self.graph:
        self.graph[to_node] = []

def dijkstra(self, start):
    """
    Find shortest paths from start node using
    Dijkstra's algorithm.

    Args:
        start: The starting node

    Returns:
        tuple: (distances, paths) where:
            - distances: Shortest distances
            - paths: Shortest paths
    """
    if start not in self.graph:
        raise KeyError(
            f"Start node '{start}' not in graph"
        )

    # Initialize distances to infinity
    distances = {
        node: float('infinity')
        for node in self.graph
```

186

```
        }
        distances[start] = 0

        # Priority queue to store (distance, node)
        pq = [(0, start)]

        # Track shortest paths
        paths = {start: [start]}

        while pq:
            current_distance, current_node = (
                heapq.heappop(pq)
            )

            # Skip if longer path found
            if current_distance > distances[current_node]:
                continue

            # Check all neighbors
            for neighbor, weight in (
                self.graph[current_node]
            ):
                distance = current_distance + weight

                # Update if shorter path found
                if distance < distances[neighbor]:
                    distances[neighbor] = distance
                    paths[neighbor] = (
                        paths[current_node] + [neighbor]
                    )
                    heapq.heappush(
                        pq, (distance, neighbor)
                    )

        return distances, paths

# Example usage
if __name__ == "__main__":
    # Create graph representing US city network
    g = Graph()
```

```
# Add edges (from_city, to_city, distance)
g.add_edge('Dallas', 'Chicago', 920)
g.add_edge('Dallas', 'Memphis', 410)
g.add_edge('Chicago', 'Boston', 850)
g.add_edge('Memphis', 'Atlanta', 335)
g.add_edge('Memphis', 'Chicago', 480)
g.add_edge('Atlanta', 'Miami', 610)
g.add_edge('Atlanta', 'Boston', 1070)
g.add_edge('Boston', 'Miami', 1450)

# Run Dijkstra's algorithm from Dallas
start_node = 'Dallas'
distances, paths = g.dijkstra(start_node)

# Print results
print(f"Shortest distances from {start_node}:")
for node, distance in distances.items():
    print(f"  To {node}: {distance} miles")

print("\nShortest paths:")
for node, path in paths.items():
    if node != start_node:
        print(
            f"  To {node}: {' -> '.join(path)} "
            f"(distance: {distances[node]} miles)"
        )
```

Next I will add the same data and test cases to test this implementation. You will notice that the code to test the routine is larger than the routine itself.

```
def test_dijkstra():
    # Test Case 1: Simple path
    # Verify basic shortest path functionality
    g1 = Graph()
    g1.add_edge('Dallas', 'Chicago', 920)
    g1.add_edge('Dallas', 'Memphis', 410)
```

```python
g1.add_edge('Chicago', 'Boston', 850)
g1.add_edge('Memphis', 'Boston', 1200)
g1.add_edge('Memphis', 'Chicago', 480)

distances, paths = g1.dijkstra('Dallas')
assert distances == {
    'Dallas': 0,
    'Chicago': 890,
    'Memphis': 410,
    'Boston': 1740
}, "Test case 1 distances failed"
assert paths == {
    'Dallas': ['Dallas'],
    'Chicago': ['Dallas', 'Memphis', 'Chicago'],
    'Memphis': ['Dallas', 'Memphis'],
    'Boston': ['Dallas', 'Memphis', 'Chicago', 'Boston']
}, "Test case 1 paths failed"
print("Test case 1 passed!")


# Test Case 2: Disconnected graph
# Check handling of unreachable nodes
g2 = Graph()
g2.add_edge('Dallas', 'Chicago', 920)
g2.add_edge('Atlanta', 'Miami', 610)

distances, paths = g2.dijkstra('Dallas')
assert distances['Chicago'] == 920, (
    "Test case 2 reachable distance failed"
)
assert distances['Atlanta'] == float('infinity'), (
    "Test case 2 unreachable distance failed"
)
assert distances['Miami'] == float('infinity'), (
    "Test case 2 unreachable distance failed"
)
assert (
    'Atlanta' not in paths and
    'Miami' not in paths
), "Test case 2 unreachable paths failed"
print("Test case 2 passed!")
```

```
# Test Case 3: Cyclic graph
# Verify handling of graph with cycles
g3 = Graph()
g3.add_edge('Dallas', 'Chicago', 920)
g3.add_edge('Chicago', 'Atlanta', 590)
g3.add_edge('Atlanta', 'Dallas', 780)
g3.add_edge('Chicago', 'Boston', 850)

distances, paths = g3.dijkstra('Dallas')
assert distances == {
    'Dallas': 0,
    'Chicago': 920,
    'Atlanta': 1510,
    'Boston': 1770
}, "Test case 3 distances failed"
assert paths['Boston'] == [
    'Dallas', 'Chicago', 'Boston'
], "Test case 3 paths failed"
print("Test case 3 passed!")

# Test Case 4: Multiple paths to same destination
# Check shortest path selection
g4 = Graph()
g4.add_edge('Dallas', 'Chicago', 920)
g4.add_edge('Dallas', 'Memphis', 410)
g4.add_edge('Chicago', 'Boston', 850)
g4.add_edge('Memphis', 'Boston', 1400)
g4.add_edge('Dallas', 'Boston', 1800)

distances, paths = g4.dijkstra('Dallas')
assert distances['Boston'] == 1770, (
    "Test case 4 distance failed"
)
assert paths['Boston'] == [
    'Dallas', 'Chicago', 'Boston'
], "Test case 4 path failed"
print("Test case 4 passed!")

# Test Case 5: Large weights
```

```
# Test algorithm with large number values
g5 = Graph()
g5.add_edge('Dallas', 'Chicago', 1000000)
g5.add_edge('Chicago', 'Boston', 2000000)

distances, paths = g5.dijkstra('Dallas')
assert distances['Boston'] == 3000000, (
    "Test case 5 large weights failed"
)
print("Test case 5 passed!")

print("\nAll test cases passed successfully! Your "
        "implementation handles:")
print("Basic shortest path finding")
print("Disconnected graphs")
print("Cyclic graphs")
print("Multiple paths to same destination")
print("Large weight values")

if __name__ == "__main__":
    test_dijkstra()
```

Performance Characteristics

Time Complexity: $O((V + E) \log V)$ with binary heap

Space Complexity: $O(V)$

Key Tips

Dijkstra's algorithm is used to build route planning for many food delivery services. Typically, the edges are streets, weights are travel times based on distance, speed, and traffic. This is all the data needed to pick the quickest route. Here's a simplified version:

```
def find_fastest_delivery_route(restaurants, customer,
traffic_data):
    graph = Graph()

    # Add roads with current traffic conditions
    for road, traffic in traffic_data.items():
        start, end = road
        time = calculate_travel_time(traffic)
        graph.add_edge(start, end, time)

    # Find fastest route from restaurant to customer
    distances, path = graph.dijkstra(restaurants)
    return path[customer]
```

Pro Tips

If you are asked for an example of a greedy algorithm in your interview, answer with this one and explain why it is greedy: It makes locally optimal choices and never reconsiders those choices. Because of this, it prunes bad paths early, reducing the search space.

Use Priority Queue for Better Performance:

```
# Instead of searching for minimum distance each time
heapq.heappush(pq, (distance, node))
```

Early Stopping:

```
def dijkstra_with_target(self, start, target):
    # Stop when we reach our target
    if current_node == target:
        return distances[target]
```

Two Pointers

Core Concept

The Two Pointers technique uses two pointers to solve array-related problems more efficiently, typically reducing time complexity from $O(n^2)$ to $O(n)$. Mastering this pattern will be like having a secret weapon. Two Pointers come in two versions: Opposite Direction Pointers and Same Direction Pointers. Both have their place.

In the diagram below, we are looking for two numbers whose sum is 9. First, we move pointer 2 down because 1+10 is larger than the target. Next, we move pointer 2 up because 1+6 is less than our target. Finally, we find 3+6=9.

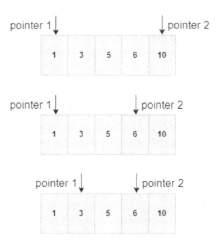

Opposite Direction Pointers

This is the most common pattern I use, especially for sorted arrays.

Python Implementation

```python
# Two Sum II
def findTwoSum(numbers, target):
    left, right = 0, len(numbers) - 1

    while left < right:
        current_sum = numbers[left] + numbers[right]
        if current_sum == target:
            return [left + 1, right + 1]  # 1-based indexing
        elif current_sum < target:
            left += 1
        else:
            right -= 1

    return []  # No solution found
```

Same Direction Pointers (Fast and Slow/Hare & Tortoise Algorithm)

This pattern is perfect for cyclic linked list and array problems. Here's an example often used to detect cycles in a linked list. The algorithm starts with two pointers set to the head of a linked list. In each loop, the fast pointer will move twice as fast as the slow pointer. So, the slow pointer will move one spot, and the fast pointer will move two spots.

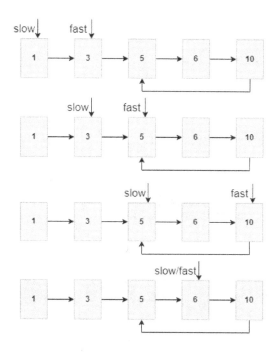

This algorithm will determine if a cycle is present by either the fast pointer reaching a null value, meaning no cycle is present, or the slow pointer and the fast pointer becoming the same value, meaning that a cycle is present.

Python Implementation

```
# Remove Duplicates from Sorted Array
def removeDuplicates(nums):
    if not nums:
        return 0

    slow = 0  # Points to last unique element

    for fast in range(1, len(nums)):
        if nums[fast] != nums[slow]:
```

```
        slow += 1
        nums[slow] = nums[fast]

    return slow + 1
```

Three Pointers

Here's a slightly more advanced pattern being used to sort colors. This is the Dutch National Flag problem proposed by Edsger Dijkstra (yes, the same Dijkstra!). The problem is as follows:

Dutch National Flag (printed in greyscale? Its 3 bars of red, white, and blue.)

You are given **n** balls of color red, white, or blue arranged in a line in random order. You have to arrange all the balls such that the balls with the same colors are adjacent to the order of the balls, with the order of the colors being red, white, and blue. All red balls come first, then all white balls, then all blue balls.

Now that you see the pattern of using two points see if you can write a three-point solution to this problem. The code is below:

Python Implementation

```python
# Sort Colors (Dutch National Flag problem)
def sortColors(nums):
    low = curr = 0
    high = len(nums) - 1

    while curr <= high:
        if nums[curr] == 0:
            nums[low], nums[curr] = nums[curr], nums[low]
            low += 1
            curr += 1
        elif nums[curr] == 2:
            nums[curr], nums[high] = nums[high], nums[curr]
            high -= 1
        else:
            curr += 1
```

This algorithm runs in O(n) time with O(1) space complexity, making it highly efficient. It's a beautiful example of how three-pointers can solve what might initially seem like a sorting problem requiring O(n log n) time.

Key Tips

Pattern Recognition: Before diving into code, I always try to identify if it's an:

- Opposite direction problem (like two sum)
- Same direction problem (like remove duplicates)
- Three-pointer problem (like the Dutch flag)

Time/Space Complexity:

- Most two-pointer solutions run in O(n) time.
- Usually achieve O(1) extra space
- Much better than naive $O(n^2)$ solutions

When to Use:

- Sorted array problems
- Palindrome problems
- Reversal problems
- Cyclic array problems
- Sliding window variations

Mastering the Two-Pointer technique takes practice. I suggest starting with simpler problems like Two Sum (which we solved above) and gradually working your way up to more complex ones like Container With Most Water. The pattern will become second nature with practice! I have included several two-pointer problems for you in the Practice Coding Problems chapter.

Pro Tips

Initialization Patterns:

```
# Common initialization patterns I use
left, right = 0, len(arr) - 1  # Opposite ends
slow = fast = 0  # Same start point
slow, fast = 0, 1  # Adjacent start points
```

Boundary Conditions:

```
# Key conditions to check
while left < right:  # For opposite direction
while fast < len(arr):  # For same direction
while slow < fast:  # For gap maintenance
```

Movement Rules:

```
# When to move pointers
if condition:
    left += 1  # Move left pointer right
    right -= 1  # Move right pointer left
```

Common Interview Questions

Palindrome Check:

```python
def isPalindrome(s: str) -> bool:
    left, right = 0, len(s) - 1

    while left < right:
        # Skip non-alphanumeric characters
        while left < right and not s[left].isalnum():
            left += 1
        while left < right and not s[right].isalnum():
            right -= 1

        if s[left].lower() != s[right].lower():
            return False

        left += 1
        right -= 1

    return True
```

Container With Most Water:

```python
def maxArea(height: List[int]) -> int:
    left, right = 0, len(height) - 1
    max_area = 0

    while left < right:
        width = right - left
        max_area = max(max_area, width * min(height[left],
        height[right]))

        if height[left] < height[right]:
            left += 1
        else:
            right -= 1

    return max_area
```

Sliding Window

Core Concept

The sliding window technique, a simple yet powerful tool, is used in array/string processing problems where an operation is performed on a specific window size of an array or linked list. The method uses two pointers to create a "window" that slides through an array/string, expanding or contracting based on certain conditions. It typically transforms $O(n^2)$ brute force solutions into $O(n)$ solutions. Below, we will cover both Fixed Window Size implementations and Variable Window Size implementations.

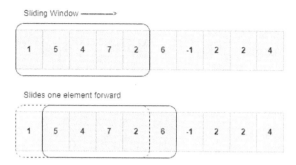

Here's a check-list to use when solving sliding window problems:

- One of the key steps in solving sliding window problems is to meticulously identify window bounds (start, end). This attention to detail is crucial for the success of the sliding window technique.
- Define window state (what to track)
- Determine window movement conditions.
- Handle state updates efficiently.
- Consider edge cases

Fixed Window Size

Let's start with a more straightforward example: **Find the maximum sum of a subarray of size k:**

I've included several helpful test cases for catching bugs in a sliding window implementation.

Basic Cases

- Regular arrays with clear maximum sums
- Edge cases where the window size equals the array length
- Arrays smaller than the window size

Edge Cases

- Empty arrays
- Single-element arrays
- Window size of 1
- Window size equal to array length

Special Cases

- All negative numbers
- Alternating positive and negative numbers
- Large numbers (testing for overflow)
- Repeating numbers

Python Implementation

```python
def maxSumSubarray(arr: List[int], k: int) -> int:
    if not arr or len(arr) < k:
        return -1

    # Compute sum of first window
    window_sum = sum(arr[:k])
    max_sum = window_sum

    # Slide window and update max_sum
    for i in range(k, len(arr)):
        window_sum = window_sum + arr[i] - arr[i - k]
        max_sum = max(max_sum, window_sum)

    return max_sum

def test_sliding_window():
    # Test case 1: Basic case
    arr1 = [1, 4, 2, 10, 2, 3, 1, 0, 20]
    k1 = 4
```

```
print(f"Test 1: Window size {k1}")
print(f"Array: {arr1}")
print(f"Expected: 24 (sum of window [2, 3, 1, 0])")
print(f"Result: {maxSumSubarray(arr1, k1)}\n")

# Test case 2: Window size equals array length
arr2 = [1, 4, 2, 10]
k2 = 4
print(f"Test 2: Window equals array size")
print(f"Array: {arr2}")
print(f"Expected: 17")
print(f"Result: {maxSumSubarray(arr2, k2)}\n")

# Test case 3: Small array
arr3 = [1, 2]
k3 = 3
print(f"Test 3: Array smaller than window")
print(f"Array: {arr3}")
print(f"Expected: -1")
print(f"Result: {maxSumSubarray(arr3, k3)}\n")

# Run tests
test_sliding_window()
```

Variable Window Size

I often use a more complex example in interviews: **Find the longest substring with no repeating characters**. See if you can write the test cases for these.

Python Implementation

```
def lengthOfLongestSubstring(s: str) -> int:
    char_index = {}
```

```
max_length = 0
window_start = 0

for window_end in range(len(s)):
    # If we've seen this character before in our current
    window
    if (s[window_end] in char_index and
        char_index[s[window_end]] >= window_start):
        window_start = char_index[s[window_end]] + 1
    else:
        max_length = max(
            max_length,
            window_end - window_start + 1
        )

    char_index[s[window_end]] = window_end

return max_length
```

Performance Characteristics

Time Complexity: Usually O(n)

Space Complexity: O(1) to O(k) where k is window size

Key Tips

Start with a **Fixed Size** window. It is usually simpler to implement. Move on to **Variable** and **Dynamic Size** windows with conditional resizing to optimize for your problem.

Be sure to set up your tests to check for edge cases.

Always test window boundaries:

```
def test_boundaries(arr, k):
    # Test first window
    first_window = maxSumSubarray(arr[:k], k)
    # Test last window
    last_window = maxSumSubarray(arr[-k:], k)
```

Check for performance with large arrays:

```
def test_performance():
    large_arr = [i % 100 for i in range(1000000)]
    k = 1000
    start_time = time.time()
    result = maxSumSubarray(large_arr, k)
    end_time = time.time()
    print(f"Time taken: {end_time - start_time} seconds")
```

Run these tests regularly as you modify your code. A test suite will save you countless hours of debugging and give you confidence in your sliding window implementations.

Pro Tips

Window State Management:

```
# Common pattern I use for state tracking
window_sum = 0  # For sum-based problems
window_chars = {}  # For character frequency
max_seen = float('-inf')  # For maximum calculations
min_seen = float('inf')  # For minimum calculations
```

Common Window Operations:

```
# Adding to window
window_sum += arr[window_end]
```

```
window_chars[s[window_end]] = window_chars.get(s[window_end],
0) + 1

# Removing from window
window_sum -= arr[window_start]
window_chars[s[window_start]] -= 1
```

Window Size Calculations:

```
current_window_size = window_end - window_start + 1
```

With practice, sliding windows become second nature. The key is to visualize the window sliding through the data and consider what information you need to maintain at each step. Keep practicing, and don't get discouraged if it takes time to master. These patterns will become powerful tools in your programming toolkit.

Common Interview Questions

Here are the common interview problems you will likely see using a sliding window as a solution. Take some time now to work on each of them and see if you can solve them using a sliding window technique.

- Maximum sum subarray of size k
- Longest substring with k distinct characters
- Minimum window substring
- Maximum consecutive ones III in a string

Backtracking (N-Queens Problem)

Core Concept

Think of backtracking like finding your way through a maze - you explore a path until you either reach your goal or hit a dead end. If you hit a dead end, you "backtrack" to your last decision point and try a different route.

Let's look at backtracking through a classic example question you might face: The N-Queens problem. **We need to place N queens on an NxN chessboard so that no two queens threaten each other.**

For example, for a 4x4-sized chessboard, here is a valid solution:

N-Queens Problem

How will you solve this using backtracking? First, we place a queen and then iterate through the board, placing another queen. We test if the new queen placement violates a rule (no queens threaten each other). If it does, we remove the last queen placed, backtrack to our last known good position, and go forward.

Let's look at what the code below is doing. Here, we try to place a queen in each column working down. At each step, if we hit a condition with a queen that violates the rules, we remove that queen, backtrack, and try a new combination at that level until we have attempted all valid combinations. Once we have found a solution for a level, we go to the next level. Once we find a solution to placing all four queens, we stop.

Let's walk through it step by step; see the flowchart below, from top to bottom and left to right.

1. Start at top left (0,0), placing a queen and checking safety with is_safe().
2. Recursively try placing queens in each subsequent column.
3. For each column, test every row position until finding a safe placement.
4. If no safe placement exists in a column, backtrack to the previous column and try the next row position.
5. When backtracking from the first queen, move it to the next row position (0,1) and repeat the process.
6. Continue until all queens are placed (solution found) or all possibilities exhausted.

A valid solution is our four queens located at [(0, 1), (1, 3), (2, 0), (3, 2)]. This will be output from our solution as [[0, 0, 1, 0], [1, 0, 0, 0], [0, 0, 0, 1], [0, 1, 0, 0]], which maps each row of our chessboard from top to bottom and whether the space contains a queen or is empty.

N-Queens Problem

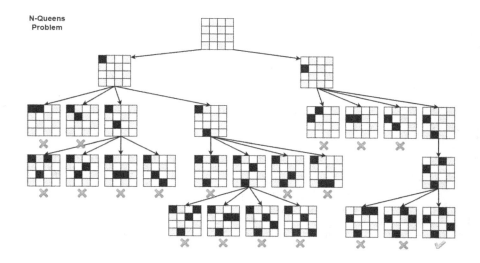

How would you write thorough unit tests to test whether this produces an optimal solution? Could there be more than one optimal solution? There is an edge case that this code will not handle. Can you determine what that is? I have commented on every step of the code below to explain what is happening in each step.

Python Implementation

```python
def solve_n_queens(n):
    # Tests if queen location violates rules
    def is_safe(board, row, col):
        # Check row on left side
        for j in range(col):
            if board[row][j] == 1:
                return False

        # Check upper diagonal on left side
        for i, j in zip(range(row, -1, -1),
                        range(col, -1, -1)):
            if board[i][j] == 1:
```

```
            return False

    # Check lower diagonal on left side
    for i, j in zip(range(row, n, 1),
                    range(col, -1, -1)):
        if board[i][j] == 1:
            return False

    return True

def solve_util(board, col):
    # Base case: all queens placed
    if col >= n:
        return True

    # Try placing queen in each row of current column
    for i in range(n):
        # Check if queen can be placed
        if is_safe(board, i, col):
            # Place the queen
            board[i][col] = 1

            # Recur to place rest of queens
            if solve_util(board, col + 1):
                return True

            # Backtrack if no solution found
            board[i][col] = 0

    # No solution with current configuration
    return False

# Initialize empty chessboard
board = [[0 for x in range(n)] for y in range(n)]

# Start solving from leftmost column
if solve_util(board, 0) == False:
    print("Solution does not exist")
    return False
```

```
    # Return solution
    return board

result = solve_n_queens(4)
print(result)
```

This results in:

```
[[0, 0, 1, 0],
 [1, 0, 0, 0],
 [0, 0, 0, 1],
 [0, 1, 0, 0]]
```

Expanded Implementation

I have expanded the implementation for thoroughness for N-Queens, as you might be asked to do in an interview. Let me walk you through what I've added here:

I've created a proper NQueens class with static methods, making it more maintainable and testable - something I learned is crucial when working with algorithmic problems.

The test suite covers several vital scenarios:

· Edge case: 1x1 board (has a solution)
· Edge case: 2x2 and 3x3 boards (no solutions)
· Typical case: 4x4 board (first interesting case with solutions)
· Larger case: 8x8 board (classic chess board size)

Validation test: checking that no queens threaten each other

I've added a visualization helper that converts the numeric board representation to a more readable format using 'Q' for queens and "." for empty spaces.

If you run this code, you'll see something like this for a 4x4 solution:

```
.Q..
...Q
Q...
..Q.
```

This testing approach allows us to catch the edge cases. The original implementation does not handle a 1x1 board case properly; this testing suite would catch that.

```
import unittest

class NQueens:
    @staticmethod
    def solve_n_queens(n):
        def is_safe(board, row, col):
            # Check row on left side
            for j in range(col):
                if board[row][j] == 1:
                    return False

            # Check upper diagonal on left side
            for i, j in zip(range(row, -1, -1),
                            range(col, -1, -1)):
                if board[i][j] == 1:
                    return False

            # Check lower diagonal on left side
            for i, j in zip(range(row, n, 1),
                            range(col, -1, -1)):
                if board[i][j] == 1:
                    return False

            return True
```

```python
    def solve_util(board, col):
        # Base case: all queens placed
        if col >= n:
            return True

        for i in range(n):
            # Check if queen can be placed
            if is_safe(board, i, col):
                # Place the queen
                board[i][col] = 1

                # Recur to place rest of the queens
                if solve_util(board, col + 1):
                    return True

                # Remove queen if no solution found
                board[i][col] = 0

        # No solution with current configuration
        return False

    # Initialize board
    board = [[0 for x in range(n)] for y in range(n)]

    if not solve_util(board, 0):
        return None

    return board

@staticmethod
def format_board(board):
    # Return None if no solution
    if board is None:
        return None
    # Convert board to readable format
    return [''.join(['Q' if cell == 1 else '.'
                for cell in row])
            for row in board]

class TestNQueens(unittest.TestCase):
```

```python
def setUp(self):
    # Initialize solver
    self.solver = NQueens()

def test_1x1_board(self):
    """Test case for 1x1 board - should have one solution"""
    result = self.solver.solve_n_queens(1)
    self.assertIsNotNone(result)
    self.assertEqual(len(result), 1)
    self.assertEqual(result[0][0], 1)

def test_2x2_board(self):
    """Test case for 2x2 board - should have no solution"""
    result = self.solver.solve_n_queens(2)
    self.assertIsNone(result)

def test_3x3_board(self):
    """Test case for 3x3 board - should have no solution"""
    result = self.solver.solve_n_queens(3)
    self.assertIsNone(result)

def test_4x4_board(self):
    """Test case for 4x4 board - should have a solution"""
    result = self.solver.solve_n_queens(4)
    self.assertIsNotNone(result)
    formatted = self.solver.format_board(result)
    # One of the possible solutions for 4x4
    self.assertEqual(len(formatted), 4)
    self.assertEqual(sum(row.count('Q')
                         for row in formatted), 4)

def test_8x8_board(self):
    """Test case for 8x8 board - should have a solution"""
    result = self.solver.solve_n_queens(8)
    self.assertIsNotNone(result)
    formatted = self.solver.format_board(result)
    self.assertEqual(len(formatted), 8)
    self.assertEqual(sum(row.count('Q')
                         for row in formatted), 8)
```

```python
    def test_queen_threats(self):
        """Test that no queens threaten each other"""
        n = 4
        result = self.solver.solve_n_queens(n)
        self.assertIsNotNone(result)

        # Check row threats
        for row in result:
            self.assertEqual(sum(row), 1)

        # Check column threats
        for j in range(n):
            self.assertEqual(sum(result[i][j]
                                 for i in range(n)), 1)

        # Check diagonal threats
        for i in range(n):
            for j in range(n):
                if result[i][j] == 1:
                    # Check diagonals from queen's position
                    for k in range(1, n):
                        # Check upper-right diagonal
                        if i-k >= 0 and j+k < n:
                            self.assertEqual(result[i-k][j+k], 0)
                        # Check lower-right diagonal
                        if i+k < n and j+k < n:
                            self.assertEqual(result[i+k][j+k], 0)

def visualize_solution(board):
    """Helper function to visualize board solution"""
    if board is None:
        return "No solution exists"

    # Format the board
    formatted = NQueens.format_board(board)
    return '\n'.join(formatted)

if __name__ == '__main__':
    # Example usage and visualization
    print("Testing different board sizes:")
```

```python
for n in [1, 2, 3, 4, 8]:
    print(f"\nTesting {n}x{n} board:")
    solution = NQueens.solve_n_queens(n)
    print(visualize_solution(solution))

# Run the unit tests
unittest.main(argv=['first-arg-is-ignored'],
              exit=False)
```

This will output:

```
Testing different board sizes:

Testing 1x1 board:
Q

Testing 2x2 board:
No solution exists

Testing 3x3 board:
No solution exists

Testing 4x4 board:
..Q.
Q...
...Q
.Q..

Testing 8x8 board:
Q.......
......Q.
....Q...
.......Q
.Q......
...Q....
.....Q..
..Q.....
......
-----------------------------------------------------------------
```

```
Ran 6 tests in 0.001s
```

Performance Characteristics

Time Complexity: approximately $O(N!)$ because of the branching nature

Space Complexity: is $O(N)$ for the recursion stack and board representation

Key Tips

Here are the elements that make backtracking work on this problem. Without these, backtracking would not be a good solver for our problem.

- A way to make choices (placing queens in our example)
- A way to validate choices (checking if queens threaten each other)
- A way to undo choices (removing queens when we hit a dead end)
- A clear goal condition (all queens placed successfully)

Pro Tips

Start with a clear state representation For N-Queens, I use a simple array where queensPos[row] = column to indicate a queen's position. This makes checking validity much cleaner.

Verbalize your pruning strategy Don't just code - explain how you're avoiding unnecessary branches.

Draw it out For your on site interview, draw out the first few steps of solving 4-Queens on the whiteboard before writing any code. Discuss the pruning strategy involved in backtracking.

Practice generating examples Interviewers might ask, "How many solu-

217

tions exist for 8-Queens?" Know that there are 92 distinct solutions (but only 12 if you account for symmetry).

Don't forget to revert state One bug I've seen many candidates make: not resetting the state properly when backtracking. Always undo your choices!

Inefficient validity checking Checking if a queen placement is valid can be done in $O(N)$ time, but I've seen candidates use $O(N^2)$ approaches unnecessarily.

Missing base cases Make sure you clearly define when to stop recursing and when to add solutions to your result set.

Common Interview Questions

The Classic N-Queens Problem. This is the quintessential backtracking question: Place N queens on an N×N chessboard so no two queens attack each other. The interviewer was looking for:

- Clear understanding of the constraints (queens can't share rows, columns, or diagonals)
- A recursive solution with proper state tracking
- Efficient pruning of invalid paths

Sudoku Solver. Another favorite! You'll need to implement an algorithm to solve a partially filled Sudoku grid. I've found that interviewers watch closely for:

- How you handle constraint checking
- Your approach to representing the board
- Your strategy for trying values and backtracking

Word Search in a Grid. Given a 2D board and a word, find if the word exists in the grid. Practice this pattern until you are good at it.

- You'll typically use DFS with backtracking
- Marking visited cells without extra space is a typical follow-up question

Permutations and Combinations. "Generate all permutations of a string" or "find all combinations that sum to target" are common variations. The key insight I've found helpful:

- Understand the difference between permutations (order matters) and combinations (order doesn't)
- Know how to avoid duplicates when needed

Typical Follow-Up Questions

Optimization Techniques

- "How would you optimize your solution?"
- "What if the constraints were different?"
- For N-Queens, you might be asked if bitwise operations could be used to speed up validity checking.

Iterative vs. Recursive Approaches

- Convert your recursive solution to an iterative one using a stack
- Discuss the trade-offs between the approaches

Interviews aren't just about getting the right answer—they're about demonstrating your systematic problem-solving approach.

Trie Data Structure

Core Concept

Next, we will tackle the Trie (pronounced "try") data structure. This is an efficient algorithm for working with strings. It is particularly useful for autocomplete in a desktop or web application.

A Trie is a tree-like data structure that stores strings in a way that makes prefix-based operations extremely efficient. It is essentially an n-ary tree where each node represents a character and each path from the root to a node forms a string. Leaf nodes store the keys while the remaining nodes match a prefix.

The key features that make Tries special are:

- Each node can have multiple children (up to 26 for lowercase English letters)
- Words sharing the same prefix share the same initial nodes
- Each node typically has a boolean flag indicating if it's the end of a word

Trie Data Structure

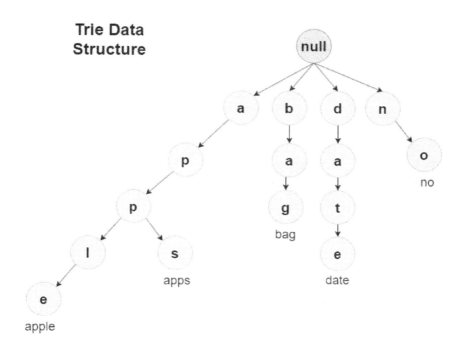

Python Implementation

```python
class TrieNode:
    """
    A node in the Trie data structure.

    Each node contains a dictionary mapping characters to
    child nodes and a flag for end of word.
    """
    def __init__(self):
        # Dictionary mapping characters to child nodes
        self.children = {}
        # Flag to mark end of a word
        self.is_end = False

class Trie:
```

```python
    """
    A Trie (prefix tree) implementation for efficient word
    storage and retrieval.
    """
    def __init__(self):
        # Initialize with empty root node
        self.root = TrieNode()

    def insert(self, word: str) -> None:
        """
        Insert a word into the trie.

        Args:
            word (str): The word to insert
        """
        # Start from the root node
        node = self.root

        # Traverse the trie character by character
        for char in word:
            # Create node if character doesn't exist
            if char not in node.children:
                node.children[char] = TrieNode()
            # Move to the child node
            node = node.children[char]

        # Mark the end of the word
        node.is_end = True

    def search(self, word: str) -> bool:
        """
        Search for a word in the trie.

        Args:
            word (str): The word to search for

        Returns:
            bool: True if word exists, False otherwise
        """
        # Start from the root node
```

```
        node = self.root

        # Traverse the trie character by character
        for char in word:
            # Word not in trie if character doesn't exist
            if char not in node.children:
                return False
            # Move to the child node
            node = node.children[char]

        # Check if this path forms a complete word
        return node.is_end

    def startsWith(self, prefix: str) -> bool:
        """
        Check if any word starts with the given prefix.

        Args:
            prefix (str): The prefix to check

        Returns:
            bool: True if prefix exists, False otherwise
        """
        # Start from the root node
        node = self.root

        # Traverse the trie character by character
        for char in prefix:
            # Prefix not in trie if character doesn't exist
            if char not in node.children:
                return False
            # Move to the child node
            node = node.children[char]

        # Return True if prefix path exists
        return True
```

Here is how you would insert words into Trie and do a search for those words,

```
# Creating a trie and inserting words
trie = Trie()
trie.insert("apple")
trie.insert("app")
trie.insert("apricot")

print(trie.search("apple"))      # True
print(trie.search("app"))        # True
print(trie.search("appl"))       # False
print(trie.startsWith("app"))    # True
```

Performance Characteristics

Time Complexity: $O(m)$ time complexity, where m is the length of the prefix, regardless of how many words are stored.

Space Complexity: However, the space complexity gets large fairly quickly: *O(ALPHABET_SIZE * m * n)* for n words. For an English alphabet with 26 letters, 10,000 words and a prefix of 3, the number of nodes will be 78,000.

Key Tips

Some key things to remember about Tries:

- Time complexity for operations is O(m), where m is the length of the word
- Space complexity can be significant - O(ALPHABET_SIZE * m * n) for n words
- They're particularly useful for prefix-based operations like autocomplete
- The trade-off between using a hash map vs array for children depends on your specific use case. This question comes up repeatedly.

- Master recursion first: If your recursion is shaky, Tries will be challenging. Spend a weekend just on recursive Trie operation

Common Interview Questions

Implement a basic Trie data structure

This is the classic starter question.

```
class TrieNode:
    def __init__(self):
        self.children = {}  # Map from character to TrieNode
        self.is_end = False

class Trie:
    def __init__(self):
        self.root = TrieNode()

    def insert(self, word):
        # Your implementation

    def search(self, word):
        # Your implementation

    def starts_with(self, prefix):
        # Your implementation
```

Interviewers are looking for clarity in how you handle:

- Child node management
- Word termination marking
- Traversal logic

Implement autocomplete / word suggestions

The key is to start with a working prefix search, then gather all words under that prefix node:

```
def get_all_words_with_prefix(self, prefix):
    # First find the node that represents the prefix
    # Then traverse from that node to collect all complete words
```

Solve a word search in a matrix (Boggle solver)

This combines Tries with backtracking. You solve it by:

- Build a Trie with a list of dictionary words
- For each cell in the board, try to find words starting there
- Use backtracking to explore adjacent cells

Longest common prefix: "Find the longest common prefix among a set of strings."

Replace words: "Given a dictionary of roots and a sentence, replace each word with its root if it exists."

Typical Follow-Up Questions

Space-Time Analysis

Be ready to explain:

- Time complexity for insert/search/delete: O(L) where L is word length
- Space complexity: O(N*L) for N words of average length L
- Why a Trie might be more efficient than a hash table for certain operations

Optimization Questions: "How would you reduce the memory footprint of your Trie?"

Your answer can include:

- Using compressed Tries (called a Radix Tree or a Patricia Trie)
- Alphabet-specific optimizations (e.g., utilizing arrays instead of maps

for limited character sets)

Real-World Applications: "In what scenarios would you use a Trie over other data structures?"

Have solid examples ready to go so you don't have to thing about this one:

- Autocomplete systems
- IP routing (longest prefix matching)
- Spell checkers
- Genomic sequence searches

Topological Sort

Core Concept

Here we are going to cover two methods for doing topological sorting, using **DFS** and **Kahn's Algorithm**.

Topological sorting is an algorithm best used for mapping dependency relationships, such as A must happen before B. B has a prior dependency on A. For instance, you may run into build dependencies while trying to compile your program, but a crucial version of a library is missing. A typical example is a university that has a dependency of taking Calculus I before you are allowed to enroll in Calculus II. We map these dependencies using a Topological sort in a directed graph.

You may have heard of DAGs, or directed acyclic graphs, which are directed graphs with no cycles. The directed graph in a topology sort is essentially the same, meaning that a graph that can be topologically sorted is by definition a DAG as topological sorting is only possible on graphs with no directed cycles (circular dependencies).

A topological sort of a directed graph is a linear ordering of its vertices such that for every directed edge u → v, vertex u comes before vertex v in the ordering. Think of it like planning your college courses - you need to take Calculus I before Calculus II. Here you can see the difference between an unsorted graph and a sorted graph.

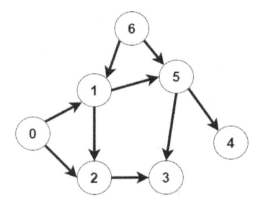

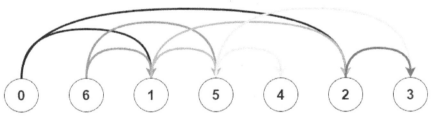

Note the two sorting implementations, both DFS, which you already know, and Kahn's algorithm, which is a special implementation of BFS.

Python Implementation

```
from collections import defaultdict, deque

class Graph:
    """
```

A graph implementation with topological sorting.

Implements directed graph with two topological sorting
algorithms: Kahn's (BFS) and DFS-based approach.

Attributes:
    graph (defaultdict): Adjacency list of the graph
    V (int): Number of vertices in the graph

Note:
    - Graph must be a DAG for topological sort
    - Vertices are integers from 0 to V-1
    """

```python
def __init__(self, vertices):
    """

    Initialize graph with vertices.

    Args:
        vertices (int): Number of vertices
    """
    self.graph = defaultdict(list)
    self.V = vertices

def add_edge(self, u, v):
    """

    Add directed edge from u to v.

    Args:
        u (int): Source vertex
        v (int): Destination vertex
    """
    self.graph[u].append(v)

def topological_sort_kahn(self):
    """

    Perform topological sort using Kahn's algorithm.

    Returns:
        list: Sorted vertices or empty list if cycle exists
```

```
        """
        # Calculate in-degree of all vertices
        in_degree = [0] * self.V
        for i in self.graph:
            for j in self.graph[i]:
                in_degree[j] += 1

        # Add vertices with 0 in-degree to queue
        queue = deque()
        for i in range(self.V):
            if in_degree[i] == 0:
                queue.append(i)

        result = []
        while queue:
            vertex = queue.popleft()
            result.append(vertex)

            # Reduce in-degree of adjacent vertices
            for neighbor in self.graph[vertex]:
                in_degree[neighbor] -= 1
                if in_degree[neighbor] == 0:
                    queue.append(neighbor)

        # Check for cycle
        return result if len(result) == self.V else []

    def topological_sort_dfs(self):
        """
        Perform topological sort using DFS algorithm.

        Returns:
            list: Topologically sorted list of vertices
        """
        visited = [False] * self.V
        stack = []

        def dfs(v):
            """

            Helper function for DFS traversal.
```

```
        Args:
            v (int): Current vertex
        """
        visited[v] = True
        for neighbor in self.graph[v]:
            if not visited[neighbor]:
                dfs(neighbor)
        stack.insert(0, v)

    # Run DFS on all unvisited vertices
    for vertex in range(self.V):
        if not visited[vertex]:
            dfs(vertex)

    return stack
```

Let me show you a practical example to demonstrate this concept with the class prerequisites for registration.

```
# Creating a course prerequisite graph
g = Graph(6)  # 6 courses numbered 0 to 5

# Adding prerequisites (edges)
g.add_edge(5, 2)  # Algorithms requires Data Structures
g.add_edge(5, 0)  # Algorithms requires Programming Basics
g.add_edge(4, 0)  # Advanced Programming requires Programming
Basics
g.add_edge(4, 1)  # Advanced Programming requires Computer
Architecture
g.add_edge(2, 3)  # Data Structures requires Discrete Math
g.add_edge(3, 1)  # Discrete Math requires Computer Architecture

# Get course order using Kahn's algorithm
course_order = g.topological_sort_kahn()
print("Course order:", course_order)

# Get course order using BFS
course_order = g.topological_sort_dfs()
```

```
print("Course order:", course_order)
```

Running this will return:

```
Course order: [5, 4, 2, 3, 1, 0]
Course order: [4, 5, 2, 0, 3, 1]
```

Why would the two ordering algorithms return a different sort order? Does it matter?

Performance Characteristics

Time Complexity: $O(V + E)$ for both approaches

Space Complexity: $O(V)$ for both approaches

Key Tips

- It only works on Directed Acyclic Graphs (DAGs) – if there's a cycle, you can't have a valid ordering
- The solution isn't always unique – there can be multiple valid orderings
- Kahn's algorithm has the bonus of being able to detect cycles

Common Interview Questions

Course Schedule Problems: This one appears in various forms, but the classic version is: "Given n courses and prerequisites (course A must be taken before course B), determine if it's possible to finish all courses."

- Build an adjacency list representation
- Use DFS or Khan's to detect cycles
- If there's a cycle, it's impossible to create a valid schedule

Alien Dictionary: "Given a sorted dictionary of an alien language, find the order of characters."

The trick is to:

- Compare adjacent words to extract character ordering rules
- Build a graph where edges represent "comes before" relationships
- Run topological sort to get the character ordering

Job Scheduling with Dependencies: "Given a set of jobs with dependencies, find a sequence to complete all jobs." To solve, you should

- Represent jobs as nodes and dependencies as directed edges
- Handle cases where multiple valid orderings exist
- Identify impossible scenarios (dependency cycles

> **Know the difference between BFS and DFS approaches.** Being able to implement both and discuss their trade-offs shows depth of understanding. I prefer Kahn's algorithm for its straightforward cycle detection, but know both so you can implemented them successfully in interviews.

Bucket Sort

Core Concept

Bucket Sort is also a small, elegant algorithm. If we go back to organizing our music collection, you would first organize them by genre (the buckets) and then arrange each genres section individually. Its is essentially a type of divide and conquer.

To implement bucket sort, do the following in order:

- Create a set of buckets (usually implemented as arrays or lists)
- Distribute the elements into these buckets based on their values
- Sort each bucket individually (typically using another sorting algorithm)
- Concatenate all buckets in order

Python Implementation

```python
def bucket_sort(arr):
    # Return empty array if input is empty
    if not arr:
        return arr

    # Create buckets using array length as bucket count
    max_val, min_val = max(arr), min(arr)
    bucket_count = len(arr)
    buckets = [[] for _ in range(bucket_count)]

    # Distribute elements into buckets
    for num in arr:
        # Calculate bucket index for this element
        index = int((num - min_val) * (bucket_count - 1) /
                (max_val - min_val))
        buckets[index].append(num)

    # Sort individual buckets
    for bucket in buckets:
        bucket.sort()

    # Concatenate all buckets into final result
    sorted_arr = []
    for bucket in buckets:
        sorted_arr.extend(bucket)

    return sorted_arr

# Example usage
```

```
arr = [0.897, 0.565, 0.656, 0.1234, 0.665, 0.3434]
sorted_arr = bucket_sort(arr)
print(sorted_arr)
```

What happens to our sort for edge cases, such as when all elements are the same or when there is a huge gap between values? Go test it now and determine what type of validation check you need to make in your code and test cases.

Performance Characteristics

Time Complexity: The time complexity of bucket sort is $O(n + k)$ in the average case, where:

- n is the number of elements to be sorted
- k is the number of buckets

However, to fully understand bucket sort's efficiency, we need to look at each step:

- Creating buckets: $O(k)$ time to initialize k buckets
- Distributing elements: $O(n)$ time to place n elements into their appropriate buckets
- Sorting individual buckets, depends on:
- The distribution of the elements
- The sorting algorithm used for each bucket
- The number of elements per bucket
- Concatenating buckets: $O(k)$ time to combine k buckets

The best case for Bucket sort is $O(n + k)$, so near linear performance. But in its worst case, it is $O(n^2)$, such as when all items are put into a single bucket and then you use a quadratic sorting algorithm for that bucket, like insertion sort.

Space Complexity: $O(n + k)$.

Key Tips

If the problem mentions a range or uniform distribution, bucket sort should immediately come to mind.

Be ready to discuss space complexity (usually O(n+k)) and when bucket sort might not be ideal (when k is very large).

Sometimes interviewers will follow up by asking what you'd do if the range becomes very large or unknown – pivot to comparison-based sorts like quicksort or merge sort.

Common Interview Questions

Here are three common bucket sort interview questions you're likely to encounter:

Sort an Array of Integers in a Known Range. This is the quintessential bucket sort question I've seen in countless interviews: "Given an array of integers where all elements are in range [0, k], sort the array in O(n) time."

- Example: Input: [3, 1, 4, 2, 5, 0, 3] with k=5 Output: [0, 1, 2, 3, 3, 4, 5]
- This directly tests if you recognize when to apply bucket sort - when elements are uniformly distributed in a known range, bucket sort achieves O(n) time complexity, beating comparison-based sorts.

A solid approach would be:

```
def bucket_sort(arr, k):
    # Create k+1 buckets (for numbers 0 to k)
```

```
count = [0] * (k + 1)

# Count occurrences of each element
for num in arr:
    count[num] += 1

# Reconstruct the sorted array
sorted_arr = []
for i in range(k + 1):
    sorted_arr.extend([i] * count[i])

return sorted_arr
```

Sort Floating-Point Numbers in Range [0,1]. "Sort an array of n floating-point numbers that are uniformly distributed over [0, 1)."

- Input: [0.42, 0.15, 0.73, 0.29, 0.53, 0.01]
- Output: [0.01, 0.15, 0.29, 0.42, 0.53, 0.73]
- This tests if you understand when and how to apply bucket sort to non-integer data and how to handle collisions within buckets.

A typical solution would involve:

```
def bucket_sort_float(arr):
    n = len(arr)
    buckets = [[] for _ in range(n)]

    # Place elements into buckets
    for num in arr:
        bucket_idx = int(n * num)
        buckets[bucket_idx].append(num)

    # Sort individual buckets
    for bucket in buckets:
        # Can use insertion sort for small buckets
        bucket.sort()
```

```
# Concatenate all buckets
result = []
for bucket in buckets:
    result.extend(bucket)

return result
```

Sort Nearly-Sorted Array (K-Sorted Array). "Sort an array where each element is at most k positions away from its sorted position."

- Input: [2, 1, 3, 5, 4, 7, 6], k=2
- Output: [1, 2, 3, 4, 5, 6, 7]
- While this can be solved with a heap, a bucket-based approach can achieve $O(n)$ time if k is small and fixed. This tests your ability to adapt sorting algorithms to specific constraints.

Here's an approach using k+1 sized buckets:

```
from collections import deque

def k_sort(arr, k):
    # Get length of input array
    n = len(arr)
    result = []

    # Create buckets for possible values
    min_val, max_val = min(arr), max(arr)
    buckets = [deque() for _ in range(k+1)]

    # Process elements in order
    for i in range(n):
        # Place elements in appropriate buckets
        bucket_idx = min(k, i)
        buckets[bucket_idx].append(arr[i])

        # Extract when k+1 buckets are filled
        if i >= k:
```

```
    # Find minimum non-empty bucket
    min_bucket = min(
        range(k+1),
        key=lambda x: float('inf')
        if not buckets[x] else buckets[x][0]
    )
    result.append(buckets[min_bucket].popleft())

# Extract remaining elements
while any(buckets):
    min_bucket = min(
        range(k+1),
        key=lambda x: float('inf')
        if not buckets[x] else buckets[x][0]
    )
    result.append(buckets[min_bucket].popleft())

return result
```

Quickselect

Core Concept

We are going to spend extra time on Quickselect as the likelihood of it coming up in an interview is very high.

Quickselect combines partitioning like Quicksort with a clever optimization that only explores the parts we actually need. Think of Quickselect like finding the median height of a group of students in a classroom - instead of fully sorting everyone, you just need to find the person who has exactly k people shorter than them.

Here is how Quickselect works:

- Choose a pivot element (in our implementation, we're using the last element)
- Partition the array around this pivot (smaller elements to the left,

larger to the right)
- Check if we found our k-th element:
- If the pivot index is k, we're done!
- If k is smaller, look in the left portion
- If k is larger, look in the right portion

Here is a visual example: Given at Initial array of [7, 5, 4, 3, 2, 8, 1] find the 3rd smallest element. We are choosing the last item in the array in consideration to be our pivot element then comparing with the array from left to right:

1. 7 is greater than 1, so we swap them and mark 1 as discarded because we know it is the 1st position. Rinse and repeat.
2. For the second step our pivot is 7 and we compare are previous numbers looking to items greater than seven to move to the right. 8 is larger than 7 so we swap them and mark them both as discarded.
3. Our next pivot is 2, the first number we consider, 5, is larger, so we swap them and mark the 2 as discarded.
4. Next, 5 has no items larger than it, so we discard it.
5. Our next pivot is 3, 4 is larger so we swap them, mark the 4 as discarded and find 3 is our smallest element.

Quickselect

| 7 | 5 | 4 | 3 | 2 | 8 | 1 |

Pivot is 1

| 1 | 5 | 4 | 3 | 2 | 8 | 7 |

Pivot is 7

| 1 | 5 | 4 | 3 | 2 | 7 | 8 |

Pivot is 2

| 1 | 2 | 4 | 3 | 5 | 7 | 8 |

Pivot is 5

| 1 | 2 | 4 | 3 | 5 | 7 | 8 |

Pivot is 3

| 1 | 2 | 3 | 4 | 5 | 7 | 8 |

3 is 3rd Smallest Element

Array in consideration   Discarded array

The partitioning step is where the real efficiency comes from. Just like Quicksort, we're moving elements around the pivot, but unlike Quicksort, we only recurse on one side of the partition.

In all three implementations I've provided, we're using the same example: finding the 3rd smallest element (**k=2 since we're using 0-based indexing**) in the array [3, 2, 1, 5, 6, 4].

Let's trace through one iteration:

```
Initial array: [3, 2, 1, 5, 6, 4]
Choose pivot (4)
After partitioning: [3, 2, 1, 4, 6, 5]
                             ^ now the pivot is at index 3
We want k=2, which is smaller than 3, so now we only look at
[3, 2, 1]
```

Lets walk though what happens during the first partition step by step in the code:

- We choose the last element with value 4 as our pivot.
- We start with storeIndex = 0 and iterate through the array:

```
Current array: [3, 2, 1, 5, 6, 4]  (pivot = 4 is at the end)
storeIndex = 0

i=0: arr[0]=3 < 4? Yes → swap arr[0] with arr[storeIndex] →
[3, 2, 1, 5, 6, 4] (no change)
     increment storeIndex to 1

i=1: arr[1]=2 < 4? Yes → swap arr[1] with arr[storeIndex] →
[3, 2, 1, 5, 6, 4] (no change)
     increment storeIndex to 2

i=2: arr[2]=1 < 4? Yes → swap arr[2] with arr[storeIndex] →
[3, 2, 1, 5, 6, 4] (no change)
     increment storeIndex to 3

i=3: arr[3]=5 < 4? No → do nothing
i=4: arr[4]=6 < 4? No → do nothing

After iterating, storeIndex = 3
```

Final step - put the pivot in its correct position by swapping arr[right] with arr[storeIndex]:

- Swap arr[5] (value 4) with arr[3] (value 5)
- Result: [3, 2, 1, 4, 6, 5]

In a standard Quickselect, the ordering of elements on either side of the pivot isn't guaranteed to be sorted - just that everything to the left is smaller than the pivot and everything to the right is greater.

This is a common point of confusion. What's important is that after partitioning:

- The pivot (value 4) is at index 3

- Everything to the left is less than 4
- Everything to the right is greater than 4

Common partitioning schemes, that is selecting an item to pivot on include both Lomuto (last element of the array as the pivot) and Hoare (first element of the array as the pivot) partitioning schemes.

Python Implementation

```python
def quickselect(arr, k):
    def partition(left, right, pivot_index):
        pivot_value = arr[pivot_index]
        # Move pivot to the end
        arr[pivot_index], arr[right] = arr[right],
        arr[pivot_index]

        store_index = left
        for i in range(left, right):
            if arr[i] < pivot_value:
                arr[store_index], arr[i] = arr[i],
                arr[store_index]
                store_index += 1

        # Move pivot to its final place
        arr[right], arr[store_index] = arr[store_index],
        arr[right]
        return store_index

    def select(left, right, k):
        if left == right:
            return arr[left]

        # Choose pivot (using middle element for simplicity)
        pivot_index = (left + right) // 2
        pivot_index = partition(left, right, pivot_index)

        if k == pivot_index:
```

```
            return arr[k]
        elif k < pivot_index:
            return select(left, pivot_index - 1, k)
        else:
            return select(pivot_index + 1, right, k)

    return select(0, len(arr) - 1, k)

# Example usage with detailed steps
def demo_quickselect():
    arr = [3, 2, 1, 5, 6, 4]
    k = 2  # Find 3rd smallest element (0-based index)

    print("Original array:", arr)
    result = quickselect(arr, k)
    print(f"The {k+1}th smallest element is: {result}")
    print("Note: Array may be partially sorted after running
    quickselect:", arr)

if __name__ == "__main__":
    demo_quickselect()
```

Running this will return:

```
Original array: [3, 2, 1, 5, 6, 4]
The 3th smallest element is: 3
Note: Array may be partially sorted after running quickselect:
[1, 2, 3, 4, 5, 6]
```

Performance Characteristics

Time Complexity: The time complexity is $O(n)$ on average, which is pretty remarkable when you think about it - we can find the kth element without fully sorting the array! In the worst case, it's $O(n^2)$, but this is rare with good pivot selection.

Space Complexity: $O(n)$

Consider using a random pivot selection for better average-case performance, especially if you suspect the input might be partially sorted.

Common Interview Questions

Compare and contrast Quickselect with Quicksort They'll want to see if you understand that Quickselect uses the same partitioning strategy but only recursively processes one partition (average $O(n)$ vs Quicksort's $O(n \log n)$). Explain the efficiency difference between the two.

When would you use Quickselect over other selection algorithms?

- When you need just the kth element, not a full sorting
- When average-case performance matters more than worst-case guarantees
- When working with large datasets where in-place algorithms are preferred

Find the kth largest element in an unsorted array This is probably THE most common Quickselect coding question. The trick here is understanding that finding the kth largest element is the same as finding the (n-k)th smallest element.

Find the median of an unsorted array The median is just the (n/2)th element in the sorted array.

Find the top k frequent elements in an array This is more advanced – you'll need to count frequencies first, then use Quickselect on the frequency counts.

Typical Follow-up Questions

These are the curveballs that often come after you've solved the initial problem:

How would you improve Quickselect for arrays with many duplicates? Three-way partitioning is the key here (elements less than, equal to, and greater than the pivot).

Can Quickselect be implemented iteratively? Yes, and they might ask you to convert your recursive solution to an iterative one.

How would you handle very large arrays that don't fit in memory? This is where external selection algorithms come in - you might discuss approaches like external merge selection.

What's the relationship between Quickselect and the median-of-medians algorithm? This is an advanced question - median-of-medians guarantees O(n) worst-case performance, unlike standard Quickselect.

Key Tips

Practice tracing through the algorithm verbally - Interviewers appreciate when you can walk through how the partitioning works step by step.

Be ready to implement different pivot selection strategies - Discuss discussing random pivoting or other pivoting strategies.

Know common optimizations - Like using insertion sort for small subarrays or the "median of three" pivot selection, which I describe below.

Understand the practical tradeoffs - I got great feedback once when I discussed when I'd choose Quickselect over heap-based approaches in real systems.

Interviews are evaluating your thought process as much as they are your final code, and this is a great topic to talk on. I've seen candidates get offers despite not perfectly solving every problem because they communicated their thinking clearly.

Pro Tips

Partition Strategy: All versions above use the same basic partition strategy, but each language has its own elegant way of handling the swaps:

- Python: tuple unpacking
- Java: explicit swap method
- C++: std::swap

Pivot Selection: I've chosen the middle element as pivot for simplicity, but in real-world applications, you might want to use:

```
pivot_index = random.randint(left, right)
```

Extras: Partitioning Strategy

Here we are going to cover the median-of-three partitioning to move your knowledge of Quickselect from average to outstanding. This technique will fundamentally change how you approach quicksort implementations, and it's one of those clever algorithmic improvements that demonstrates how small changes can yield significant performance gains.

The standard quicksort algorithm has a critical weakness: if you always pick the first (or last) element as the pivot, and your data is already sorted or reverse-sorted, you'll get the worst-case $O(n^2)$ performance. This happens because each partition operation produces one empty subarray and one with n-1 elements.

Median of three partitioning addresses this vulnerability by making a more intelligent pivot selection:

- Select three elements from the array: typically the first, middle, and last elements
- Find the median value among these three elements
- Use this median value as the pivot for partitioning

For example, if we have an array [10, 80, 30, 90, 40] and choose the first (10), middle (30), and last (40) elements, the median is 30, which becomes our pivot.

```
def median_of_three(arr, low, high):
    mid = (low + high) // 2

    # Find median of first, middle, and last elements
    if arr[low] > arr[mid]:
        arr[low], arr[mid] = arr[mid], arr[low]
    if arr[mid] > arr[high]:
        arr[mid], arr[high] = arr[high], arr[mid]
    if arr[low] > arr[mid]:
        arr[low], arr[mid] = arr[mid], arr[low]

    # Return the median as pivot (usually at position high-1)
    arr[mid], arr[high-1] = arr[high-1], arr[mid]
    return arr[high-1]
```

This will avoid the worst case on sorted data, where you are given nearly-sorted datasets. This will also give your production systems more predictable performance across varying patterns. And, finally, it will add protection against malicious inputs. With median of threes, the time and space complexity of best/average, and worst case remains. However, now the worst case is very unlikely to happen in practice.

For larger systems, you can extend this and use Median of nine, were sampling nine values can provide an even better pivot, or combining median of three with some randomness to add robustness.

Prefix Sum

Core Concept

The prefix sum (cumulative sum) is refreshingly straightforward: for an array A, the prefix sum array P contains the sum of all elements up to each position. So P[i] equals the sum of elements A[0] + A[1] + ... + A[i].

What makes this special is that once we've computed this prefix array (in just one pass!), we can find the sum of any subarray from index i to j in constant time using sum(A[i..j]) = P[j] − P[i−1] (with a slight adjustment for i=0).

Given an array A of length n:

The prefix sum array P has the same length as n

```
P[i] = A[0] + A[1] + ... + A[i]
```

After computing the prefix sum array, you can calculate the sum of any contiguous subarray from index i to j in O(1) time using:

```
sum(A[i..j]) = P[j] - P[i-1]
```

For the edge case where i = 0, the formula simplifies to sum(A[0..j]) = P[j].

This transforms a problem that would typically require O(n) time (iterating through elements i to j) into an O(1) operation after an initial O(n) preprocessing step.

Let me give you an example:

With this original array, [3, 1, 4, 1, 5], the prefix becomes [3, 4, 8, 9, 14], so finding the sum from index 1 to 3 is just prefix[3]—prefix[0] = 9 - 3 = 6, which matches 1 + 4 + 1 = 6.

The prefix array of [3, 4, 8, 9, 14] is built by adding each number in order from the left. We start with the first number, 3. Next, we add the second number, 1, to get 4. Next, we add the third number, 4, to get 8, until each number in the new array is the sum of all numbers that came before it in the original array. Now, we have an array of prefixes we can use to do calculations quickly.

Python Implementation

```python
def build_prefix_sum(arr):
    n = len(arr)
    prefix_sum = [0] * n
    prefix_sum[0] = arr[0]

    for i in range(1, n):
        prefix_sum[i] = prefix_sum[i-1] + arr[i]

    return prefix_sum

def range_sum(prefix_sum, i, j):
    if i == 0:
        return prefix_sum[j]
    else:
        return prefix_sum[j] - prefix_sum[i-1]

# Example usage
arr = [3, 1, 4, 1, 5, 9, 2, 6]
prefix = build_prefix_sum(arr)
print(f"Original array: {arr}")
print(f"Prefix sum array: {prefix}")
print(f"Sum of elements from index 2 to 5: {range_sum(prefix,
2, 5)}")
```

Performance Characteristics

Time Complexity: Building the prefix sum array: O(n). Querying the sum of a range: O(1)

Space Complexity: Prefix sum array: O(n)

Key Tips

Zero-Indexing: Be careful with zero-indexing when calculating range sums. The formula is P[j] - P[i-1] when i > 0, but just P[j] when i = 0.

Handling Edge Cases: To simplify edge case handling, sometimes creating a prefix array with length n+1 is helpful, where the first element is 0. This way, the range sum formula becomes P[j+1] - P[i] for all ranges.

In-Place Calculation: If memory is a concern, you can calculate the prefix sum in-place, modifying the original array.

Numerical Stability: Know integer overflows in large arrays with potentially large sums. Use long integers when necessary.

Preprocessing: Prefix sums are a preprocessing technique. The time spent building the array is amortized across multiple queries.

Pro Tips

2D Prefix Sums: The concept extends to 2D arrays (matrices). With a 2D prefix sum matrix, you can calculate the sum of any rectangular submatrix in O(1) time.

Difference Arrays: The inverse operation of prefix sum is the difference array (sometimes called delta encoding). If you need to perform range updates (add a value to a range of indices), difference arrays can be combined with prefix sums for efficient solutions.

Sliding Window + Prefix Sum: Prefix sums can optimize many sliding window problems, especially when the window size is variable.

Prefix XOR: The concept isn't limited to sums. Prefix XOR arrays are useful for problems involving XOR operations on subarrays.

Prefix Min/Max: Similar to prefix sums, you can create prefix minimum or maximum arrays for range minimum/maximum queries.

Monotonic Queues: When combined with monotonic queues, prefix sums can efficiently solve sliding window minimum/maximum problems.

Common Interview Questions

Subarray Sum Equals K: Given an array of integers and a target value K, find the number of continuous subarrays whose sum equals K.

Maximum Subarray Sum: Find the contiguous subarray within an array with the largest sum.

Range Sum Query – Immutable: Design a data structure that efficiently handles multiple range sum queries on a fixed array.

Subarray Sum Divisible by K: Count the number of continuous subarrays whose sum is divisible by K.

Product of Array Except Self: Compute an array where each element is the product of all elements in the original array except the element at that position.

Count Number of Nice Subarrays: Count the subarrays with exactly k odd numbers.

Path Sum III: Count the number of paths in a binary tree where the sum of values along the path equals a given sum.

Continuous Subarray Sum: Check if the array has a continuous subarray of size at least 2 that sums up to a multiple of k.

Monotonic Stack

Core Concept

A monotonic stack maintains elements in either strictly increasing or strictly decreasing order. As we process elements, we remove them from the stack until we can maintain this monotonic property before pushing the new element.

The beauty of monotonic stacks is that they allow us to efficiently find the "next greater/smaller element" or "previous greater/smaller element" for each element in an array in O(n) time. This pattern comes up surprisingly often in interview questions and real-world problems.

Python Implementation

Let's implement a monotonic increasing stack to find the next greater element for each element in an array:

```python
def next_greater_element(nums):
    # Initialize result with -1 for no greater element
    result = [-1] * len(nums)
    stack = []  # Monotonic stack

    for i in range(len(nums)):
```

```
    # Pop and update for elements smaller than current
    while stack and nums[i] > nums[stack[-1]]:
        popped_index = stack.pop()
        result[popped_index] = nums[i]

    # Push current index to stack
    stack.append(i)

  return result

# Example usage
nums = [4, 5, 2, 10, 8]
print(next_greater_element(nums))
```

This implementation maintains a stack of indices (rather than values), allowing us to update our result array easily.

Performance Characteristics

Time Complexity: O(n), where n is the length of the input array. Although we have nested loops, each element is pushed and popped at most once, so the amortized time complexity is linear.

Space Complexity: O(n) in the worst case when all elements must be stored in the stack.

Key Tips

Direction Matters: Depending on the problem, you might need to traverse the array from left to right or right to left.

Stack Content: You can store either values or indices in the stack. Storing indices is often more flexible as it allows you to reference the original array.

Variations: You might need a monotonically increasing or monotonically decreasing stack based on the problem requirements.

Circular Arrays: For problems involving circular arrays, you can iterate through the array twice (use the modulo operation for indexing).

Pro Tips

Visualize the Process: After each operation, drawing out the stack state helps one understand how elements flow through.

Pattern Recognition: Monotonic stacks are particularly useful for problems involving "next greater/smaller" or "previous greater/smaller" elements.

Combined with Binary Search: Some advanced problems combine monotonic stacks with binary search for robust solutions.

Dynamic Programming: Monotonic stacks can sometimes simplify dynamic programming solutions by efficiently finding specific boundaries.

Practice Tracing: Before coding, practice tracing the algorithm on paper first. I can't emphasize this enough - it saved me in multiple interviews!

Common Interview Questions

Next/Previous Greater/Smaller Element: Find the next greater element for each element in an array. We covered this implementation above.

Daily Temperatures: Given an array of daily temperatures, return an array where each day tells you how many days you need to wait until a warmer day.

```
def daily_temperatures(temperatures):
    n = len(temperatures)
    result = [0] * n
    stack = []

    for i in range(n):
        while stack and temperatures[i] >
        temperatures[stack[-1]]:
            prev_day = stack.pop()
            result[prev_day] = i - prev_day
        stack.append(i)

    return result

# Example
temps = [73, 74, 75, 71, 69, 72, 76, 73]
print(daily_temperatures(temps)) # Output: [1, 1, 4, 2, 1, 1,
0, 0]
```

Largest Rectangle in Histogram: Find the area of the largest rectangle in a histogram.

```
def largest_rectangle_area(heights):
    stack = []
    max_area = 0
    i = 0

    while i < len(heights):
        # Push if stack empty or height increasing
        if not stack or heights[stack[-1]] <= heights[i]:
            stack.append(i)
            i += 1
        else:
            # Calculate area with stack top as smallest bar
            top = stack.pop()

            # Calculate width
            width = i if not stack else i - stack[-1] - 1
```

```
        # Update max area
        max_area = max(max_area, heights[top] * width)

    # Process remaining stack elements
    while stack:
        top = stack.pop()
        width = i if not stack else i - stack[-1] - 1
        max_area = max(max_area, heights[top] * width)

    return max_area

# Example usage
heights = [2, 1, 5, 6, 2, 3]
print(largest_rectangle_area(heights))
```

Trapping Rain Water: Calculate how much water can be trapped between the bars.

```
def trap(height):
    if not height:
        return 0

    n = len(height)
    left_max = [0] * n
    right_max = [0] * n

    # Fill left_max
    left_max[0] = height[0]
    for i in range(1, n):
        left_max[i] = max(left_max[i-1], height[i])

    # Fill right_max
    right_max[n-1] = height[n-1]
    for i in range(n-2, -1, -1):
        right_max[i] = max(right_max[i+1], height[i])

    # Calculate trapped water
    water = 0
```

```
    for i in range(n):
        water += min(left_max[i], right_max[i]) - height[i]

    return water

# Example
height = [0, 1, 0, 2, 1, 0, 1, 3, 2, 1, 2, 1]
print(trap(height))  # Output: 6
```

Union Find

Core Concept

Union Find (also called Disjoint Set Union or DSU) is a data structure that keeps track of elements split into one or more disjoint sets. It provides near-constant-time operations to:

- **Find**: Determine which set an element belongs to
- **Union**: Join two sets together

Think of it like managing friend groups at a party. Initially, everyone is alone. As people meet, their circles merge. Union Find helps us efficiently track who's in which social circle.

The key insight is using a tree structure where each element points to its parent, with the root of the tree representing the set's representative element.

Python Implementation

```
class UnionFind:
    def __init__(self, n):
```

```python
        # Initial parent, each is own set
        self.parent = list(range(n))
        # Rank for balancing tree
        self.rank = [0] * n
        # Count of disjoint sets
        self.count = n

    def find(self, x):
        # Path compression
        if self.parent[x] != x:
            self.parent[x] = self.find(self.parent[x])
        return self.parent[x]

    def union(self, x, y):
        # Find set roots
        root_x = self.find(x)
        root_y = self.find(y)

        # Already in same set
        if root_x == root_y:
            return False

        # Union by rank
        if self.rank[root_x] < self.rank[root_y]:
            self.parent[root_x] = root_y
        elif self.rank[root_x] > self.rank[root_y]:
            self.parent[root_y] = root_x
        else:
            # Equal ranks
            self.parent[root_y] = root_x
            self.rank[root_x] += 1

        # Decrease set count
        self.count -= 1
        return True

    def is_connected(self, x, y):
        # Check same set
        return self.find(x) == self.find(y)
```

I've added three comprehensive test cases to demonstrate the UnionFind data structure in action:

1. **Friend Circles Test**: This test shows how to use the UnionFind to identify social groups among students, based on their friendship connections.
2. **Network Connectivity Test**: This test demonstrates how to determine whether all computers in a network can communicate with each other and identifies isolated network components.
3. **Dynamic Connectivity Test**: This test illustrates the dynamic nature of the data structure by adding connections over time and tracking how the connectivity changes.

Each test includes detailed sample data and step-by-step output to help visualize how the UnionFind operations work. The examples cover both practical applications and demonstrate all the key features of the implementation, including:

- Path compression
- Union by rank
- Tracking the count of disjoint sets
- Checking connectivity between elements

If you run short on time, a short initialization and check to see if it is connected will give you a count of disjointed sets.

```
def main():
    # Initialize with 10 elements
    uf = UnionFind(10)

    # Connect elements
    uf.union(0, 1)
    uf.union(1, 2)
    uf.union(3, 4)
```

```
# Check connections
print(uf.is_connected(0, 2))  # True
print(uf.is_connected(0, 4))  # False

# Disjoint sets count
print(uf.count)  # 7

if __name__ == "__main__":
    main()
```

Performance Characteristics

Time Complexity:
By Operation
Construction - O(n)
Find - O(α(n)) - Almost constant
Union - O(α(n)) - Almost constant
Is Connected - O(α(n)) - Almost constant
Here, α(n) is the inverse **Ackermann function**, which grows incredibly slowly. It can be considered a constant (≤ 4 for any reasonable input size) for all practical purposes.

Space Complexity
The space complexity is O(n) for storing the parent and rank arrays.

Key Tips

Always use both optimizations (path compression and union by rank) for optimal performance.

Initialize carefully - every element starts as its own set.

Check if elements are in the same set before performing a union.

Use 0-indexing or adjust accordingly - the implementations above assume elements are numbered 0 to n-1.

Tracking the size of each set instead of ranking can be helpful for some problems.

Pro Tips

Weighted Union Find: Instead of using rank, you can use the size of each set to decide which becomes the parent. This can be more intuitive in some cases.

```
# Inside the UnionFind class, replace rank with size
def __init__(self, n):
    self.parent = list(range(n))
    self.size = [1] * n  # Each set initially has size 1
    self.count = n

def union(self, x, y):
    root_x = self.find(x)
    root_y = self.find(y)

    if root_x == root_y:
        return False

    # Attach smaller tree to the root of larger tree
    if self.size[root_x] < self.size[root_y]:
        self.parent[root_x] = root_y
        self.size[root_y] += self.size[root_x]
    else:
        self.parent[root_y] = root_x
        self.size[root_x] += self.size[root_y]

    self.count -= 1
    return True
```

Component Extraction: Get all elements in a specific set:

```
def get_component(self, x):
    root = self.find(x)
    return [i for i in range(len(self.parent))
            if self.find(i) == root]
```

Lazy Union Find: In some applications, you can defer the find operations until needed, which can be more efficient.

Dynamic Union Find: If you need to add elements dynamically, you can use a map or dictionary instead of arrays.

Path Halving/Splitting: Alternative path compression techniques that require less memory writes but achieve similar performance.

Common Interview Questions

Number of Connected Components in an Undirected Graph

Given n nodes labeled 0 to n-1 and a list of undirected edges, find the number of connected components.

```
def count_components(n, edges):
    uf = UnionFind(n)
    for u, v in edges:
        uf.union(u, v)
    return uf.count
```

Friend Circles

Given a matrix where Mi = 1 if person i and person j are friends, find the total number of friend circles.

```
def friend_circles(M):
    n = len(M)
    uf = UnionFind(n)
```

```
for i in range(n):
    for j in range(i+1, n):
        if M[i][j] == 1:
            uf.union(i, j)

return uf.count
```

Redundant Connection

One extra edge was added in a graph that started as a tree. Find that edge.

```
def find_redundant_connection(edges):
    n = len(edges)
    uf = UnionFind(n + 1)

    for u, v in edges:
        if not uf.union(u, v):
            return [u, v]

    return []
```

Accounts Merge

Given a list of accounts where each element is a list [name, email1, email2, ...], merge accounts if they belong to the same person (two accounts belong to the same person if they share an email).

Minimum Spanning Tree (Kruskal's Algorithm)

Find the minimum weight tree that connects all nodes in a weighted undirected graph.

```
def kruskal_mst(n, edges):
    # Sort edges by weight
    edges.sort(key=lambda x: x[2])

    uf = UnionFind(n)
    mst = []
```

```
for u, v, weight in edges:
    if uf.union(u, v):
        mst.append((u, v, weight))

        # Early termination when we have n-1 edges
        if len(mst) == n - 1:
            break

return mst
```

Regions Cut By Slashes

Given an n x n grid where each cell is either empty or contains a forward slash ('/') or a backslash (''), find the number of regions the grid is split into.

> Union Find shines in problems involving connected components, equivalence relations, or whenever you need to join sets and query membership efficiently. Master these patterns, and your toolkit will have a robust algorithm.

Prim's Algorithm (Minimum Spanning Trees)

Core Concept

Prim's algorithm finds the minimum spanning tree (MST) of a **weighted, connected, undirected graph**. Think of it as finding the most economical way to connect all points in a network while using the least total "cost" (or weight).

The beauty of Prim's approach is its greedy nature: it grows the MST one edge at a time, always choosing the lowest-weight edge that connects a vertex in the tree to a vertex outside the tree. This simple idea produces optimal results every time!

The steps are:

1. Start with any vertex as a single-vertex tree.
2. Repeatedly add the minimum-weight edge that connects the tree to a vertex not yet in the tree.
3. Continue until all vertices are included

Python Implementation

```
import heapq

def prims_algorithm(graph):
    """
    Find minimum spanning tree using Prim's algorithm.

    Builds a minimum spanning tree (MST) by greedily selecting
    the lowest-weight edge that connects a vertex in the MST
    to a vertex outside the MST.

    Args:
        graph: Dictionary representing an adjacency list with
        weights
                {node: [(neighbor, weight), ...], ...}

    Returns:
        List of tuples (u, v, weight) representing edges in the MST

    Time Complexity:
        O(E log V) where E is the number of edges and V is
        the number of vertices

    Space Complexity:
        O(E + V) for storing the priority queue and tracking
        vertices

    Example:
        >>> graph = {
        ...     'A': [('B', 2), ('C', 3)],
        ...     'B': [('A', 2), ('C', 1), ('D', 1)],
```

```
...      'C': [('A', 3), ('B', 1), ('D', 2)],
...      'D': [('B', 1), ('C', 2)]
... }
>>> prims_algorithm(graph)
[('A', 'B', 2), ('B', 'C', 1), ('B', 'D', 1)]
"""
# Start with first vertex
start_vertex = list(graph.keys())[0]

# Track MST vertices and edges
mst_vertices = {start_vertex}
mst_edges = []

# Priority queue of edges
edges = [(weight, start_vertex, neighbor)
         for neighbor, weight in graph[start_vertex]]
heapq.heapify(edges)

# Process edges while not all vertices included
while edges and len(mst_vertices) < len(graph):
    weight, u, v = heapq.heappop(edges)

    # Add edge if it connects new vertex
    if v not in mst_vertices:
        mst_vertices.add(v)
        mst_edges.append((u, v, weight))

        # Add new candidate edges
        for neighbor, w in graph[v]:
            if neighbor not in mst_vertices:
                heapq.heappush(edges, (w, v, neighbor))

    return mst_edges

# Example usage
if __name__ == "__main__":
    graph = {
        'A': [('B', 2), ('D', 1)],
        'B': [('A', 2), ('D', 2), ('C', 3)],
        'C': [('B', 3), ('D', 4)],
```

```
    'D': [('A', 1), ('B', 2), ('C', 4)]
}

mst = prims_algorithm(graph)
print("Minimum Spanning Tree edges:")
for u, v, weight in mst:
    print(f"{u} -- {v} : {weight}")
```

Performance Characteristics

Time Complexity:

- With an adjacency matrix and array-based selection: $O(V^2)$
- With an adjacency list and binary heap: $O(E \log V)$
- With an adjacency list and Fibonacci heap: $O(E + V \log V)$

Where V is the number of vertices and E is the number of edges.

Space Complexity:

- O(V) is used to track visited vertices.
- O(E) for the priority queue in the worst case

The implementation choice depends on your graph's density. For dense graphs ($E \approx V^2$), the matrix approach works well. The adjacency list with a heap is much more efficient for sparse graphs.

Key Tips

These tips helped me avoid common pitfalls when implementing Prim's algorithm:

Initialization matters: Always start with a valid vertex and initialize your data structures properly.

Priority queue optimization: Use decrease-key operations if available in your language's priority queue implementation.

Graph representation: Choose between an adjacency matrix or list based on your graph's density.

Handle disconnected graphs: Prim's assumes a connected graph. If your graph might be disconnected, run the algorithm for each component.

Edge case handling: Don't forget to handle graphs with just 1 or 0 vertices as exceptional cases.

Pro Tips

Custom comparators: When edge weights have multiple criteria, use custom comparators in your priority queue.

Lazy deletion: Instead of removing edges from the priority queue when a vertex is added to the MST, use a lazy approach by checking if the destination is already in the MST when you dequeue an edge.

Dynamic graphs: For changing graphs, consider modified versions of Prim's that can efficiently update an existing MST.

Memory optimization: Consider a sparse matrix representation or compressed data structures for extremely large graphs.

Parallelization: Certain parts of Prim's algorithm can be parallelized for significant performance gains on multi-core systems.

Common Interview Questions

Compare Prim's and Kruskal's algorithms: When would you choose one?

Correctness proof: Explain why Prim's algorithm always finds the minimum spanning tree.

Modifications: How would you modify Prim's algorithm to find the maximum spanning tree?

Applications: What are real-world applications of minimum spanning trees?

Edge weights: How would you handle negative edge weights in Prim's algorithm?

Implementation challenge: Implement Prim's algorithm with a specific time/space complexity constraint.

Distributed version: How would you implement Prim's algorithm in a distributed environment?

> Understanding the underlying principles is more important than memorizing code.

Kruskal's Algorithm

If you struggle with graph algorithms, they are just picking the cheapest roads to connect all cities.

Core Concept

Kruskal's algorithm finds the Minimum Spanning Tree (MST) of a **weighted, connected, undirected graph** – essentially the cheapest way to connect all vertices. Think of it as finding the most economical way to build roads between cities where you want to minimize total construction costs while ensuring everyone can reach everyone else.

The algorithm follows a refreshingly straightforward approach:

1. Sort all edges by weight (cost)
2. Start with an empty graph.
3. Add edges one by one (smallest weight first)
4. Skip any edge that would create a cycle.
5. Stop when you've added n-1 edges (where n is the number of vertices)

This greedy strategy always produces the optimal solution.

Python Implementation

```python
class DisjointSet:
    """
    Disjoint-Set (Union-Find) data structure
    implementation.

    Efficiently tracks disjoint sets with path
    compression and union by rank optimizations
    for near-constant time operations.

    Attributes:
        parent (list): Parent pointers for each
            element
        rank (list): Rank of each set to optimize
            union operations
    """
```

```python
def __init__(self, n):
    # Initialize parent and rank lists
    self.parent = list(range(n))
    self.rank = [0] * n

def find(self, x):
    """
    Find the representative of the set
    containing element x.

    Args:
        x (int): Element to find

    Returns:
        int: Representative of x's set

    Time Complexity: Oα((n)) amortized
    """
    if self.parent[x] != x:
        # Path compression
        self.parent[x] = self.find(
            self.parent[x]
        )
    return self.parent[x]

def union(self, x, y):
    """
    Merge the sets containing elements x
    and y.

    Args:
        x (int): First element
        y (int): Second element

    Returns:
        bool: True if x and y were in
            different sets (union performed),
            False if they were already in
            the same set
```

```
    Time Complexity: Oα((n)) amortized
    """
    # Find roots of x and y
    root_x = self.find(x)
    root_y = self.find(y)

    # Check if already in same set
    if root_x == root_y:
        return False

    # Union by rank
    if self.rank[root_x] < self.rank[root_y]:
        self.parent[root_x] = root_y
    elif self.rank[root_x] > self.rank[root_y]:
        self.parent[root_y] = root_x
    else:
        # Ranks are equal, arbitrarily choose
        # one as root
        self.parent[root_y] = root_x
        self.rank[root_x] += 1

    return True


def kruskal(graph, vertices):
    """
    Find minimum spanning tree using
    Kruskal's algorithm.

    Builds a minimum spanning tree by
    adding edges in order of increasing
    weight, skipping edges that would
    create cycles.

    Args:
        graph (list): Adjacency list of the
            form [[(v, weight),...],...]
            where graph[u] contains edges
            from u
        vertices (int): Number of vertices
```

```
        in the graph

Returns:
    tuple: (mst, total_weight) where:
        - mst is list of (u, v, weight)
            tuples representing MST edges
        - total_weight is the sum of all
            edge weights in the MST

Time Complexity: O(E log E)
Space Complexity: O(V + E)
"""
# Create a list of all edges
edges = []
for u in range(vertices):
    for v, weight in graph[u]:
        # Add each edge only once
        if u < v:
            edges.append((weight, u, v))

# Sort edges by weight
edges.sort()

# Initialize disjoint set
ds = DisjointSet(vertices)

mst = []
mst_weight = 0

# Process edges in order of increasing
# weight
for weight, u, v in edges:
    # If including this edge doesn't
    # create a cycle
    if ds.union(u, v):
        mst.append((u, v, weight))
        mst_weight += weight

        # Stop when we have V-1 edges
        if len(mst) == vertices - 1:
```

```
            break

    return mst, mst_weight


# Example usage
if __name__ == "__main__":
    # Example graph: adjacency list with
    # (neighbor, weight) pairs
    vertices = 6
    graph = [[] for _ in range(vertices)]

    # Add edges: (u, v, weight)
    edges = [
        (0, 1, 4), (0, 2, 3), (1, 2, 1),
        (1, 3, 2), (2, 3, 4), (2, 4, 3),
        (3, 4, 2), (3, 5, 1), (4, 5, 3)
    ]

    for u, v, w in edges:
        # Undirected graph
        graph[u].append((v, w))
        graph[v].append((u, w))

    mst, total_weight = kruskal(graph, vertices)

    print("Edges in the MST:")
    for u, v, w in mst:
        print(f"{u} -- {v} == {w}")
    print(f"Total MST weight: {total_weight}")
```

Performance Characteristics

Time Complexity: O(E log E) or O(E log V)

- Sorting E edges takes O(E log E)
- Union-Find operations take O(E log V) with path compression and union by rank

- Since E can be at most V^2, log E is at most 2 log V, so $O(E \log V)$ dominates

Space Complexity: $O(E + V)$

- $O(E)$ for storing the edges
- $O(V)$ for the disjoint set data structure

In my experience, understanding these complexities has been crucial for explaining algorithm choices in system design interviews.

Key Tips

Continually optimize Union-Find: Implement path compression and union by rank for near-constant time operations.

Handle undirected edges carefully: In an undirected graph, add each edge only once to your sorting list to avoid duplicate work.

Early termination: The algorithm can stop once you've added n-1 edges to the MST, which can provide significant speedups.

Edge cases: Be prepared to handle disconnected graphs and empty graphs (you'll get a minimum spanning forest).

Pro Tips

Know when to use Prim's instead: For dense graphs where E approaches V^2, Prim's algorithm with a binary heap can be more efficient ($O(E \log V)$).

Custom Union-Find optimizations: In high-performance scenarios, consider "path halving" or "path splitting" techniques to further optimize your Union-Find.

Memory optimization: If memory is a concern, you can modify the algorithm to process edges individually without storing them all upfront.

Parallelization: The edge sorting step can be parallelized for massive graphs, and some parts of the Union-Find can be optimized for multicore processors.

Common Interview Questions

Algorithm comparison: "Compare Kruskal's and Prim's algorithms. When would you use each?" (Kruskal's is typically better for sparse graphs, Prim's for dense graphs)

Disconnected graphs: "What does Kruskal's algorithm produce for a disconnected graph?" (A minimum spanning forest)

Maximum spanning tree: "How would you modify Kruskal's to find the maximum spanning tree?" (Sort edges in descending order instead of ascending)

Efficiency for sparse graphs: "How would you implement Kruskal's for a graph with millions of vertices but few edges?" (Focus on efficient Union-Find and consider streaming approaches)

Cycle detection: "Explain how Union-Find helps detect cycles in Kruskal's algorithm." (Two vertices already in the same set would form a cycle if connected

> Prims and Kruskal's both have a clean simplicity—**always choose the cheapest valid connection.**

Binary Manipulation

Core Concept

Binary manipulation involves directly working with the binary (base-2) representation of numbers, applying operations like AND, OR, XOR, shifts, and rotations to solve problems efficiently.

At its heart, binary manipulation is about understanding that computers store all data as sequences of bits (0s and 1s) and learning to leverage this representation. Rather than thinking about decimal values, we work directly with these bits.

The fundamental binary operations are:

- **AND (&)**: Returns 1 if both bits are 1, otherwise 0
- **OR (|)**: Returns 1 if at least one bit is 1, otherwise 0
- **XOR (^)**: Returns 1 if exactly one bit is 1, otherwise 0
- **NOT (~)**: Flips each bit (0 becomes 1, 1 becomes 0)
- **Left Shift («)**: Shifts bits to the left, effectively multiplying by powers of 2
- **Right Shift (»)**: Shifts bits to the right, effectively dividing by powers of 2

These seemingly simple operations unlock efficient solutions for problems ranging from setting/clearing/toggling individual bits to more complex operations like finding unique elements, detecting cycles, or optimizing space usage.

Python Implementation

```python
def binary_operations_demo():
    # Demonstrate binary operations with
```

```python
# sample numbers
a = 25  # 11001 in binary
b = 13  # 01101 in binary

# Print decimal and binary
# representations
print(f"a = {a} (binary: {bin(a)[2:].zfill(5)})")
print(f"b = {b} (binary: {bin(b)[2:].zfill(5)})")

# Bitwise AND operation
print(f"a & b = {a & b} (binary: {bin(a & b)[2:].zfill(5)})")

# Bitwise OR operation
print(f"a | b = {a | b} (binary: {bin(a | b)[2:].zfill(5)})")

# Bitwise XOR operation
print(f"a ^ b = {a ^ b} (binary: {bin(a ^ b)[2:].zfill(5)})")

# Bitwise NOT operation
print(f"~a = {~a} (truncated binary: {bin(~a &
0xFF)[2:].zfill(8)})")

# Left shift operation
print(f"a << 2 = {a << 2} (binary: {bin(a <<
2)[2:].zfill(7)})")

# Right shift operation
print(f"a >> 2 = {a >> 2} (binary: {bin(a >>
2)[2:].zfill(3)})")


def count_set_bits(n):
    """
    Count the number of 1s in binary
    representation of n
    """
    count = 0
    while n:
        # Check least significant bit
        count += n & 1
```

279

```
        # Right shift by 1
        n >>= 1
    return count


def is_power_of_two(n):
    """
    Check if n is a power of 2
    """
    # Detect single bit set
    return n > 0 and (n & (n-1)) == 0


def set_bit(n, position):
    """Set the bit at given position to 1"""
    return n | (1 << position)


def clear_bit(n, position):
    """Clear the bit at given position to 0"""
    return n & ~(1 << position)


def toggle_bit(n, position):
    """Toggle the bit at given position"""
    return n ^ (1 << position)


def is_bit_set(n, position):
    """
    Check if bit at given position is 1
    """
    return (n & (1 << position)) != 0


def find_single_number(nums):
    """
    Find single number in array where
    all others appear twice
    """
```

```
result = 0
for num in nums:
    # XOR of number with itself is 0
    result ^= num
return result
```

Performance Characteristics

Time Complexity: Most basic bit operations (AND, OR, XOR, NOT, shifts) are O(1) - constant time operations.

Space Complexity: Generally O(1) as these operations don't require additional space proportional to input size.

Binary manipulation operations have excellent performance characteristics and are often used for optimization. For operations that need to process all bits (like counting set bits), the time complexity becomes O(log n), where n is the number since an n-bit number can represent values up to 2^n.

Some algorithms that leverage binary manipulation can achieve dramatic improvements over naive solutions.

Key Tips

Sign Implications: Be careful with signed integers. Right, shifts on negative numbers may behave differently depending on the language (arithmetic vs. logical shift).

Boundary Values: When working with binary, always consider edge cases like:

- 0 (all bits are 0)
- -1 (all bits are 1 in two's complement)
- Maximum/minimum values of the data type

Use Built-ins When Available: Many languages offer optimized built-in functions for common operations:

- Python: bin(), int.bit_length(), int.bit_count() (Python 3.10+)
- Java: Integer.bitCount(), Integer.numberOfLeadingZeros()
- C++: std::bitset, ___builtin_popcount(), ___builtin_ctz()

Mask Technique: Create masks to isolate specific bits:

- Get last n bits: x & ((1 « n) - 1)
- Get bits from position i to j: (x » i) & ((1 « (j-i+1)) - 1)

Bit Testing: To test if the ith bit is set: (n & (1 « i)) != 0

Pro Tips

Clear LSB: Clear the least significant set bit with n & (n-1).

```
# Clear rightmost set bit
n = n & (n-1)
```

Isolate LSB: Isolate the least significant set bit with n & -n or n & (~n + 1).

```
# Isolate rightmost set bit
rightmost_bit = n & -n
```

Swap Without Temp Variable:

```
# Swap a and b without temporary variable
a = a ^ b
b = a ^ b
a = a ^ b
```

Calculate XOR from 0 to n Efficiently:

```
def xor_from_0_to_n(n):
    """Compute XOR of all numbers from 0 to n without loop"""
    remainder = n % 4
    if remainder == 0:
        return n
    elif remainder == 1:
        return 1
    elif remainder == 2:
        return n + 1
    else:  # remainder == 3
        return 0
```

Off-by-One Trick: Check if a number is one less than a power of 2:

```
# Check if n is one less than a power of 2
def is_one_less_than_power_of_two(n):
    return n > 0 and (n & (n + 1)) == 0
```

Flip Bits in a Range: Using XOR with a mask.

```
# Flip bits from position i to j
def flip_bits_in_range(n, i, j):
    # Create mask with 1s from position i to j
    mask = ((1 << (j - i + 1)) - 1) << i
    return n ^ mask
```

Common Interview Questions

Find the Missing Number

Problem: Find the missing number in an array containing n distinct numbers taken from 0, 1, 2, ..., n.

```
def find_missing_number(nums):
    n = len(nums)
    expected_sum = n * (n + 1) // 2
    actual_sum = sum(nums)
    return expected_sum - actual_sum

# Alternative bit manipulation approach
def find_missing_number_xor(nums):
    result = len(nums)
    for i, num in enumerate(nums):
        result ^= i ^ num
    return result
```

Count Bits

Problem: Count the number of bits that must be flipped to convert integer A to integer B.

```
def count_bits_to_flip(a, b):
    # XOR gives 1 for bits that are different
    xor_result = a ^ b
    # Count the set bits in the XOR result
    return count_set_bits(xor_result)
```

Power of Four

Problem: Determine if a given integer is a power of 4 without using loops.

```
def is_power_of_four(n):
    # Check if positive and power of 2
    if n <= 0 or (n & (n-1)) != 0:
        return False

    # Check set bit at even positions
    # 0x55555555 is 01010101...01 in binary
    return (n & 0x55555555) != 0
```

Maximum Subarray XOR

Problem: Find the maximum XOR value of any subarray in a given array.

```
def max_subarray_xor(nums):
    if not nums:
        return 0

    max_xor = float('-inf')
    prefix_xor = 0

    for num in nums:
        prefix_xor ^= num
        max_xor = max(max_xor, prefix_xor)

        curr_xor = prefix_xor
        for i in range(len(nums)):
            curr_xor ^= nums[i]
            max_xor = max(max_xor, curr_xor)

    return max_xor
```

Sum of Two Integers Without Using +/-

Problem: Calculate the sum of two integers without using the + or - operators.

```
def add_without_plus(a, b):
    while b != 0:
        # Carry is AND, shifted by 1
        carry = (a & b) << 1
        # Sum is XOR
        a = a ^ b
        b = carry
    return a
```

Find the Single Number III

Problem: Find those two numbers in an array where all numbers appear twice except for two numbers that appear only once.

```
def find_two_single_numbers(nums):
    # Get XOR of all numbers
    xor_all = 0
    for num in nums:
        xor_all ^= num

    # Find a bit where the two unique numbers differ
    # (rightmost set bit)
    diff_bit = xor_all & -xor_all

    # Separate numbers into two groups based on the diff bit
    num1 = 0
    for num in nums:
        if num & diff_bit:
            num1 ^= num

    # The other number is XOR of num1 and xor_all
    num2 = xor_all ^ num1

    return [num1, num2]
```

Reverse Bits

Problem: Reverse the bits of a 32-bit unsigned integer.

```
def reverse_bits(n):
    result = 0
    for i in range(32):
        result <<= 1
        result |= (n & 1)
        n >>= 1
    return result
```

Bitwise AND of Range

Problem: Find the bitwise AND of all numbers in the range [m, n].

```
def range_bitwise_and(m, n):
    # Count the number of shifts needed to make m and n equal
```

```
shift = 0
while m < n:
    m >>= 1
    n >>= 1
    shift += 1

# Shift back to get the common prefix
return m << shift
```

Mastering binary manipulation takes practice. These techniques often feel unintuitive initially, but they become powerful tools in your programming arsenal with time—practice, practice, practice.

Floyd's Algorithm

Core Concept

Floyd's algorithm (also known as Floyd-Warshall) finds the shortest paths between all pairs of vertices in a weighted graph. Unlike Dijkstra's algorithm, which works from a single source, Floyd's algorithm gives you a complete picture of the distances between every node.

Floyd's algorithm iteratively improves the shortest path estimate between each pair of vertices by considering whether an intermediate vertex provides a shorter route.

It's based on a simple insight: if the shortest path from vertex A to vertex B passes through vertex C, then it must be composed of the shortest path from A to C followed by the shortest path from C to B.

Python Implementation

```python
def floyd_warshall(graph):
    """
    Compute all-pairs shortest paths using
    Floyd-Warshall algorithm.

    Finds shortest paths between every pair
    of vertices in a weighted graph.

    Args:
        graph (list): 2D adjacency matrix with
            edge weights

    Returns:
        tuple: (distances, next_vertex, get_path)
                - distances: Shortest distances
                - next_vertex: Path matrix
                - get_path: Path reconstruction

    Time Complexity: O(V³)
    Space Complexity: O(V²)
    """
    # Number of vertices
    n = len(graph)

    # Initialize distance matrix
    dist = [row[:] for row in graph]

    # Path reconstruction matrix
    next_vertex = [
        [
            j if graph[i][j] != float('inf')
            and i != j else None
            for j in range(n)
        ] for i in range(n)
    ]

    # Floyd-Warshall core algorithm
    for k in range(n):
        for i in range(n):
            for j in range(n):
```

```
            # Check intermediate path exists
            if (dist[i][k] != float('inf') and
                dist[k][j] != float('inf')):
                # Update if shorter path found
                if dist[i][j] > dist[i][k] + dist[k][j]:
                    dist[i][j] = dist[i][k] + dist[k][j]
                    next_vertex[i][j] = next_vertex[i][k]


    def get_path(i, j):
        """
        Reconstruct shortest path between
        vertices i and j.

        Args:
            i (int): Source vertex
            j (int): Destination vertex

        Returns:
            list: Shortest path vertices
        """
        if next_vertex[i][j] is None:
            return []

        path = [i]
        while i != j:
            i = next_vertex[i][j]
            path.append(i)
        return path


    return dist, next_vertex, get_path

# Example usage
INF = float('inf')
graph = [
    [0, 5, INF, 10],
    [INF, 0, 3, INF],
    [INF, INF, 0, 1],
    [INF, INF, INF, 0]
]
```

```
# Compute shortest paths
distances, next_v, get_path = floyd_warshall(graph)

# Print distances
print("Shortest distances:")
for row in distances:
    print(row)

# Find and print path
path = get_path(0, 3)
print(f"Path from 0 to 3: {path}")
```

Performance Characteristics

Time Complexity: $O(V^3)$ where V is the number of vertices. This comes from the three nested loops that iterate through all vertices.

Space Complexity: $O(V^2)$ for storing the distance and next vertex matrices.

While $O(V^3)$ may seem high, for dense graphs and all-pairs shortest paths, this is often more efficient than running Dijkstra's algorithm V times (which would be $O(V^2 \log V + VE)$).

Key Tips

Infinity Representation: When implementing, be careful with how you represent infinity. Using MAX_VALUE or similar constants might lead to overflow during addition.

Negative Cycles: Floyd's algorithm can detect negative cycles. If any diagonal element (disti) is negative after running the algorithm, there's a negative cycle in the graph.

Path Reconstruction: The next_vertex matrix is crucial for reconstructing the actual paths, not just finding distances.

In-Place Implementation: You can implement Floyd's algorithm in place to save memory, but having separate matrices makes the code more straightforward.

Pro Tips

Transitive Closure: You can use a modified version to find the transitive closure of a directed graph by changing the relaxation condition.

Resource Constraints: In problems with multiple constraints (like flight paths with both time and cost), consider running multiple instances of Floyd's algorithm.

Dynamic Programming Insight: Understanding Floyd's algorithm as a dynamic programming solution can help you tackle problems similar to the DP approach.

Pre-processing for Repeated Queries: If you must make multiple shortest path queries on a static graph, computing all pairs' shortest paths once with Floyd's is more efficient than repeated Dijkstra runs.

Common Interview Questions

Graph Representation: How would you modify Floyd's algorithm to work with an adjacency list instead of an adjacency matrix?

Detecting Cycles: How can you use Floyd's algorithm to detect if a graph contains a negative cycle?

Optimization: Can you optimize Floyd's algorithm for sparse graphs?

Applications: Name some real-world applications where Floyd's algorithm would be more suitable than Dijkstra's or Bellman-Ford.

Variants: Explain how to modify Floyd's algorithm to find the maximum flow between all pairs of vertices.

Space Optimization: How can you reduce the space complexity of Floyd's algorithm if you only need the shortest distances and not the paths?

Parallelization: How would you parallelize Floyd's algorithm?

Median-of-Medians Algorithm

Core Concept

The Median-of-Medians algorithm (also known as BFPRT after its inventors Blum, Floyd, Pratt, Rivest, and Tarjan) is a deterministic way to find the kth smallest element in an unsorted array in O(n) time. Use it to find the kth smallest/largest element in an unsorted array—with a surprisingly clever approach that guarantees linear time complexity.

While Quickselect is excellent, its worst-case performance can degrade to $O(n^2)$ with bad pivot choices. Median-of-Medians fixes this by carefully selecting a "good enough" pivot that guarantees balanced partitioning.

The algorithm works like this:

- Divide the input array into groups of 5 elements.
- Find the median of each group of 5.
- Recursively find the median of these medians.
- Use this "median of medians" as a pivot for partitioning.
- Recursively apply the algorithm on the appropriate partition.

This approach ensures that at least 30% of elements will be less than the pivot and at least 30% greater, guaranteeing progress and a linear time complexity.

Python Implementation

I've included detailed comments to help you understand each step. Notice how we recursively find the "median of medians" to use as our pivot—this guarantees linear time complexity.

```python
def median_of_medians(arr, k):
    """
    Find kth smallest element using
    median-of-medians algorithm.

    Args:
        arr (list): Input array
        k (int): Zero-based index to find

    Returns:
        Kth smallest element

    Time Complexity: O(n)
    Space Complexity: O(n)
    """
    if len(arr) <= 5:
        # Base case: sort small arrays
        return sorted(arr)[k]

    # Find medians of 5-element groups
    medians = []
    for i in range(0, len(arr), 5):
        group = arr[i:i+5]
        group_median = sorted(group)[len(group) // 2]
        medians.append(group_median)

    # Find median of medians
    pivot = (medians[0] if len(medians) <= 1
             else median_of_medians(medians, len(medians) // 2))
```

```python
    # Partition array around pivot
    left = [x for x in arr if x < pivot]
    middle = [x for x in arr if x == pivot]
    right = [x for x in arr if x > pivot]

    # Recursively find element
    if k < len(left):
        return median_of_medians(left, k)
    elif k < len(left) + len(middle):
        return pivot
    else:
        return median_of_medians(
            right,
            k - len(left) - len(middle)
        )


# Example usage
if __name__ == "__main__":
    arr = [9, 1, 8, 2, 7, 3, 6, 4, 5]

    # Find 4th smallest element
    result = median_of_medians(arr, 3)
    print(f"4th smallest: {result}")

    # Find array median
    median_index = len(arr) // 2
    median = median_of_medians(arr, median_index)
    print(f"Median: {median}") // 5
```

Performance Characteristics

Time Complexity: O(n) in the worst case.

This is much better than quickselect's O(n²) worst-case complexity. Let me break down why:

- Finding medians of groups of 5: O(n) time (constant time per group)

- Finding the median of medians: $T(n/5)$
- Partitioning around the pivot: $O(n)$
- Recursive call on one partition: At most $T(7n/10)$ due to the guaranteed balanced split

The recurrence relation works out to $T(n) \leq T(n/5) + T(7n/10) + O(n)$, which solves to $T(n) = O(n)$.

Space Complexity: $O(n)$ due to the recursive calls and temporary arrays.

Unlike quicksort, which can become unbalanced, Median-of-Medians guarantees a somewhat balanced recursion tree, ensuring the $O(n)$ bound.

Key Tips

If you're implementing this algorithm for the first time, here's what helped me:

Group size matters: Using groups of 5 is not arbitrary! With 5 elements, we guarantee that the median of the medians is greater than or equal to at least 30% and less than or equal to at least 30% of all elements.

Handling duplicates: The "middle" partition for elements equal to the pivot is crucial for correctness, especially with duplicates.

Base case efficiency: For small arrays ($\leq$ 5 elements), just sorting is more efficient than continuing the recursion.

Understand the guarantees: The beauty of this algorithm is its worst-case guarantee, unlike randomized approaches.

Pro Tips

In-place implementation: For memory-constrained environments, you can adapt this to work in-place like quickselect, though it becomes more complex.

Real-world usage: In practice, a hybrid approach often works best—use randomized quickselect first and fall back to Median-of-Medians if you detect poor pivot choices.

Tweaking group size: While 5 is theoretically optimal, experiment with different group sizes for specific data distributions. I've seen performance improvements with group sizes of 3 or 7 in specific contexts.

Early termination: If you only need approximate results, you can terminate early after a certain recursion depth.

Common Interview Questions

Compare with Quickselect: "How does Median-of-Medians compare to Quickselect regarding average-case performance? When would you use one over the other?"

Group size reasoning: "Why do we use groups of 5 specifically? What happens if we use groups of 3 or 7?"

Finding the median: "How would you efficiently find the median of a large stream of integers?"

Implementation tradeoffs: "Can you implement an in-place version of Median-of-Medians? What are the tradeoffs?"

Performance optimization: "How would you optimize Median-of-

Medians for real-world usage?"

> This is essentially "Quickselect with insurance"—we pay a little extra up-front (finding the median of medians) to guarantee we never get stuck with a bad pivot.

Recursion with Memoization

Core Concept

Recursion with memoization combines the elegant problem-solving approach of recursive functions with a performance optimization technique called memoization.

Recursion is when a function calls itself to solve smaller instances of the same problem. Think of it as breaking down a complex problem into simpler sub-problems until you reach a base case that's trivial to solve.

Memoization is a technique for storing the results of expensive function calls and returning the cached result when the same inputs occur again. It's like taking notes during an exam so you don't have to recalculate the same answer twice.

When we combine these two concepts, we get the best of both worlds:

- The clean, intuitive design of recursive solutions
- The performance benefits of avoiding redundant calculations

Imagine you're exploring a maze with many intersecting paths. Without memoization, you might revisit the same junctions repeatedly. With memoization, you'd mark each junction as you visit it, saving yourself from wasted effort.

Let's look at how to solve the classic Fibonacci sequence problem:

Python Implementation

```
from functools import lru_cache

def fib_slow(n):
    # Naive recursive fibonacci
    if n <= 1:
        return n
    return fib_slow(n-1) + fib_slow(n-2)

def fib_memo(n, memo={}):
    # Memoized recursive fibonacci
    if n in memo:
        return memo[n]
    if n <= 1:
        return n
    memo[n] = fib_memo(n-1, memo) + fib_memo(n-2, memo)
    return memo[n]

@lru_cache(maxsize=None)
def fib_lru(n):
    # LRU cached fibonacci
    if n <= 1:
        return n
    return fib_lru(n-1) + fib_lru(n-2)

# Example usage
if __name__ == "__main__":
    print(f"Slow Fib(30): {fib_slow(30)}")
    print(f"Memoized Fib(30): {fib_memo(30)}")
    print(f"LRU Cached Fib(40): {fib_lru(40)}")
```

Performance Characteristics

The beauty of memoization lies in its dramatic impact on complexity:

Time Complexity:

- Without Memoization: $O(2^n)$ for problems like Fibonacci, making them practically unsolvable for large inputs.
- With Memoization: $O(n)$ for the same problems, each subproblem is solved exactly once.

For instance, computing fib(50):

- Without Memoization: ~1,125,899,906,842,624 recursive calls
- With Memoization: Only 50 unique calculations

Space Complexity: $O(n)$ stores computed results in the memoization table, and $O(n)$ is used for the recursion call stack.

This space trade-off is almost always worth it for the exponential time savings.

Key Tips

Identify Overlapping Subproblems: Memoization works best when your recursive function calls itself multiple times with the same argument. If each recursive call has unique parameters, memoization won't help.

Choose the Right Data Structure: For constant-time lookups, use a hash table (dictionary, HashMap, or unordered_map). Arrays might be even faster for problems with integer parameters within a known range.

Beware of Mutable Default Arguments: In Python, using memo={} as a default parameter can cause unexpected behavior because the dictionary is created only once. Consider using None and initializing inside:

```python
def recursive_func(n, memo=None):
    if memo is None:
        memo = {}
    # Rest of function...
```

Top-down vs. Bottom-up: Memoization is a top-down approach (solve bigger problems first, then cache smaller ones). Consider if a bottom-up approach (dynamic programming without recursion) might be cleaner for your specific problem.

Pro Tips

Cache Invalidation Strategy: To prevent memory bloat, consider implementing a cache eviction policy (like LRU) for long-running applications.

Thread Safety: If memoization is used in a multi-threaded environment, ensure your cache is thread-safe or use thread-local storage.

Tuple Keys for Multiple Parameters: When memoizing functions with multiple parameters, use tuples as dictionary keys:

```
def recursive_func(m, n, memo={}):
    if (m, n) in memo:
        return memo[(m, n)]
    # Calculate result
    memo[(m, n)] = result
    return result
```

Trace for Debugging: When debugging complex recursive functions, add tracing to visualize the call tree:

```
def recursive_func(n, depth=0, memo={}):
    indent = "  " * depth
    print(f"{indent}Computing f({n})")
    if n in memo:
        print(f"{indent}Found in cache: {memo[n]}")
        return memo[n]
    # Rest of function...
```

State in the Function Signature: Ensure that all states needed for the calculation are passed explicitly in the function parameters, making the memoization cleaner and more effective.

Common Interview Questions

Fibonacci Sequence: A classic starting point. Implement a function to calculate the nth Fibonacci number efficiently.

Climbing Stairs: Given n steps, how many ways can you climb if you can take 1 or 2 steps at a time?

Coin Change: Given a set of coin denominations and a target amount, what's the minimum number of coins needed to make that amount? We will see this again in the next chapter.

```python
def coin_change(coins, amount, memo={}):
    if amount in memo:
        return memo[amount]
    if amount == 0:
        return 0
    if amount < 0:
        return float('inf')

    min_coins = float('inf')
    for coin in coins:
        result = coin_change(coins, amount - coin, memo) + 1
        min_coins = min(min_coins, result)

    memo[amount] = min_coins
    return min_coins
```

Longest Common Subsequence: Find the length of the longest subsequence present in two strings. We will see this again in the next chapter.

```
def lcs(X, Y, m, n, memo=None):
    # Initialize memo dictionary if None
    if memo is None:
        memo = {}

    # Return memoized result if available
    if (m, n) in memo:
        return memo[(m, n)]

    # Base case: empty string
    if m == 0 or n == 0:
        return 0

    # If characters match, add 1 to result
    if X[m-1] == Y[n-1]:
        memo[(m, n)] = 1 + lcs(X, Y, m-1, n-1, memo)
    else:
        # Take maximum of two possible subproblems
        memo[(m, n)] = max(lcs(X, Y, m, n-1, memo),
                           lcs(X, Y, m-1, n, memo))

    return memo[(m, n)]
```

0/1 Knapsack Problem: Given weights and values of n items, put these items in a knapsack of capacity W to get the maximum total value. We will see this again in the next chapter.

Grid Paths: Count the number of paths from the top-left to the bottom-right corner of a grid, moving only right or down.

Word Break: Given a string and a dictionary of words, determine if the string can be segmented into a space-separated sequence of dictionary words. We will see this again in the next chapter.

In interviews, always discuss the naive recursive approach first, then explain how memoization dramatically improves performance. This demonstrates your understanding of both the problem-solving technique and optimization principles.

Huffman Coding Algorithm

I include this algorithm not because you will likely see it in an interview but because it contains new techniques that you can use on some edge-case questions you may run into. It also introduces another binary tree usage. Huffman coding is one of the compression methods used in Zip files.

Core Concept

Huffman coding is a lossless data compression algorithm that assigns variable-length codes to input characters based on their frequencies. The more frequent a character, the shorter its code.

The insight behind Huffman coding is that we can represent data more efficiently by using fewer bits for common characters and more bits for rare ones. It's like creating a custom shorthand where you use simple symbols for words you write often and longer symbols for those you rarely use.

At its heart, Huffman coding uses a binary tree (called a Huffman tree) where each leaf node represents a character and its frequency. The path from the root to a leaf (0 for left, 1 for right) gives the binary code for that character.

Python Implementation

```python
import heapq
from collections import defaultdict, Counter
```

```python
def build_huffman_tree(text):
    """
    Build a Huffman tree and return character codes.

    Args:
        text (str): Input text to encode

    Returns:
        dict: Dictionary mapping characters to their
            binary codes

    Time Complexity: O(n log n) where n is the number
                    of unique characters
    """
    # Count frequency of each character
    frequency = Counter(text)

    # Create a priority queue (min heap)
    heap = [[weight, [char, ""]]
            for char, weight in frequency.items()]
    heapq.heapify(heap)

    # Build Huffman Tree
    while len(heap) > 1:
        lo = heapq.heappop(heap)
        hi = heapq.heappop(heap)

        for pair in lo[1:]:
            pair[1] = '0' + pair[1]
        for pair in hi[1:]:
            pair[1] = '1' + pair[1]

        heapq.heappush(heap, [lo[0] + hi[0]] + lo[1:] +
                    hi[1:])

    # Extract codes
    huffman_codes = {char: code
                    for char, code in sorted(
                        heapq.heappop(heap)[1:])}
```

```
    return huffman_codes

def huffman_encode(text):
    """

    Encode text using Huffman coding.

    Args:
        text (str): Input text to encode

    Returns:
        tuple: (encoded_text, codes)
                - encoded_text (str): Binary string of the
                                      encoded text
                - codes (dict): Dictionary mapping
                            characters to their binary codes

    Time Complexity: O(n + k log k) where n is text
                    length and k is unique characters
    """
    codes = build_huffman_tree(text)
    encoded_text = ''.join(codes[char] for char in text)
    return encoded_text, codes

def huffman_decode(encoded_text, codes):
    """

    Decode Huffman-encoded text.

    Args:
        encoded_text (str): Binary string of the
                            encoded text
        codes (dict): Dictionary mapping characters
                    to their binary codes

    Returns:
        str: Decoded original text

    Time Complexity: O(n) where n is the length of
                    encoded_text
    """
    reversed_codes = {code: char
```

```
                        for char, code in codes.items()}
    current_code = ""
    decoded_text = ""

    for bit in encoded_text:
        current_code += bit
        if current_code in reversed_codes:
            decoded_text += reversed_codes[current_code]
            current_code = ""

    return decoded_text

# Example usage
text = "this is an example for huffman encoding"
encoded, codes = huffman_encode(text)
decoded = huffman_decode(encoded, codes)
print(f"Original: {text}")
print(f"Encoded: {encoded}")
print(f"Decoded: {decoded}")
print(f"Compression ratio: {len(encoded)/(len(text)*8):.2f}")
```

Performance Characteristics

Time Complexity:

- Building the frequency table: O(n) where n is the length of the input text
- Building the Huffman tree: O(k log k) where k is the number of unique characters
- Encoding the text: O(n)
- Overall: O(n + k log k), which is effectively O(n) for most practical applications since k is usually bounded

Space Complexity:

- Frequency table: O(k)

- Priority queue: $O(k)$
- Huffman tree: $O(k)$
- Huffman codes table: $O(k)$
- Overall: $O(k)$

Key Tips

Always sort by frequency: The algorithm first processes least frequent items.

Use a priority queue: This data structure is perfect for Huffman coding as it efficiently gives us the two nodes with the lowest frequency.

Prefix property: Huffman codes are prefix-free, meaning no code is a prefix of another. This makes decoding unambiguous.

Balance check: While Huffman trees don't have to be balanced, extremely unbalanced trees can lead to inefficient codes. If your frequency distribution is very skewed, consider other compression methods.

Single character case: Handle the special case where your input has only one unique character - you can't build a proper binary tree in this case.

Pro Tips

Adaptive Huffman coding: Consider using adaptive Huffman coding for streaming data where frequencies are unknown in advance.

Canonical Huffman codes maintain the same code lengths but reassign the bit patterns to make encoding/decoding faster.

Huffman with memory: Consider modeling character probabilities based on preceding characters (like in PPM compression) for text compression.

Code serialization: When storing Huffman-compressed data, you must also store the code table or the tree structure to enable decompression.

Pre-calculated tables: For standard applications (like ASCII text), you can use pre-calculated Huffman tables based on typical frequency distributions.

Common Interview Questions

How would you handle a case where all characters have the same frequency?

Answer: In this case, Huffman coding would generate codes of equal length (similar to fixed-length coding), and the compression benefit would be minimal.

How would you implement Huffman coding for a streaming application where you can't see all the data simultaneously?

Answer: You would use Adaptive Huffman coding (also called Dynamic Huffman coding), which adjusts the coding tree as new characters are processed.

What's the worst-case scenario for Huffman coding in terms of compression ratio?

Answer: The worst case is when all symbols occur with equal frequency, resulting in codes of equal length and minimal compression.

How would you modify the algorithm to handle Unicode text efficiently?

Answer: You would treat each Unicode code point as a symbol, possibly using a hybrid approach for common vs rare characters or implementing a two-stage compression.

Compare Huffman coding with other compression techniques like LZW or arithmetic coding.

Answer: Huffman is more straightforward but less efficient than arithmetic coding for highly skewed distributions. LZW captures repeated patterns better than character-based Huffman.

I still struggle with this algorithm each time I see it. Visualize the tree-building process step by step, and you will do well. Drawing out the frequency table by hand will also help you master it.

Red-Black Tree Algorithm

Core Concept

A Red-Black tree is a self-balancing binary search tree where each node has a color (red or black) and satisfies these properties:

1. Every node is either red or black.
2. The root is black.
3. All leaf nodes (NIL) are black.
4. If a node is red, both its children are black.
5. Every path from root to leaf contains the same number of black nodes.

These properties ensure the tree remains relatively balanced, guaranteeing O(log n) operations.

Python Implementation

```
class Node:
    def __init__(self, key):
        # Initialize node with key and default properties
        self.key = key
        self.left = None
        self.right = None
```

```python
        self.parent = None
        self.color = "RED"  # New nodes are always red


class RedBlackTree:
    def __init__(self):
        # Create sentinel NIL node
        self.NIL = Node(0)
        self.NIL.color = "BLACK"
        self.NIL.left = None
        self.NIL.right = None
        self.root = self.NIL

    def insert(self, key):
        # Create new node
        node = Node(key)
        node.left = self.NIL
        node.right = self.NIL

        y = None
        x = self.root

        # Find position for new node
        while x != self.NIL:
            y = x
            if node.key < x.key:
              x = x.left
            else:
                x = x.right

        # Set parent of node
        node.parent = y

        # If tree is empty, make node the root
        if y is None:
            self.root = node
            node.color = "BLACK"  # Root must be black
            return
        # Otherwise, link node to its parent
        elif node.key < y.key:
```

```
        y.left = node
    else:
        y.right = node

    # If grandparent is None, return
    if node.parent.parent is None:
        return

    # Fix the tree to maintain Red-Black properties
    self._fix_insert(node)

def _fix_insert(self, k):
    # Fix Red-Black Tree properties after insertion
    while k.parent and k.parent.color == "RED":
        # If parent is right child of grandparent
        if k.parent == k.parent.parent.right:
            u = k.parent.parent.left  # uncle

            # Case 1: Uncle is red
            if u.color == "RED":
                u.color = "BLACK"
                k.parent.color = "BLACK"
                k.parent.parent.color = "RED"
                k = k.parent.parent
            else:
                # Case 2: Uncle is black and k is left child
                if k == k.parent.left:
                    k = k.parent
                    self._right_rotate(k)

                # Case 3: Uncle is black and k is right child
                k.parent.color = "BLACK"
                k.parent.parent.color = "RED"
                self._left_rotate(k.parent.parent)
        else:
            # If parent is left child of grandparent
            u = k.parent.parent.right  # uncle

            # Case 1: Uncle is red
            if u.color == "RED":
```

```
            u.color = "BLACK"
            k.parent.color = "BLACK"
            k.parent.parent.color = "RED"
            k = k.parent.parent
        else:
            # Case 2: Uncle is black and k is right child
            if k == k.parent.right:
                k = k.parent
                self._left_rotate(k)

            # Case 3: Uncle is black and k is left child
            k.parent.color = "BLACK"
            k.parent.parent.color = "RED"
            self._right_rotate(k.parent.parent)

    # If k is the root, break
    if k == self.root:
        break

# Root must be black
self.root.color = "BLACK"

def _left_rotate(self, x):
    # Perform left rotation
    y = x.right
    x.right = y.left

    if y.left != self.NIL:
        y.left.parent = x

    y.parent = x.parent

    if x.parent is None:
        self.root = y
    elif x == x.parent.left:
        x.parent.left = y
    else:
        x.parent.right = y

    y.left = x
```

```python
        x.parent = y

    def _right_rotate(self, x):
        # Perform right rotation
        y = x.left
        x.left = y.right

        if y.right != self.NIL:
            y.right.parent = x

        y.parent = x.parent

        if x.parent is None:
            self.root = y
        elif x == x.parent.right:
            x.parent.right = y
        else:
            x.parent.left = y

        y.right = x
        x.parent = y

    def in_order_traversal(self, node):
        # Perform in-order traversal
        result = []
        if node != self.NIL:
            result = self.in_order_traversal(node.left)
            result.append((node.key, node.color))
            result += self.in_order_traversal(node.right)
        return result

    def search(self, key):
        # Search for a key in the tree
        return self._search_helper(self.root, key)

    def _search_helper(self, node, key):
        # Helper function for search
        if node == self.NIL or key == node.key:
            return node
```

```
        if key < node.key:
            return self._search_helper(node.left, key)
        return self._search_helper(node.right, key)

# Example usage
if __name__ == "__main__":
    rb_tree = RedBlackTree()
    keys = [7, 3, 18, 10, 22, 8, 11, 26]

    for key in keys:
        rb_tree.insert(key)

    print("In-order traversal of the Red-Black Tree:")
    print(rb_tree.in_order_traversal(rb_tree.root))

    # Find a key
    key_to_find = 10
    found_node = rb_tree.search(key_to_find)
    if found_node != rb_tree.NIL:
        print(f"Found key {key_to_find}, color: "
            f"{found_node.color}")
    else:
        print(f"Key {key_to_find} not found")
```

Performance Characteristics

By Operation - Average Case - Worst Case

Search - O(log n) - O(log n)

Insert - O(log n) - O(log n)

Delete - O(log n) - O(log n)

Space - O(n) - O(n)

The Red-Black tree guarantees O(log n) performance for all operations, even in worst-case scenarios, unlike regular BSTs that can degrade to O(n).

Key Tips

Red-Black trees are preferred in applications requiring predictable performance.

Always follow the key properties when implementing:

- New nodes are always inserted as RED.
- The fixing operations (rotations and recoloring) ensure a balance is maintained.
- NIL nodes are considered BLACK
- Time complexity for all operations is guaranteed to be O(log n)

Pro Tips

- Red-Black trees are used in standard libraries like Java's TreeMap, C++'s std::map, and Linux kernel's completely fair scheduler.
- For deletion, similar but more complex rebalancing is required.
- When implementing, separate the standard BST operations from the Red-Black specific balancing.
- Consider using sentinel nodes (NIL) to simplify boundary conditions.
- In practice, Red-Black trees outperform AVL trees for insertion-heavy workloads.

Typical Interview Questions

What is the maximum possible height of a Red-Black tree with n nodes?

- $2 \log_2(n+1)$ nodes, approximately twice the height of a perfectly balanced tree

When would you use a Red-Black tree over other data structures?

- When you need guaranteed O(log n) operations
- For ordered maps/sets with frequent modifications
- When implementation complexity is acceptable for the performance benefits

How do you handle rebalancing after insertion in a Red-Black tree?

- Identify the case based on the uncle's color and node placement.
- Perform rotations and/or color changes as needed.
- Propagate fixes up the tree until the root or until no violations exist

Ford-Fulkerson Algorithm (Edmonds-Karp)

Core Concept

The Ford-Fulkerson algorithm solves the maximum flow problem in a flow network. It finds the maximum flow that can be sent from a source node to a sink node through a directed graph where each edge has a capacity.

The algorithm works by:

1. Starting with zero flow
2. Repeatedly finding an augmenting path (a path from source to sink with available capacity)
3. Augmenting flow along this path (increasing flow by the minimum residual capacity along the route)
4. Terminating when no more augmenting paths exist

The Edmonds-Karp implementation uses BFS to find the shortest augmenting path, which provides better complexity guarantees.

Python Implementation

```python
from collections import defaultdict, deque

class Graph:
    def __init__(self, vertices):
        # Initialize graph with vertices
        self.vertices = vertices
        self.graph = defaultdict(list)
        self.flow = {}
        self.capacity = defaultdict(int)

    def add_edge(self, u, v, capacity):
        # Add forward edge
        self.graph[u].append(v)
        # Add backward edge for residual graph
        self.graph[v].append(u)
        # Initialize flow to 0
        self.flow[(u, v)] = 0
        self.flow[(v, u)] = 0
        # Store capacity
        self.capacity[(u, v)] = capacity

    def bfs(self, source, sink, parent):
        # Use BFS to find augmenting path
        visited = [False] * self.vertices
        queue = deque()

        queue.append(source)
        visited[source] = True

        while queue:
            u = queue.popleft()

            for v in self.graph[u]:
                # If not visited and there is residual capacity
                residual_capacity = (self.capacity[(u, v)] -
                              self.flow[(u, v)])
                if not visited[v] and residual_capacity > 0:
                    queue.append(v)
                    visited[v] = True
                    parent[v] = u
```

```python
        # Return True if sink is reached, otherwise False
        return visited[sink]

    def edmonds_karp(self, source, sink):
        parent = [-1] * self.vertices
        max_flow = 0

        # Augment flow while there is an augmenting path
        while self.bfs(source, sink, parent):
            # Find minimum residual capacity along the path
            path_flow = float("Inf")
            s = sink
            while s != source:
                path_flow = min(
                    path_flow,
                    self.capacity[(parent[s], s)] -
                    self.flow[(parent[s], s)])
                s = parent[s]

            # Augment flow along the path
            max_flow += path_flow
            v = sink
            while v != source:
                u = parent[v]
                self.flow[(u, v)] += path_flow
                self.flow[(v, u)] -= path_flow  # Update backward
                edge
                v = parent[v]

        return max_flow

    def print_flow(self):
        print("Edge \tFlow/Capacity")
        for i in range(self.vertices):
            for j in self.graph[i]:
                # Only print forward edges
                if self.capacity[(i, j)] > 0:
                    print(f"{i} -> {j} \t{self.flow[(i, j)]}/"
                        f"{self.capacity[(i, j)]}")
```

```
# Example usage
if __name__ == "__main__":
    # Create a graph with 6 vertices
    g = Graph(6)

    # Add edges with capacities
    g.add_edge(0, 1, 16)
    g.add_edge(0, 2, 13)
    g.add_edge(1, 2, 10)
    g.add_edge(1, 3, 12)
    g.add_edge(2, 1, 4)
    g.add_edge(2, 4, 14)
    g.add_edge(3, 2, 9)
    g.add_edge(3, 5, 20)
    g.add_edge(4, 3, 7)
    g.add_edge(4, 5, 4)

    source = 0
    sink = 5

    # Find the maximum flow
    max_flow = g.edmonds_karp(source, sink)

    print(f"Maximum flow from {source} to {sink}: {max_flow}")
    g.print_flow()
```

Performance Characteristics

Ford-Fulkerson

Time Complexity: $O(E \times maxFlow)$

Space Complexity: $O(V^2)$

Edmonds-Karp (BFS)

Time Complexity: $O(V \times E^2)$

Space Complexity: $O(V^2)$

Dinic's Algorithm

Time Complexity: $O(V^2 \times E)$

Space Complexity: $O(V^2)$

E is the number of edges, V is the number of vertices, and maxFlow is the maximum flow value.

Key Tips

Choose the correct implementation based on your network:

- Edmonds-Karp for general graphs
- Dinic's Algorithm (not shown) for better performance on large networks

Keep in mind:

- The residual graph is crucial to the algorithm's correctness.
- Always initialize all flows to zero.
- The maximum flow equals the minimum cut (Max-Flow Min-Cut Theorem).
- Bidirectional edges can be represented as two separate edges.

Pro Tips

- Implement the algorithm using adjacency lists for sparse graphs.
- Use capacity scaling for better practical performance.
- Apply the Push-Relabel algorithm for large, dense graphs.
- Handle multiple sources/sinks by adding a super-source/super-sink.
- In bipartite graphs, maximum flow equals maximum bipartite matching.
- Preflow-push algorithms often outperform Ford-Fulkerson in practice.
- Use int arrays instead of maps for flow/capacity in performance-

critical applications.

Typical Interview Questions

What is the difference between Ford-Fulkerson and Edmonds-Karp algorithms?

- Ford-Fulkerson is a general method that finds augmenting paths using any search method.
- Edmonds-Karp specifically uses BFS to find the shortest augmenting path.
- Edmonds-Karp has a guaranteed polynomial time complexity of $O(V \times E^2)$.

How would you find the minimum cut in a network?

- Run Ford-Fulkerson to find maximum flow.
- Perform a reachability analysis from the source in the residual graph.
- Edges from reachable to non-reachable vertices form the minimum cut.

How do you handle multiple source/sink nodes?

- Create a super-source connected to all sources with infinite capacity.
- Create a super-sink with all sinks connected to it with infinite capacity.
- Run Ford-Fulkerson on the modified graph.

What is the relationship between maximum flow and minimum cut?

- The Max-Flow Min-Cut theorem states that the maximum flow value equals the capacity of the minimum cut.
- This forms the basis for many network flow applications.

In which real-world applications is Ford-Fulkerson used?

- Network traffic routing.
- Bipartite matching (job assignments).

Image segmentation

- Airline scheduling.
- Baseball elimination problem (If you are a fan of the Brad Pitt/Jonah Hill movie Moneyball, head to Wikipedia and read up on this; it is a classic problem.).

Array Mutation

An array mutation is where a new value recursively updates all values in an array. These sometimes appear as coding problems in interviews but more often in online tests like Codesignal. You should be familiar with the pattern and how to solve it.

Here is an example problem:

Given an integer n and an array a of length n, your task is to apply the following mutation to a:

- Array a mutates into a new array b of length n.
- For each i from 0 to n - 1, b[i] = a[i - 1] + a[i] + a[i + 1].
- If some element in the sum a[i - 1] + a[i] + a[i + 1] does not exist, it should be set to 0. For example, b[0] should be equal to 0 + a[0] + a[1].

Example

For n = 5 and a = [4, 0, 1, -2, 3], the output should be solution(n, a) = [4, 5, -1, 2, 1].

- b[0] = 0 + a[0] + a[1] = 0 + 4 + 0 = 4
- b[1] = a[0] + a[1] + a[2] = 4 + 0 + 1 = 5

- $b[2] = a[1] + a[2] + a[3] = 0 + 1 + (-2) = -1$
- $b[3] = a[2] + a[3] + a[4] = 1 + (-2) + 3 = 2$
- $b[4] = a[3] + a[4] + 0 = (-2) + 3 + 0 = 1$

So, the resulting array after the mutation will be [4, 5, -1, 2, 1].

Core Concept

We solve this with the Three-Element Sum pattern. This problem involves creating a new array in which each element is the sum of three consecutive elements from the original array—the current element plus its left and right neighbors. The tricky part is handling the edges of the array where a neighbor might not exist.

Think of it as a small sliding window moving through the array, gathering values. For positions at the edges (first and last elements), we treat the "missing" elements as zeros.

Python Implementation

```python
def array_mutation(n, a):
    b = [0] * n

    for i in range(n):
        # Left neighbor (or 0 if out of bounds)
        left = a[i-1] if i > 0 else 0

        # Current element
        current = a[i]

        # Right neighbor (or 0 if out of bounds)
        right = a[i+1] if i < n-1 else 0

        # Sum all three values
        b[i] = left + current + right
```

```
    return b

# Example
a = [4, 0, 1, -2, 3]
n = len(a)
print(array_mutation(n, a))  # [4, 5, -1, 2, 1]
```

Performance Characteristics

Time Complexity: O(n) - We iterate through the array exactly once, performing constant-time operations for each element.

Space Complexity: O(n) - We create a new array of the same size as the input.

Key Tips

Handle boundaries carefully: Always check array boundaries when accessing elements at i−1 or i+1.

Reuse the original array: If allowed, you can optimize space by reusing the original array (though this will modify it).

Consider using a single loop: Notice how we consolidated the logic into a single loop for clarity and efficiency.

Look for patterns. In this case, each new value is determined by a clear pattern (the sum of three consecutive elements).

Pro Tips

One-liner: If you're comfortable with list comprehension, it makes for a for a concise solution:

```
def solution(n, a):
    return [(0 if i-1 < 0 else a[i-1]) + a[i] + (0 if i+1 >= n
    else a[i+1]) for i in range(n)]
```

Handle potential overflow: Watch for integer overflow when summing values in real-world applications with large integers.

Consider using padding: Another approach is to conceptually "pad" the array with zeros at both ends, which can simplify the logic:

```
def solution(n, a):
    padded = [0] + a + [0]  # Add zeros at both ends
    return [padded[i] + padded[i+1] + padded[i+2] for i in
    range(n)]
```

Memory efficiency: If working with vast arrays, consider generating elements of the result on-demand rather than storing the entire result array.

Common Interview Questions

Variation: How would you modify your solution if the window size is a parameter k instead of fixed at 3?

Optimization: Can you solve this problem without using extra space (in place)?

Extension: What if we need to find the maximum value in each three-element window instead of summing?

Complexity challenge: Can you optimize this for very large arrays where memory usage is a concern?

Real-world application: How might this problem apply to signal processing or data smoothing? (Hint: This is essentially a convolution operation with a [1,1,1]kernel)

7

Practice Coding Problems

Work through these 75 problems more than once to become comfortable with the solution patterns.

1. Arrays & Hashing: Character Pattern Matching

Problem: Two strings follow the same character pattern if a bijective mapping (one-to-one correspondence) exists between the characters of the first string and the characters of the second string. Write a function that determines if two strings have the same character pattern.

Example:

```
Input: str1 = "abba", str2 = "deed"
Output: true
Explanation: 'a' maps to 'd', 'b' maps to 'e'

Input: str1 = "aaaa", str2 = "bbbb"
Output: true
Explanation: 'a' maps to 'b'

Input: str1 = "abcd", str2 = "aabb"
Output: false
Explanation: No valid mapping exists - both 'c' and 'd' would
```

need to map to the same character

```
Input: str1 = "abba", str2 = "abcd"
Output: false
Explanation: No valid mapping exists - 'a' cannot map to both
'a' and 'd'
```

Approach:

1. Check if the strings have the same length.
2. Use two hashmaps to track character mappings:
   - First map tracks str1 → str2 mappings
   - Second map tracks str2 → str1 mappings (ensuring bijection)
3. Iterate through both strings simultaneously:
   - If a character isn't mapped yet, create mappings in both directions.
   - If a character is already mapped, verify the mapping is consistent.
4. Return true if all mappings are consistent

2. Arrays & Hashing: Product Price Pairing

Problem: A retail marketplace needs to match a customer's budget by finding a pair of products that exactly match a specific price. Given an array of product prices and a target budget, return the indices of two prices that add up to the target budget. Assume there is exactly one solution, and each price can only be used once.

Example:

```
Input: prices = [23, 45, 12, 18, 7], budget = 30
Output: [0, 4]
Explanation: The prices at indices 0 and 4 add up exactly to
the budget: 23 + 7 = 30

Input: prices = [150, 24, 79, 50, 88, 345, 3], budget = 200
Output: [0, 3]
```

```
Explanation: The prices at indices 0 and 3 add up exactly to
the budget: 150 + 50 = 200
```

Approach: Use a hash map to track prices already seen:

1. Create an empty hash map to store price values and their indices.
2. Iterate through the array of prices.
3. Calculate the complement needed (budget - current price) for each price.
4. If the complement exists in our hash map, return the current price indices and its complement.
5. Otherwise, add the current price to the hash map and continue.

3. Arrays & Hashing: Vocabulary Pattern Clusters

Problem: Given an array of strings, group all strings that share identical letter distributions (where strings are considered in the same group if they contain the same letters regardless of order). Return the groups in any order.

Example:

```
Input: ["eat", "tea", "tan", "ate", "nat", "bat"]
Output: [["eat", "tea", "ate"], ["tan", "nat"], ["bat"]]

Input: ["listen", "silent", "enlist", "hello"]
Output: [["listen", "silent", "enlist"], ["hello"]]
```

Approach:

1. Create a hash map where:
   - The key is a unique identifier for each letter distribution (sorted string).
   - The value is a list of words with that distribution.
2. Iterate through each string in the input array.

3. Generate the key by sorting the characters in the string.

4. Append the current string to the list in the map for that key.

5. Return all the groups from the hash map.

4. Heap/Priority Queue: Trending Hashtag Analysis

Problem: A social media analytics platform needs to identify trending topics. Given an array of hashtags used in posts over the last hour and a number k, return the k most frequently used hashtags. If multiple hashtags have the same frequency, any can be included in the result to meet the count of k.

Example:

```
Input: hashtags = ["tech", "coding", "tech", "career",
"coding", "tech", "lifestyle"], k = 2
Output: ["tech", "coding"]
Explanation: "tech" appears 3 times, "coding" appears 2 times,
and others appear once.

Input: hashtags = ["travel", "food", "travel", "photography",
"food", "travel", "travel", "food", "vacation"], k = 3
Output: ["travel", "food", "photography"]
Explanation: "travel" appears 4 times, "food" appears 3 times,
others appear once.
```

Approach:

1. Count the frequency of each hashtag using a hash map.

2. Use a heap (priority queue) to maintain the k most frequent hashtags:
   - Create a min-heap of size k
   - For each hashtag-frequency pair, add to the heap
   - If heap size exceeds k, remove the least frequent element.

3. Extract the hashtags from the heap to get the result.

5. Arrays & Hashing: Supply Network Resilience Calculator

Problem: You oversee a factory network where each factory contributes a specific daily production value to the supply chain. Your task is to assess the network's resilience by calculating each factory's total production if that factory were removed from the network.

Given an array production where production[i] represents the daily production of factory i, return an array resilience where resilience[i] is the product of all productions except for production[i].

Your solution must run in O(n) time complexity and use only O(1) extra space (not counting the output array).

Example:

```
Input: production = [4, 2, 3, 5]
Output: resilience = [30, 60, 40, 24]
Explanation:
For factory 0: 2 * 3 * 5 = 30
For factory 1: 4 * 3 * 5 = 60
For factory 2: 4 * 2 * 5 = 40
For factory 3: 4 * 2 * 3 = 24
```

Approach:

1. Create a result array initialized with 1s
2. Perform two passes through the array:
   - First pass: Calculate the running product from left to right and store it in the result array
   - Second pass: Calculate the running product from right to left and multiply it with the existing values in the result array.
3. Return the result array

6. Sliding Window: Optimal Document Segment

Problem: You are analyzing document segments containing specific tokens. Given a document string document and a token string tokens, find the shortest substring in the document that includes all characters from tokens, including duplicates.

For a substring to be valid, each character in tokens must occur in the substring at least as many times as it occurs in tokens. Return the shortest valid substring. If multiple valid substrings have the same length, return the one that appears first in the document. If no valid substring exists, return an empty string.

Example:

```
Input: document = "ADOBECODEBANC", tokens = "ABC"
Output: "BANC"
Explanation: "BANC" contains at least one 'A', one 'B', and one
'C'.
```

Another example:

```
Input: document = "aabcbcdbca", tokens = "abcd"
Output: "dbca"
Explanation: "dbca" is the shortest substring containing all
characters in "abcd".
```

Approach:

1. Create a frequency counter for characters in tokens.
2. Maintain a sliding window with left and right pointers.
3. Expand the window until all token requirements are met.
4. Once a valid window is found, shrink it from the left while keeping it valid.
5. Track the shortest valid window.
6. Continue this process until the end of the document.

7. Sliding Window: Extrema Product

Problem: In market analysis, a useful volatility indicator is the product of the highest and lowest prices within a trading window. Given an array of prices representing stock prices over consecutive time intervals and a window size of k, calculate the product of the maximum and minimum prices for each sliding window.

Return an array containing these extrema products for each window.

Example:

```
Input: prices = [2, 5, 1, 8, 3, 4, 6, 7], k = 3
Output: [5, 8, 8, 24, 18, 28]
Explanation:
Window [2, 5, 1] → max = 5, min = 1, product = 5
Window [5, 1, 8] → max = 8, min = 1, product = 8
Window [1, 8, 3] → max = 8, min = 1, product = 8
Window [8, 3, 4] → max = 8, min = 3, product = 24
Window [3, 4, 6] → max = 6, min = 3, product = 18
Window [4, 6, 7] → max = 7, min = 4, product = 28
```

Approach:

1. Use two deques, one for tracking potential maximums and one for tracking potential minimums.
2. Both deques will store indices, not values.
3. For each new element:

- Remove elements from the back of the max deque that are smaller than the current element.
- Remove elements larger than the current element from the back of the min deque.
- Add the current index to both deques.
- Remove elements from the front of both deques outside the current window.
- Calculate the product using the values at the front of both deques.

8. Arrays & Hashing: Longest Palindromic Substring

Problem: Find the longest substring that reads the same forward and backward.

```
Input: "babad"
Output: "bab" or "aba"

Input: "cbbd"
Output: "bb"

Input: "racecar"
Output: "racecar"

Input: "forgeeksskeegfor"
Output: "geeksskeeg"

Input: "a"
Output: "a"

Input: "aacabdkacaa"
Output: "aca"
```

Approach: The "expand around center" approach treats each position in the string as a potential palindrome center:

1. For each position i in the string:
   - Check for odd-length palindromes with single character center at position i.
   - Check for even-length palindromes with centers between positions i and i+1.

2. For each center type, expand outward simultaneously in both directions:
   - Continue expanding as long as characters at both ends match.
   - When expansion stops, record the palindrome if it's longer than the previous ones.

333

3. This method handles both odd and even-length palindromes.
4. After checking all positions, return the longest palindrome found.

9. Arrays & Hashing: Two Sum

Problem: Find indices of two numbers that add up to a target value.

```
Input: nums = [2,7,11,15], target = 9
Output: [0,1]
```

Approach: The hash map solution works by:

1. Create a hash map to store values and their indices.
2. Iterate through the array once
3. For each element:
   - Calculate the complement needed (target - current element)
   - Check if the complement already exists in the hash map
   - If found, return the current index and store the complement's index
   - If not found, store the current element and its index.
4. This allows finding the pair in a single pass

10. Trees: Level Order Traversal

Problem: Return values of a binary tree's nodes level by level, from left to right.

```
Input: [3,9,20,null,null,15,7]
Output: [[3],[9,20],[15,7]]
```

Approach: The queue-based BFS approach ensures level-by-level processing:

1. Use a queue to track nodes waiting to be processed.

2. Initialize the queue with the root node.

3. Process nodes level by level:

- At each level, determine the number of nodes (queue size)
- Create a list of the current level's values.
- For each node at the current level:
  - Remove it from the queue
  - Add its value to the current level's list
  - Add any children to the queue (left then right)
  - Add completed level list to the results

11. Dynamic Programming: Fibonacci with Memoization

Problem: Calculate the nth Fibonacci number efficiently.

```
Input: n = 6
Output: 8
```

Approach: The solution shows both recursive (with memoization) and iterative approaches. Attempt both.

Recursive with memoization:

- Create a cache (array or hash map) to store computed values.
- Check the cache before calculating any Fibonacci number.
- Store each new result in the cache.
- Base cases: $F(0)=0$, $F(1)=1$.
- Recursively compute $F(n) = F(n-1) + F(n-2)$.

Iterative approach:

- Create an array to store all values from $F(0)$ to $F(n)$.

- Initialize F[0]=0, F[1]=1.
- Calculate each F[i] = F[i-1] + F[i-2] in order.
- Return F[n].

12. Graphs: Number of Islands

Problem: Count the number of islands in a 2D grid.

```
Input: Grid with 1s (land) and 0s (water)
Output: Number of distinct islands

Example Input (20x20 grid):
[
  [0,0,0,0,0,0,0,0,0,0,0,0,0,0,0,0,0,0,0,0],
  [0,1,1,1,0,0,0,0,0,0,0,0,0,1,1,1,1,0,0,0],
  [0,1,1,1,0,0,0,0,0,0,0,0,0,1,1,1,1,0,0,0],
  [0,1,1,0,0,0,0,0,0,0,0,0,0,1,1,1,1,0,0,0],
  [0,0,0,0,0,0,0,0,0,0,0,0,0,0,0,0,0,0,0,0],
  [0,0,0,0,0,1,0,0,0,0,0,0,0,0,0,0,0,0,0,0],
  [0,0,0,0,1,1,1,0,0,0,0,0,0,0,0,0,0,0,0,0],
  [0,0,0,0,0,1,0,0,0,0,0,0,0,0,0,0,0,0,0,0],
  [0,0,0,0,0,0,0,0,0,0,0,0,0,0,0,0,0,0,0,0],
  [0,0,0,0,0,0,0,0,0,0,0,0,0,0,0,0,0,0,0,0],
  [0,0,0,0,0,0,0,0,0,0,1,1,0,0,0,0,0,0,0,0],
  [0,0,0,0,0,0,0,0,0,0,1,1,0,0,0,0,0,0,0,0],
  [0,0,0,0,0,0,0,0,0,0,0,0,0,0,0,0,0,0,0,0],
  [0,0,0,0,0,0,0,0,0,0,0,0,0,0,0,0,0,0,0,0],
  [0,0,0,0,0,0,0,0,0,0,0,0,0,0,1,1,1,0,0,0],
  [0,0,0,0,0,0,0,0,0,0,0,0,0,0,1,1,1,0,0,0],
  [0,0,0,0,0,0,0,0,0,0,0,0,0,0,1,1,1,0,0,0],
  [0,0,0,0,0,0,0,0,0,0,0,0,0,0,0,0,0,0,0,0],
  [0,0,0,0,0,0,0,0,0,0,0,0,0,0,0,0,0,0,0,0],
  [0,0,0,0,0,0,0,0,0,0,0,0,0,0,0,0,0,0,0,0]
]

Output: 5
```

Approach: DFS efficiently identifies and counts islands:

1. Initialize island counter to 0.
2. Iterate through each cell in the grid.
3. When land ('1') is found:
   - Increment island counter.
   - Use DFS to mark all connected land cells as visited.
4. DFS procedure:
   - Mark the current cell as visited (change to '0').
   - Recursively explore adjacent cells (up, down, left, right).
   - Skip cells out of bounds or water ('0').
5. Each DFS call explores and marks an entire island.
6. Return final counter value.

13. Arrays & Hashing: First Non-Repeating Character

Problem: Find the first non-repeating character in a string.

```
Input: "allapples"
Output: 7` (index of 'e')
```

Approach: The hash map frequency counting operates in two phases:

First pass - build frequency map:

- Create a hash map for character counts.
- Iterate through the string.
- Increment the count for each character encountered.

Second pass - find non-repeating character:

- Iterate through the string in the original order.
- Check each character's frequency in the map.
- Return index of the first character with frequency 1.
- Return -1 if none exists.

14. Linked List: Reverse a Linked List

Problem: Reverse a singly linked list.

```
Input: [1,2,3,4,5]
Output: [5,4,3,2,1]
```

Approach: The three-pointer iterative solution:

1. Initialize three pointers:
   - prev: set to null
   - current: set to head
   - next: will be used temporarily.
2. Reverse links while traversing:
   - Store next node (next = current.next)
   - reverse current pointer (current.next = prev)
   - Advance prev pointer (prev = current)
   - Advance current pointer (current = next)
3. Continue until the current becomes null.
4. Return prev as the new head

15. Heap/Priority Queue: Balanced Network Traffic

Problem: Design a load balancer that distributes network traffic among servers based on their current load. A new request should be assigned to the least loaded server when it arrives. If multiple servers have the same load, choose the one that idles the longest.

Example:

```
Input: [Request(id=1, size=5), Request(id=2, size=2),
Request(id=3, size=7)]
       Servers: [Server(id=1, capacity=10), Server(id=2,
       capacity=8)]
```

338

```
Output: [(1,1), (2,2), (1,3)] // (server_id, request_id)
```

Approach: Use a min-heap to keep track of servers based on their current load and last active time. For each request, extract the least loaded server, assign the request, and reinsert the server with the updated load.

16. Graphs: Dependency Resolver

Problem: Implement a dependency resolver that determines the order in which tasks should be executed based on their dependencies. Each task has a unique ID and a list of prerequisite tasks that must be completed before it.

Example:

```
Input: tasks = {
    "A": [],
    "B": ["A"],
    "C": ["A"],
    "D": ["B", "C"],
}
Output: ["A", "B", "C", "D"] or ["A", "C", "B", "D"] (both are
valid)
```

Approach: This is a topological sorting problem. Use Kahn's algorithm (BFS) or a depth-first search approach to find a valid ordering that respects all dependencies.

17. Intelligent Cache System

Problem: Design a cache with a custom eviction policy that considers both frequency and recency of access. The cache should have a fixed capacity and evict the least valuable items when full.

Example:

```
cache = IntelligentCache(capacity=3)
cache.put(1, "A")
// Cache: {1: "A"}
cache.put(2, "B")
// Cache: {1: "A", 2: "B"}
cache.get(1)
// Returns "A", Cache: {1: "A", 2: "B"} (1's frequency
increases)
cache.put(3, "C")
// Cache: {1: "A", 2: "B", 3: "C"}
cache.put(4, "D")
// Cache is full, evict least valuable item (2), Cache: {1:
"A", 3: "C", 4: "D"}
```

Approach: Combine frequency and recency using a score function. Maintain a priority queue or sorted structure to find the item with the lowest score for eviction efficiently.

18. Trees: Text Editor Line Tracker

Problem: Implement a data structure for a text editor that efficiently tracks line numbers as text is inserted and deleted. The editor should support operations to insert text, delete text, and find the line number for a given position in the document.

  Example:

```
// Initialize editor with empty text
LineTracker editor = new LineTracker();

// Insert text with newlines
editor.insert(0, "Hello\nWorld\nHow are you?");

// Get line number for position
editor.getLineNumber(0);  // Returns 1 (first line)
editor.getLineNumber(7);  // Returns 2 (second line)
editor.getLineNumber(15); // Returns 3 (third line)
```

```
// Delete text across a line break
editor.delete(5, 7);        // Delete "World\n" leaving
"Hello\nHow are you?"

// Get updated line numbers
editor.getLineNumber(7);   // Returns 2 (now on the second line)
```

Approach: Use a balanced tree structure (like a red-black or AVL tree) to track line breaks efficiently. Each node in the tree represents a line break and stores the character position of that break.

19. Sliding Window: Message Rate Limiter

Problem: Implement a rate limiter restricting the number of messages a user can send in a given time window. Each user can send at most N messages in any window of T seconds.

Example:

```
RateLimiter limiter = new RateLimiter(2, 10); // 2 messages per
10 seconds
limiter.canSend("user1", 0); // returns true
limiter.canSend("user1", 1); // returns true
limiter.canSend("user1", 2); // returns false
limiter.canSend("user2", 2); // returns true
limiter.canSend("user1", 11); // returns true (new window)
```

Approach: Use a sliding window approach with a queue to track message timestamps for each user. When checking if a user can send a message, remove messages outside the current time window and then check if adding a new message would exceed the limit.

20. Heap/Priority Queue: Evidence Processing Queue

Problem: A law office has numerous evidence items for a high-profile case. Each piece of evidence has three attributes: importance (1-100), processing time (hours), and an expiration date (days from now). The legal team must process evidence before expiration, prioritizing based on a score calculated as: (importance/processing_time) * (1/days_until_expiration). Create an algorithm that determines the optimal processing order to maximize the value of evidence processed before expiration.

Example:

```
Input:
evidence = [
    {"id": "E1", "importance": 80, "processing_time": 4,
    "days_until_expiration": 3},
    {"id": "E2", "importance": 90, "processing_time": 6,
    "days_until_expiration": 5},
    {"id": "E3", "importance": 40, "processing_time": 2,
    "days_until_expiration": 1},
    {"id": "E4", "importance": 70, "processing_time": 3,
    "days_until_expiration": 2}
]
available_hours_per_day = 8

Output: ["E3", "E4", "E1", "E2"]
```

Approach: Use a max heap to prioritize evidence processing. Calculate the priority score for each item, process the highest-priority items first, and recalculate scores as time passes.

21: Arrays & Hashing: Circular Array Rotation Sequence

Problem: You are given a circular array of integers and a set of queries. For each query, you must simulate rotating the array in a specific number of positions and then return the element to a given index.

Input:

- An array of integers arr
- A list of queries, where each query is a pair

```
[rotations, index]
```

- rotations: The number of positions to rotate the array to the right
- index: The index to query after rotation

Example:

```
arr = [3, 7, 1, 9, 5]
queries = [[2, 1], [4, 3], [0, 2]]
```

Expected Output:

```
[3, 3, 1]
```

Explanation:

- Query 1: After rotating 2 positions right, the array becomes [5, 3, 7, 1, 9]. Element at index 1 is 3.
- Query 2: After rotating 4 positions right, the array becomes [7, 1, 9, 5, 3]. Element at index 3 is 5.
- Query 3: With 0 rotations, the array remains [3, 7, 1, 9, 5]. The element at index 2 is 1.

Approach: We can solve this without actually rotating the array. The key insight is that after rotating a circular array of length n by k positions, the element originally at index i will be at index $(i - k)$ % n (with a proper modulo to handle negative values).

Alternatively, we can compute where an element will end up after rotation: if we want to find the element at index i after k rotations, it will be the element originally at position (i + k) % n.

22. Greedy Algorithm: Optimized Task Scheduler

Problem: You must implement a task scheduler that processes tasks with cooldown periods.

A character represents each task. After executing a task, there must be a cooldown period of n time units before the same task can be executed again. Different tasks can be executed without cooldown constraints.

Your goal is to find the minimum time required to execute all given tasks.

Input:

- An array of tasks where each element is a character representing a task
- An integer n representing the cooldown period

Example:

```
tasks = ['A', 'A', 'B', 'C', 'A', 'B']
n = 2

Expected Output: 7
```

Explanation: One optimal sequence is A -> B -> C -> idle -> A -> B -> A, which takes 7-time units. The 'idle' is necessary because we need to wait for the cooldown period for task 'A'.

Approach:

1. Count the frequency of each task.
2. Use a max heap to always process the most frequent tasks first.
3. Use a queue to track when tasks become available again after the cooldown.
4. Process tasks until both the heap and queue are empty.

23. Greedy Algorithm: Interval Coverage Optimization

Problem: You're given a list of time intervals [start, end] that need coverage by a team. Each team member can cover any number of intervals, but they have a "shift time" constraint - they can only work for a continuous period of K hours. You must determine the minimum number of team members required to cover all intervals.

Example:

```
intervals = [[1, 3], [2, 5], [6, 8], [8, 10], [11, 12]]
K = 5
```

Expected output: 2

Explanation:

- Team member 1 covers from 1 to 6 (intervals [1,3], [2,5])
- Team member 2 covers from 6 to 12 (intervals [6,8], [8,10], [11,12])

Approach:

1. Sort the intervals by start time.
2. Use a greedy approach with a simulation of assigning team members.
3. For. each team member, try to cover as many intervals as possible within their K-hour shift.
4. The key insight is to start each team member's shift at the earliest uncovered interval.

24. Graphs: Dynamic Maze Flood Fill

Problem: You are given a maze represented as a 2D grid where:

- 0 represents an empty cell.
- 1 represents a wall.

- 2 represents water.

Water can flood through empty cells. After each minute, water floods into all adjacent empty cells (up, down, left, right). You need to determine how many minutes it takes for water to reach a target cell from (startX, startY) to (targetX, targetY).

If water cannot reach the target, return -1.

Example:

```
maze = [
     [0, 0, 0, 0],
     [1, 1, 0, 1],
     [0, 2, 0, 0],
     [0, 1, 1, 0]
]
startX = 2, startY = 1
targetX = 0, targetY = 0
```

Expected output: 3

Approach:

The problem can be solved using Breadth-First Search (BFS):

1. Start from the water source cell.
2. Use BFS to simulate the water flooding, keeping track of the time (minutes).
3. For each cell, explore all four adjacent cells (up, down, left, right).
4. Return the time when water reaches the target cell.
5. If the queue is empty and the target hasn't been reached, return -1.

This approach guarantees the minimum time to reach the target since BFS explores all cells that can be reached in 1 minute before exploring cells that take 2 minutes, and so on.

25. Heap/Priority Queue: Adaptive Resource Scheduler

Problem: Implement a task scheduler system with adaptive resource allocation. You're given a list of tasks, each with:

- id: unique task identifier.
- priority: integer from 1-10.
- resource_needs: the amount of resources needed.
- deadline: the time by which the task should be completed.

The scheduler must determine task execution order, maximizing resource utilization while respecting priorities and deadlines. If two tasks have the same priority, choose the one with the earlier deadline.

Example:

```
tasks = [
    {"id": "T1", "priority": 3, "resource_needs": 5,
    "deadline": 10},
    {"id": "T2", "priority": 5, "resource_needs": 3,
    "deadline": 5},
    {"id": "T3", "priority": 2, "resource_needs": 2,
    "deadline": 7},
    {"id": "T4", "priority": 5, "resource_needs": 1,
    "deadline": 3}
]
```

Expected output: ["T4", "T2", "T1", "T3"]

Approach:

1. Sort tasks by priority (descending)
2. For tasks with equal priority, sort by deadline (ascending)
3. Process tasks in this order
4. Maintain a timeline of resource allocation to track utilization.
5. For each task, check if it can be completed before its deadline based on current resource allocation.

6. Return the ordered list of task IDs

26. Graphs: Distributed Cache Consistency

Problem: You're building a distributed caching system where each node must maintain consistency with others. Given:

- n cache nodes (numbered 0 to n-1)
- A sequence of operations: (node_id, key, value, timestamp)
- Different propagation delays between nodes

Determine the final state of all cache nodes after all operations are processed.

Example:

```
nodes = 3
operations = [
    (0, "x", 10, 1),   # Node 0 sets x=10 at time 1
    (1, "y", 20, 2),   # Node 1 sets y=20 at time 2
    (2, "x", 30, 3),   # Node 2 sets x=30 at time 3
    (0, "y", 40, 4)    # Node 0 sets y=40 at time 4
]
delays = [
    [0, 2, 3],   # Delays from node 0 to others
    [2, 0, 1],   # Delays from node 1 to others
    [3, 1, 0]    # Delays from node 2 to others
]

Expected output:
[{"x": 30, "y": 40}, {"x": 30, "y": 40}, {"x": 30, "y": 40}]
```

Approach:

1. Simulate the propagation of each operation across all nodes.
2. Process operations in timestamp order at each node
3. For conflicting operations on the same key, use the "last writer wins"

strategy based on the operation timestamp.

4. Track when each operation arrives at each node, considering propagation delays.

5. Determine the final state of each node's cache after all operations have been processed.

27. Arrays & Hashing: Maximum Subarray With Target Sum

Problem: Given an array of integers and a target sum, find the maximum-length subarray that sums exactly to the target value.

Example:

```
nums = [1, -1, 5, -2, 3, 0, 2, -4, 1]
target = 3
```

Expected output: 4 (the subarray [5, -2, 3, -3] has sum 3 and length 4)

Approach:

1. Use dynamic programming with a prefix sum approach.

2. Maintain a hash map where keys are cumulative sums and values are the earliest indices where those sums occur.

3. Calculate the cumulative sum for each position and check if (current_sum - target) exists in the map.

4. If it exists, calculate the length of the potential subarray and update the maximum length.

5. Return the maximum length found

28. Sliding Window: K-Nearest Neighbors

Problem: You have a stream of two-dimensional points arriving in time order. Implement a sliding window algorithm to find the K nearest neighbors to the origin (0,0) within the last N points observed.

Example:

```
points = [(1, 2), (3, 4), (0, 1), (5, 2), (2, 0), (1, 5), (3,
1)]
window_size = 5
k = 3
```

Expected output: $[(2, 0), (0, 1), (3, 1)]$

Approach:

1. Maintain a max heap of size K containing the current K nearest points.
2. Maintain a sliding window of the most recent N points.
3. When a new point arrives:
   a. Add it to the sliding window.
   b. If the window exceeds size N, remove the oldest point.
   c. If the oldest point was in the heap, rebuild the heap.
   d. Attempt to add the new point to the heap if it's closer than the farthest point.
4. The heap will always contain the K nearest points in the current window.

29. Backtracking: Matrix Circuit

Problem: Create a function determining if a robot can complete a circuit in a matrix. The matrix is represented as a grid where:

- 0 represents a path the robot can traverse.
- 1 represents a wall the robot cannot cross.

The robot can only move in four directions: up, down, left, and right. A circuit is valid if:

1. The robot starts at a valid position (value 0).
2. The robot can return to its starting position after visiting at least 3

other unique cells.

3. The robot must only travel through valid cells (value 0).

Example input:

```
matrix = [
    [0, 1, 0, 0],
    [0, 0, 0, 1],
    [1, 1, 0, 0],
    [0, 0, 0, 0]
]
start_row = 0
start_col = 0
```

Approach:

1. Use depth-first search (DFS) to explore all possible paths from the starting position.
2. Keep track of visited cells to avoid revisiting them.
3. When we reach back to the starting position, check if we've visited at least 3 other unique cells.
4. If yes, return true; otherwise, continue searching.
5. If all possible paths are explored and none form a valid circuit, return false

30. Dynamic Programming: Artwork Gallery Heist

Problem: An art thief plans a heist at a gallery where artworks are displayed in a row of exhibition rooms. Each room contains artwork with a specific monetary value. Due to the gallery's security system, an alarm will trigger if the thief steals from two adjacent rooms.

Given an array representing the value of the artwork in each room, determine the maximum total value the thief can steal without triggering any alarms.

Example:

```
Input: [5, 2, 9, 11, 3]
Output: 17
Explanation: Steal from rooms 0, 2, and 4 (values 5, 9, and 3)

Input: [2, 7, 9, 3, 1]
Output: 12
Explanation: Steal from rooms 0, 2, and 4 (values 2, 9, and 1)
```

Approach:

Use dynamic programming:

1. Define DP[i] as the maximum value that can be stolen up to the i-th room
2. For each room, either:
   - Skip the current room: DP[i-1]
   - Take the current room plus maximum value from two rooms back: DP[i-2] + values[i]
3. Recurrence relation: DP[i] = max(DP[i-1], DP[i-2] + values[i])
4. Base cases: DP[0] = values[0], DP[1] = max(values[0], values[1])

31. Sliding Window: Range Duplicate Finder

Problem:

Given an array of integers, determine if there are any duplicate values within a sliding window of size k.

Write a function that returns true if at least one pair of duplicate values exists within any k-length subarray and false otherwise.

Examples:

```
Input: nums = [1, 2, 3, 4, 1], k = 3
Output: false
Explanation: No duplicates exist within any 3-element subarray.
```

```
Input: nums = [5, 1, 4, 1, 7], k = 3
Output: true
Explanation: [1, 4, 1] contains a duplicate (1).

Input: nums = [3, 3, 3], k = 2
Output: true
Explanation: Any 2-element subarray contains a duplicate (3).
```

Approach:

Use a sliding window with a hash set:

1. Maintain a set containing elements within the current window.
2. Check if each new element is already in the set.
3. If the window size exceeds k, remove the oldest element.
4. Return true as soon as a duplicate is found within the window

32. Stack: Temperature Forecast Analysis

Problem:

Weather forecasters need to analyze temperature trends. Given an array of predicted daily temperatures, return an array where each element represents how many days from that day until a warmer temperature occurs. If no warmer temperature is expected, return 0 for that position.

Examples:

```
Input: [73, 74, 75, 71, 69, 72, 76, 73]
Output: [1, 1, 4, 2, 1, 1, 0, 0]

Input: [30, 30, 30, 30]
Output: [0, 0, 0, 0]

Input: [55, 38, 53, 81, 61, 93, 97, 32, 43]
Output: [3, 1, 1, 2, 1, 1, 0, 1, 0]
```

Approach:

Use a monotonic stack to track indices:

1. Initialize an array to store results (filled with zeros)
2. Create a stack to store indices of temperatures.
3. For each temperature from left to right:

- While the stack is not empty, and the current temperature is greater than the temperature at the stack top:
- Pop index from the stack
- Set result at popped index to current day minus popped index.
- Push the current index onto the stack

33. Two Pointers: Scenic Skyline Viewpoints

Problem:
A city planner is designing a linear park along a street with buildings of various heights. The planner wants to place two viewing platforms to maximize the scenic viewing area between them. The viewing area is calculated as the distance between the platforms multiplied by the height of the shorter platform.

Given an array of integers representing building heights along the street, find the maximum possible viewing area that can be achieved by selecting any two buildings for platforms.

Examples:

```
Input: [1, 8, 6, 2, 5, 4, 8, 3, 7]
Output: 49
Explanation: The optimal platforms are at positions 1 and 8
(heights 8 and 7), with area = 7 * 7 = 49

Input: [4, 3, 2, 1, 4]
Output: 16
Explanation: The optimal platforms are at positions 0 and 4
(both height 4), with area = 4 * 4 = 16
```

```
Input: [1, 2, 1]
Output: 2
Explanation: The optimal platforms are at positions 0 and 2
(both height 1), with area = 1 * 2 = 2
```

Approach:

Use a two-pointer technique:

1. Place one pointer at the leftmost building and another at the right-most.
2. Calculate the viewing area using the current pointers.
3. Move the pointer pointing to the shorter building inward (since moving the taller one would only decrease the area)
4. Keep track of the maximum area seen so far.
5. Repeat until the pointers meet.

34. Two Pointers: Mountain Valley Rainwater Collection

Problem: After a rainstorm, water collects in the valleys between mountains of different heights. Given an array of integers representing the mountain heights, calculate the total water volume trapped between the mountains after the rain.

Each unit of width between adjacent mountains can hold water up to the height of the shorter of the two mountains. Water cannot flow off the edges of the terrain.

Example:

```
Input: [0, 1, 0, 2, 1, 0, 1, 3, 2, 1, 2, 1]
Output: 6
Explanation: The structure traps water in several locations for
6 units.
```

```
Input: [4, 2, 0, 3, 2, 5]
Output: 9
Explanation: Water trapped: 2 units between heights 4 and 3, 3
units between heights 3 and 5, and 4 units between heights 2
and 5.
```

Approach: Use a two-pointer technique:

1. Initialize pointers at the start and end of the array
2. Track maximum heights from both left and right sides
3. Always move the pointer with the smaller height inward.
4. If current height < maximum seen from that side, water is trapped at that position
5. Otherwise, update the maximum height for that side.
6. Continue until pointers meet.

35. Greedy Algorithms: Maximum Property Value Appreciation

Problem: A real estate investor wants to maximize profit by buying a property on one day and selling it on a future day. Given an array of property values over consecutive days, determine the maximum profit the investor can achieve. If no profit can be made, return 0.

Example:

```
Input: [7, 1, 5, 3, 6, 4]
Output: 5
Explanation: Buy on day 2 (price = 1), sell on day 5 (price =
6), and profit = 6 - 1 = 5.

Input: [7, 6, 4, 3, 1]
Output: 0
Explanation: No profit can be made as prices are continuously
decreasing.
```

Approach:

1. Track the minimum property value seen so far.
2. Calculate the potential profit for each day if we sell on that day.
3. Update the maximum profit if the current potential profit is higher.
4. Return the maximum profit at the end.

36. Arrays & Hashing: Frequency Threshold Detection

Problem: Given an array of integers and a threshold value k, determine if any element appears at least k times in the array.

Example:

```
Input: nums = [1, 2, 3, 1, 2, 3], k = 2
Output: true
Explanation: 1, 2, and 3 appear twice, meeting the threshold.

Input: nums = [1, 2, 3, 4, 5], k = 2
Output: false
Explanation: No integer appears more than once.

Input: nums = [5, 5, 5, 2, 1], k = 3
Output: true
Explanation: 5 appears three times, meeting the threshold.
```

Approach:

1. Use a hash map (dictionary) to count the occurrences of each element.
2. Iterate through the array, incrementing the count for each element.
3. Check if any element's count reaches the threshold k
4. Return true as soon as an element meets the threshold; otherwise, return false

37. Arrays & Hashing: X-Sudoku Validator

Problem: X-Sudoku is a variant of Sudoku with additional diagonal constraints. Given a 9×9 grid with filled and unfilled cells (unfilled represented by '0'), determine if it follows these rules:

1. Each row must contain no duplicate digits 1-9
2. Each column must contain no duplicate digits 1-9
3. Each of the nine 3×3 sub-grids must contain no duplicate digits 1-9
4. The two main diagonals (top-left to bottom-right and top-right to bottom-left) must each contain no duplicate digits 1-9

Example:

```
Input:
[
  [5,3,0,0,7,0,0,0,0],
  [6,0,0,1,9,5,0,0,0],
  [0,9,8,0,0,0,0,6,0],
  [8,0,0,0,6,0,0,0,3],
  [4,0,0,8,0,3,0,0,1],
  [7,0,0,0,2,0,0,0,6],
  [0,6,0,0,0,0,2,8,0],
  [0,0,0,4,1,9,0,0,5],
  [0,0,0,0,8,0,0,7,9]
]
Output: true

Input with a diagonal violation:
[
  [5,3,0,0,7,0,0,0,0],
  [6,0,0,1,9,5,0,0,0],
  [0,9,8,0,0,0,0,6,0],
  [8,0,0,0,6,0,0,0,3],
  [4,0,0,8,5,3,0,0,1],
  [7,0,0,0,2,0,0,0,6],
  [0,6,0,0,0,0,2,8,0],
```

358

```
    [0,0,0,4,1,9,0,0,5],
    [0,0,0,0,8,0,0,7,9]
]
Output: false
```

Approach:

1. Use sets to track seen digits for each row, column, 3×3 subgrid, and both diagonals.
2. Iterate through the grid, checking each constraint.
3. For 3×3 subgrids, calculate the index using the formula: (row/3)*3 + col/3
4. Check the main diagonal when i==j and the anti-diagonal when i+j==8.
5. Return false at first violation, true if all constraints are satisfied

38. Greedy Algorithms: Vehicle Convoy Formation

Problem: A fleet of vehicles travels along a straight highway toward a destination at position target. Each vehicle starts at a different position and maintains a constant speed. When a faster vehicle catches up to a slower one, traffic rules require it to reduce speed to match the vehicle ahead, forming a convoy. Determine how many separate convoys will exist when all vehicles reach or pass the destination.

Example:

```
Input:
target = 12
positions = [10, 8, 0, 5, 3]
speeds = [2, 4, 1, 1, 3]
Output: 3
Explanation:
- Vehicle at position 10 with speed 2 reaches the target in
```

```
(12-10)/2 = 1 time unit
- Vehicle at position 8 with speed 4 reaches the target in
(12-8)/4 = 1 time unit (forms a convoy with the first vehicle)
- Vehicle at position 0 with speed 1 reaches the target in 12
time units (forms its own convoy)
- Vehicle at position 5 with speed 1 reaches the target in 7
time units (forms its own convoy)
- Vehicle at position 3 with speed 3 reaches the target in 3
time units (forms its own convoy)

Input:
target = 100
positions = [0, 2, 4]
speeds = [4, 2, 1]
Output: 1
Explanation: All vehicles eventually form a single convoy
behind the slowest vehicle.
```

Approach:

1. Calculate the arrival time for each vehicle: time = (target - position) / speed
2. Sort the vehicles by their initial position in descending order (to process them from front to back)
3. Iterate through the sorted vehicles:
   - If a vehicle takes longer to reach the target than the previous vehicle, it forms a new convoy.
   - Otherwise, it will catch up and join the convoy ahead.
4. Count the total number of convoys

39. Stack: Maximum Productivity Zone

Problem: A productivity analyst tracks workforce efficiency across sequential workstations in a manufacturing line. Each workstation has a capacity value representing the maximum number of units it can process per hour. The analyst wants to find the most efficient continuous segment of workstations on which to focus improvement efforts. The "productivity value" of a segment is calculated as (length of segment) × (minimum capacity among those workstations).

Example:

```
Input: [2, 1, 5, 6, 2, 3]
Output: 10
Explanation: The optimal segment is workstations [1, 5, 6, 2,
3] with minimum capacity 1 and length 5, giving 1×5=5;
alternatively, [5, 6, 2] with minimum capacity 2 and length 3,
giving 2×3=6; or optimally [5, 6] with minimum capacity 5 and
length 2, giving 5×2=10.

Input: [3, 3, 3, 2, 5]
Output: 9
Explanation: The optimal segment is workstations [3, 3, 3] with
minimum capacity 3 and length 3, giving 3×3=9.
```

Approach:

1. Use a monotonically increasing stack to track indices.
2. For each workstation, while the stack is not empty, and the current capacity is less than the capacity at the stack top:
   - Pop the top element
   - Calculate the potential productivity using the popped workstation's capacity.
   - Update the maximum productivity if greater.
   - Push the current index onto the stack.
3. After processing all workstations, handle any remaining indices in the stack.
4. Return the maximum productivity found

40. Matrix Operations: Layered Security Clearance Search

Problem: In a multi-level security system, clearance codes are organized in a matrix where each row represents a security zone, and each column represents an authorization level. The matrix has the following properties:

- Each row is sorted in ascending order by clearance code.
- The first code in each row is greater than the last code in the previous row.
- You need to determine if a specific security clearance code exists in the matrix

Example:

```
Input:
matrix = [
  [1024, 1100, 1225, 1300],
  [1350, 1400, 1450, 1500],
  [2000, 2100, 2200, 2300]
]
target = 1225
Output: true

Input:
matrix = [
  [1024, 1100, 1225, 1300],
  [1350, 1400, 1450, 1500],
  [2000, 2100, 2200, 2300]
]
target = 1800
Output: false
```

Approach: Treat the 2D matrix as a single sorted array and perform a binary search:

1. Define the search space from 0 to (rows*cols-1)
2. For each middle index in the binary search, convert it to 2D coordinates using:
   - row = mid // cols
   - col = mid % cols
3. Compare the value at these coordinates with the target and adjust the search space accordingly

41. Binary Search: Document Processing Throughput

Problem: A document processing system must handle a series of document batches. Each batch contains a different number of pages. The system can process a variable number of pages per hour. If a batch has fewer pages than the system's hourly capacity, it still takes a full hour to complete (the system cannot start a new batch until the next hour begins). Given an array where each element represents the number of pages in a batch and a deadline of h hours, find the minimum processing speed (pages per hour) needed for the system to complete all batches within h hours.

Example:

```
Input: batches = [10, 20, 30], h = 6
Output: 10
Explanation:
With speed 10 pages/hour:
- First batch (10 pages): 1 hour
- Second batch (20 pages): 2 hours (needs ceiling(20/10))
- Third batch (30 pages): 3 hours (needs ceiling(30/10))
Total: 6 hours

Input: batches = [30, 11, 23, 4, 20], h = 5
Output: 30
Explanation:
With speed 30 pages/hour:
- Batch 1 (30 pages): 1 hour
- Batch 2 (11 pages): 1 hour
```

```
- Batch 3 (23 pages): 1 hour
- Batch 4 (4 pages): 1 hour
- Batch 5 (20 pages): 1 hour
Total: 5 hours
```

Approach: Use binary search to find the minimum processing speed:

1. Define a function to check if all batches can be completed in h hours with a given speed.
2. Set the search range from 1 to maximum pages in any batch.
3. For each middle value in the binary search, check if that speed allows completion within h hours.
4. If yes, try a lower speed; if no, try a higher speed.
5. Return the minimum valid processing speed.

42. Binary Search: Encrypted Circular Buffer Search

Problem: A secure communication system encrypts a sorted sequence of unique integers by "rotating" it at a random position. For example, the sequence [1,2,3,4,5] might become [3,4,5,1,2] after being rotated 2 positions. Given such a rotated sequence, find the minimum value (initially the first element before rotation).

Example:

```
Input: [4,5,6,7,0,1,2]
Output: 0
Explanation: The original sorted array was [0,1,2,4,5,6,7] and
rotated 4 positions.

Input: [11,13,15,17]
Output: 11
Explanation: The array is already in ascending order, so the
minimum is 11.
```

```
Input: [5,1,2,3,4]
Output: 1
Explanation: The original array was [1,2,3,4,5] and rotated 1
position.
```

Approach: Use a modified binary search:

1. If the array is sorted (arr[left] < arr[right]), the minimum is at the start
2. Otherwise, use binary search to locate the "rotation point."
3. In each step, compare the middle element with the rightmost element:
   - If mid > right, the rotation point is after mid.
   - If mid < right, the rotation point is before or at mid.
4. The minimum element is found when the array is sorted, or the left and right pointers converge.

43. Matrix Operations: Parallel Matrix Diagonal Sum

Problem: You are given an n×n matrix and asked to find the diagonal with the maximum sum. A diagonal can start from any cell at the top row (row 0) or the leftmost column (column 0) and move in the bottom-right direction (incrementing both row and column indices by 1) until it reaches the edge of the matrix. Return the maximum diagonal sum found.

Example:

```
Input: [
  [1, 2, 3],
  [4, 5, 6],
  [7, 8, 9]
]
Output: 15
Explanation: Diagonals starting from the top row are:
```

```
- (0,0): 1+5+9=15
- (0,1): 2+6=8
- (0,2): 3=3
Diagonals starting from the leftmost column are:
- (1,0): 4+8=12
- (2,0): 7=7
The maximum sum is 15.

Input: [
  [9, 2, 3],
  [4, 5, 1],
  [7, 1, 6]
]
Output: 16
Explanation: Maximum diagonal starts at (2,0) with sum 7+5+3=15
```

Approach: We need to calculate the sum of each possible diagonal and track the maximum. A diagonal can start either from the top row or the leftmost column. For each starting position, we traverse in the bottom-right direction until we reach the matrix boundary, adding values along the way. We maintain a running maximum to track the highest sum found.

44. Binary Search: Version-Based Configuration Store

Problem: Implement a configuration management system that stores configuration values for different application versions. The system should support these operations:

- set(feature, version, value): Sets the value of a feature for a specific version
- get(feature, version): Gets the value of a feature for a specific version. If the feature doesn't have a value for the exact version, return the value from the highest version that is less than or equal to the requested version. Return an empty string ("") if no such version exists.

Example:

```
Input:
["ConfigStore", "set", "set", "set", "get", "get", "get", "get"]
[[], ["ui.theme", 1, "dark"], ["ui.theme", 3, "light"],
["api.timeout", 2, "30s"], ["ui.theme", 2], ["ui.theme", 5],
["api.timeout", 1], ["api.retry", 1]]

Output:
[null, null, null, null, "dark", "light", "", ""]

Explanation:
ConfigStore configStore = new ConfigStore();
configStore.set("ui.theme", 1, "dark");      // Set ui.theme for
version 1 to "dark"
configStore.set("ui.theme", 3, "light");     // Set ui.theme for
version 3 to "light"
configStore.set("api.timeout", 2, "30s");    // Set api.timeout
for version 2 to "30s"
configStore.get("ui.theme", 2);              // return "dark"
(highest version <= 2 is 1)
configStore.get("ui.theme", 5);              // return "light"
(highest version <= 5 is 3)
configStore.get("api.timeout", 1);           // return "" (no
version <= 1)
configStore.get("api.retry", 1);             // return ""
(feature not found)
```

Approach: We'll store a sorted data structure of version-value pairs for each feature. When setting a value, we add or update the version in the appropriate data structure. When getting a value, we need to find the highest version that's less than or equal to the requested version, which can be done efficiently with binary search or appropriate data structures like TreeMap in Java.

45. Binary Search: Minimum Processing Power

Problem: You are given a list of tasks, each requiring a certain number of computational cycles to complete. You must design a processor with enough processing power (cycles per second) to complete all tasks within a specified time limit. If a task requires fewer computational cycles than the processor can perform in a second, the processor still spends the full second on that task (no partial seconds).

Given an array of tasks representing the required computational cycles for each task and an integer maxSeconds representing the time limit, return the minimum processor speed (in cycles per second) required to complete all tasks within the time limit.

Example:

```
Input: tasks = [10, 20, 30, 40], maxSeconds = 5
Output: 30
Explanation:
With a processing power of 24 cycles per second:
- Task 1 (10 cycles) takes ceil(10/24) = 1 second
- Task 2 (20 cycles) takes ceil(20/24) = 1 second
- Task 3 (30 cycles) takes ceil(30/24) = 2 seconds
- Task 4 (40 cycles) takes ceil(40/24) = 2 seconds
Total: 1 + 1 + 2 + 2 = 6 seconds (exceeds limit)

With a processing power of 30 cycles per second:
- Task 1 (10 cycles) takes ceil(10/30) = 1 second
- Task 2 (20 cycles) takes ceil(20/30) = 1 second
- Task 3 (30 cycles) takes ceil(30/30) = 1 second
- Task 4 (40 cycles) takes ceil(40/30) = 2 seconds
Total: 1 + 1 + 1 + 2 = 5 seconds (meets limit)

Therefore, 30 is the minimum processing power required.
```

Approach: We'll use binary search to find the minimum processing power needed. The key insight is that the time to complete a task with processing power 'p' is the ceiling(task/p). We need to find the minimum value of 'p' such that the sum of completion times for all tasks is less than or equal to maxSeconds.

46. Trees: Clone Bi1nary Tree with Connection Pointers

Problem: You are given a binary tree where each node has a left child, right child, and a "connection" pointer that can point to any node in the tree or null. Design an algorithm to create a deep copy of this tree to preserve all structural properties, including the connection pointers.

Example:

```
Original tree visualization:
      1
    /   \
   2     3
  / \     \
 4   5     6

With connections (shown as dotted lines):
1 --> 3
2 --> 5
3 --> 4
5 --> 1
6 --> 2

Output: Return a deep copy of the tree with all connections
preserved.
```

Approach: This problem requires mapping each original node to its corresponding copy. We'll solve it in two phases:

1. Create a copy of the tree structure (without connections) and build a mapping between original and copied nodes.
2. Traverse the original tree again and set the connection pointers in the copied tree based on the mapping.

47. Linked List: Rotate Linked List Around Pivot

Problem: Given a singly linked list and an integer pivot value, rearrange the list such that all nodes with values less than the pivot appear before all nodes with values greater than or equal to the pivot. The relative order of nodes in each partition should be preserved. If the pivot value doesn't exist in the list, partition the list without placing the pivot.

Example:

```
Input: 3->1->5->8->2->4, pivot = 4
Output: 3->1->2->4->5->8

Input: 7->9->3->8->5->1, pivot = 6
Output: 3->5->1->7->9->8
```

Approach: Create two separate linked lists - one for nodes with values less than the pivot and one for nodes with values greater than or equal to the pivot. Traverse the original list, placing each node in the appropriate list while maintaining the original order. Finally, connect the two lists.

48. Linked List: Interleave K Linked Lists

Problem: Given k sorted linked lists, interleave them by taking one node from each list in a round-robin fashion until all lists are empty. If a list becomes empty, skip it and continue with the remaining lists. Return the interleaved linked list.

Example:

```
Input:
List 1: 1->4->7
List 2: 2->5->8
List 3: 3->6

Output: 1->2->3->4->5->6->7->8
```

Approach: Maintain a list of pointers to the current node in each linked list. In each round, take the current node from each list, append it to the result, and move the pointer to the next node. Continue until all lists are processed.

49. Trees: Path Matching Binary Tree

Problem: Given two binary trees, check if at least one path exists from the root to a leaf in both trees that have identical values along the path. A path is a sequence of nodes starting from the root and ending at a leaf.

Example:

```
Tree 1:
    1
   / \
  2   3
 / \
4   5

Tree 2:
    1
   / \
  2   7
 / \
4   9


Output: true
Explanation: The path 1->2->4 exists in both trees with
identical values.

Tree 1:
    1
   / \
  2   3

Tree 2:
    7
```

```
      / \
     9   1
```

```
Output: false
Explanation: No matching paths exist.
```

Approach: Collect all root-to-leaf paths in both trees, then check for at least one matching path. We can use DFS to collect all paths from root to leaf nodes in each tree and then compare the collected paths.

50. Trees: Symmetric Tree Transformation

Problem: Given a binary tree, transform it into a "symmetric tree" by reflecting each subtree that isn't already symmetric. A symmetric tree is one where the left subtree is a mirror reflection of the right subtree. If a node has only one child, add a mirrored child to make it symmetric. Return the transformed tree.

Example:

```
Input:
    1
   / \
  2   3
 /     \
4       5

Output:
    1
   / \
  2   2
 / \   \
4   4   4
```

```
Explanation: The tree wasn't symmetric initially. The algorithm
mirrors node 2 and its child 4 and replaces node 3 with a
```

```
mirror of node 2.

Input:
    1
   / \
  2   2
   \   \
    3   3

Output:
    1
   / \
  2   2
 / \   \
3   3   3
```

Explanation: The top level was symmetric, but the children of node 2 weren't balanced, so a mirror child was added.

Approach: Use a post-order traversal to process each subtree from bottom to top. For each node, check if its subtrees are symmetric. If not, transform them to be symmetric by mirroring the structure.

51. Stack: Expression Tree Execution

Problem: You are given a string representing an "expression tree" in a linear format. Each character in the string is either an operand (a lowercase letter a-z representing a variable with a value 1-26) or an operator. The operators are:

- '+': Add the two values.
- '-': Subtract the second value from the first.
- '*': Multiply the two values.
- '/': Integer division of the first value by the second.
- '$': Maximum of the two values.
- '&': Minimum of the two values.

The expression follows a pre-order traversal of a binary expression tree, where each operator is followed by exactly two operands, and each operand can be another expression. Evaluate the expression and return the result.

Example:

```
Input: "+ab"
Output: 3
Explanation: 'a' has value 1, 'b' has value 2, so 1+2=3

Input: "*+ab-cd"
Output: 9
Explanation: This represents *(+(a,b),-(c,d))
- 'a'=1, 'b'=2, so +(a,b)=3
- 'c'=3, 'd'=4, so -(c,d)=-1
- *(3,-1)=-3

Input: "$*ab&cd"
Output: 4
Explanation: This represents $(*(a,b),&(c,d))
- 'a'=1, 'b'=2, so *(a,b)=2
- 'c'=3, 'd'=4, so &(c,d)=3
- $(2,3)=3 (maximum)
```

Approach: We'll use a recursive approach to parse and evaluate the expression. When we encounter an operator, we'll recursively evaluate its two operands. When we encounter a letter, we'll convert it to its corresponding value (a=1, b=2, etc.). The structure follows a pre-order traversal, which simplifies the parsing process.

52. Stack: Balanced Bracket Sequence Generator

Problem: Design a system that, given a valid bracket expression containing only brackets []{}(), generates all valid bracket expressions that can be formed by adding exactly one pair of matching brackets. A valid bracket expression is one where all brackets have matching pairs and are properly nested.

Example:

```
Input: "()"
Output: ["()()", "(())", "()[()]", "(){}", "[()]", "{()}"]
Explanation:
- Adding () outside: "()()"
- Adding () inside: "(())"
- Adding [] outside: "[()]"
- Adding {} outside: "{()}"
- Adding {} inside: "(){}"
- Adding [] inside: "()[()]"

Input: "{[]}"
Output: ["{[]}{}", "{[]}()", "{[][]}","{[{}]}", "[{[]}]",
"({[]})", ...]
```

Approach: We need to identify all positions where we can insert new bracket pairs. We can add each type of bracket pair for each position in the original expression and check if the resulting expression is valid. We'll use a stack-based approach similar to the one used to validate bracket expressions but adapted to generate new valid expressions.

53. Trees: Balanced Tree Reconstruction

Problem: Given an unbalanced binary search tree (BST), transform it into a balanced BST without changing the in-order traversal sequence of the nodes. A balanced BST has a height difference of at most 1 between the heights of every node's left and right subtrees.

Example:

```
Input:
      10
     /
    8
   /
  6
```

375

```
     /
    4
```

Output (one possible solution):

```
      6
     / \
    4    10
         /
        8
```

Explanation: The original tree is 4 feet tall, while the balanced tree is 3 feet tall.

Input:

```
      5
     / \
    3   8
   /     \
  1       9
   \
    2
```

Output (one possible solution):

```
      5
     / \
    2   9
   / \
  1   3
     /
    8
```

Explanation: The original tree is 4 feet tall, while the balanced tree is 3 feet tall.

Approach: The key insight is that a BST with a given in-order traversal can be reconstructed into a balanced tree by:

1. Performing an in-order traversal to collect all nodes in sorted order
2. Recursively select the middle element as the root and construct the

left and right subtrees from the elements before and after the middle, respectively.

54. Trees: Optimal Node Removal for Minimum Height

Problem: Given a binary tree, you are allowed to remove at most k nodes (including their subtrees) to minimize the height of the resulting tree. Return the minimum possible height after removing at most k nodes. Removing a node means removing the entire subtree rooted at that node.

Example:

```
Input:
        5
      / \
     3   6
    / \   \
   2   4   8
  /       / \
 1       7   9
k = 1

Output: 2
Explanation: Remove the node with value 8, resulting in a tree
with height 2:
        5
      / \
     3   6
    / \
   2   4
  /
 1

Input:
          10
         /  \
        5    15
       / \   / \
```

```
    3   8 12  20
   /  /      / \
  1   6     18  25
k = 2
```

```
Output: 2
Explanation: Remove nodes with values 3 and 20, resulting in a
tree with height 2:
         10
        /  \
       5    15
        \   /
         8 12
        /
       6
```

Approach: Use a combination of DFS and dynamic programming. Calculate the possible resulting tree heights for each node after removing different combinations of subtrees up to k nodes. Keep track of the minimum height achievable for each value of j ≤ k nodes removed.

55. Tries: Context-Sensitive Search Suggestion System

Problem: Implement a search suggestion system that provides contextually relevant word suggestions based on a user's typing prefix and search history. The system should maintain two Trie data structures: one for the dictionary of all available words and another for tracking the user's recent search terms. When suggesting completions, the system should prioritize words from the user's history that match the current prefix, followed by general dictionary words sorted alphabetically. Each suggested word should be returned only once.

Example:

```
Input:
addToHistory(["apple", "application", "banana", "art",
```

```
"applied", "apple"])
suggest("ap")

Output: ["apple", "application", "applied"]
Explanation: "apple" comes first because it appears in the
history (and most recently), followed by "application" and
"applied" alphabetically.

Input:
addToHistory(["code", "coffee", "coding", "coder", "cafe"])
suggest("co")

Output: ["code", "coffee", "coding", "coder"]
Explanation: All suggestions start with "co" from the history,
sorted by their order of appearance.
```

Approach: We'll implement two Trie data structures. The first will store all dictionary words, and the second will store the user's search history with timestamps or recency information. When providing suggestions, we'll first query the history trie for matches, then supplement with dictionary matches if needed. This ensures that the most contextually relevant suggestions (based on recent searches) appear first.

56. Tries: Fuzzy Word Finder

Problem: Implement a fuzzy search system that can find words in a dictionary that match a query with up to k character substitutions allowed. A character substitution is when one character in the query is replaced with a different character at the same position in a dictionary word. Return all dictionary words that match the query with at most k substitutions, sorted by the number of substitutions required (ascending), and then alphabetically.

Example:

```
Input:
dictionary = ["apple", "appeal", "banana", "append", "app",
"ape"]
query = "apple"
k = 1

Output: ["apple", "appeal", "append"]
Explanation: "apple" has 1 substitution ('e'->'a'), "appeal"
and "append" both have 1 substitution.

Input:
dictionary = ["cat", "chat", "hat", "bat", "rat", "mat"]
query = "fat"
k = 2

Output: ["bat", "cat", "hat", "mat", "rat", "chat"]
Explanation: The first 5 words have 1 substitution, and "chat"
has 2 substitutions.
```

Approach: We'll use a Trie to store and search the dictionary efficiently. We'll use a modified DFS search for fuzzy matching that allows for character substitutions. At each level of the trie, we'll consider both the exact match path and all possible substitution paths, keeping track of the number of substitutions used. We'll prune paths that exceed k substitutions.

57. Binary Search: Minimum Allocation Threshold for Equal Array Groups

Problem: You are given an array of positive integers nums and an integer k. You need to split the array into precisely k groups so that the maximum sum of any group is minimized. Return the minimum possible value for this maximum sum.

Example:

```
Input: nums = [3, 2, 4, 8, 1, 5], k = 3
Output: 9
Explanation: One optimal grouping is [3, 2, 4], [8, 1], [5]
The maximum sum is 9 (from the first group).

Input: nums = [1, 2, 3, 4, 5, 6, 7, 8, 9], k = 5
Output: 11
Explanation: One optimal grouping is [1, 2, 3, 4], [5, 6], [7],
[8], [9]
The maximum sum is 11 (from the second group).
```

Approach: This problem can be solved using a binary search on the answer space. We'll search for the minimum possible maximum sum. For each candidate threshold value, we check if splitting the array into k or fewer groups is possible where each group's sum doesn't exceed the threshold. We can try a smaller threshold; otherwise, we need a larger one. The key insight is that the answer has a monotonic property: if we can split the array with a certain threshold, we can do it with any larger threshold.

58. Binary Search: Kth Ancestral Element in Sorted Arrays

Problem: You are given m sorted integer arrays, arrays, and a positive integer k. Each array represents a family lineage with ancestors at lower indices. Define the "ancestral element" of position p as the element that appears in at least one array at position p or earlier. Your task is to find the kth smallest ancestral element across all arrays.

  Example:

```
Input: arrays = [[1, 3, 5, 7], [2, 4, 8, 9], [3, 5, 7, 11]], k
= 5
Output: 4
Explanation: The ancestral elements in ascending order are [1,
2, 3, 3, 4, 5, 5, 7, 7, 8, 9, 11].
```

The 5th ancestral element is 4.

```
Input: arrays = [[1, 5, 8], [2, 3, 6, 9]], k = 4
Output: 5
Explanation: The ancestral elements in ascending order are [1,
2, 3, 5, 6, 8, 9].
The 4th ancestral element is 5.
```

Approach: We can use binary search to find the kth ancestral element. We count how many ancestral elements are less than or equal to mid for each potential value across all arrays. If the count is less than k, we need to look for a larger value; otherwise, we look for a smaller value. The key insight is efficiently counting ancestral elements using binary search on each sorted array.

59. Graphs: Key Collection Sequence

Problem: You are in a maze represented as a 2D grid. The maze contains walls, empty spaces, keys, and locked doors. You can move in four directions (up, down, left, right) and cannot walk through walls. Keys are represented by lowercase letters ('a' through 'z'), and doors are represented by the corresponding uppercase letters ('A' through 'Z'). You can walk through a door only if you have collected the corresponding key.

The twist is that keys must be collected in alphabetical order. For example, you must collect key 'a' before key 'b', and key 'b' before key 'c', and so on.

Your starting position is marked as 'S', and you must find the minimum number of steps to collect all keys in the maze. If it's not possible to collect all keys in the correct order, return -1.

Example:

```
Input:
[
```

```
    "S.a.#",
    "##.##",
    "c.b.d"
]

Output: 8
```

Explanation:

In this example:

- You start at 'S'
- First, you need to collect key 'a'.
- Then, you need to collect key 'b'
- Then, you need to collect key 'c'
- Finally, you need to collect the key 'd'
- The minimum number of steps to collect all keys alphabetically is 8.

Approach: To solve this problem, we'll use a modified BFS (Breadth-First Search) algorithm. Since we need to collect keys alphabetically, we'll do a series of BFS searches, one for each key.

1. Identify the starting position 'S'.
2. Identify all the keys in the maze and count them.
3. For each key in alphabetical order ('a', 'b', 'c', ...), perform a BFS to find the shortest path from the current position to the key. Update the current position after collecting each key.
4. During BFS, we can only go through doors if we have collected the corresponding keys.
5. Keep track of the total number of steps taken to collect all keys.
6. If at any point we can't reach the next key, return –1.

60. Arrays & Hashing: Group Anagrams By Frequency

Problem: Given an array of strings, group all anagrams together where anagrams are strings that have the same character frequency distribution regardless of order. Return the groups in order of their first appearance in the input array.

Example:

```
Input: ["eat", "tea", "tan", "ate", "nat", "bat"] Output:
[["eat", "tea", "ate"], ["tan", "nat"], ["bat"]]
```

Approach: We can use a hash map to group the strings. We'll create a frequency counter of its characters for each string and use that as the key in our hash map. The values will be lists of strings that share the same character frequency. We'll use an ordered data structure or track the order separately to maintain the order of appearance.

61. Dynamic Programming: Maximum Product Path

Problem: You are given a grid of integers. You start at the top-left cell and aim to reach the bottom-right cell. At each step, you can only move right or down. Instead of finding the path with the maximum sum, find the path with the maximum product of values.

Example:

```
Input:
[
  [1, 3, 1],
  [2, 5, -1],
  [4, 0, 2]
]

Output: 30
```

```
Explanation: The path with maximum product is 1 -> 3 -> 5 -> 2
= 30.
```

Approach: We can use dynamic programming to solve this problem. For each cell, we need to track both the maximum and minimum product path ending at that cell (because two negatives can make a positive). For each cell (i,j), the maximum product is max(gridi * max_dpi-1, gridi * max_dpi) if gridi > 0, and max(gridi * min_dpi-1, gridi * min_dpi) if gridi < 0. We need to handle the minimum product similarly. The answer will be the maximum product at the bottom-right cell.

62. Graphs: Island Count with Restrictions

Problem: Given an m x n 2D binary grid that represents a map of '1's (land), '0's (water), and '2's (restricted areas), count the number of islands. An island is surrounded by water and is formed by connecting adjacent lands horizontally or vertically. Restricted areas ('2') cannot be part of any island.

Example:

```
Input:
[
  ["1","1","0","0","0"],
  ["1","1","0","2","0"],
  ["0","0","1","0","0"],
  ["0","2","0","1","1"]
]

Output: 3
```

Approach: We can use depth-first search (DFS) to explore each island. When we encounter a '1', we perform a DFS to mark all connected land cells as visited (changing them to '0' to avoid revisiting), ensuring not to include cells marked as '2'. After exploring one island, we increment our counter and find the next unvisited land cell.

63. Binary Search: Find Kth Element in Two Sorted Arrays

Problem: Given two sorted arrays, nums1, and nums2, of size m and n, respectively, find the kth smallest element in the union of these two arrays.

Example:

```
Input: nums1 = [1, 3, 5, 7], nums2 = [2, 4, 6], k = 4

Output: 4

Explanation: The merged array would be [1, 2, 3, 4, 5, 6, 7],
and the 4th element is 4.
```

Approach: We can use binary search to find the kth element. The key insight is to find the correct partition in both arrays such that the combined elements to the left of the partition equals k. For each mid-point in the binary search, we calculate the corresponding position in the second array and check if the partition is valid (i.e., all elements to the left are smaller than all elements to the right).

64. Stack: Evaluate Reverse Polish Notation with Custom Operations

Problem: Given an array of tokens representing an expression in Reverse Polish Notation (RPN), evaluate the expression. The valid operators are '+', '-', '*', '/', and a custom operator '^' for exponentiation. Each token is either an operator or an integer operand.

Example:

```
Input: ["4", "5", "3", "+", "*", "2", "^"]
Output: 32768
Explanation: ((5 + 3) * 4) ^ 2 = (8 * 4) ^ 2 = 32 ^ 2 = 32768
```

Approach: We can use a stack to evaluate the RPN expression. When encountering a number, push it onto the stack. When encountering an operator, pop the required number of operands from the stack, apply the operation, and push the result back to the stack. For the exponentiation operator, pop two elements where the second popped element is the base and the first is the exponent.

65. Matrix Operations: Optimal Kennel Assignment

Problem: You manage a dog kennel with n dogs and an n×n grid of kennel spaces. You have a compatibility matrix where compatibility[i][j] represents how healthy dog i gets along with dog j when placed in adjacent kennels (higher values mean better compatibility). Adjacent kennels share a wall horizontally or vertically. Design an algorithm to place all dogs in kennels to maximize the total compatibility score, the sum of compatibility values for all adjacent dog pairs.

Example:

```
Input:

compatibility = [
  [0, 5, 2, 1],
  [5, 0, 3, 8],
  [2, 3, 0, 4],
  [1, 8, 4, 0]
]

Output: 24
```

Explanation: Placing dogs in a 2×2 grid as [[0,1],[2,3]] gives compatibility sum: 5 (dogs 0,1) + 3 (dogs 1,2) + 8 (dogs 1,3) + 4 (dogs 2,3) = 20. The optimal arrangement is [[3,1],[2,0]], giving a total score of 24.

Approach: We can model this as a graph problem where each position in the kennel grid corresponds to a node, and edges represent adjacent kennel positions. We then need to find an assignment of dogs to nodes that maximizes the total compatibility. Since this is an NP-hard problem, we'll use a backtracking approach to explore all possible arrangements, pruning branches that can't lead to an optimal solution.

66. Matrix Operations: Wedding Seating Arrangement

Problem: You're organizing a wedding with n guests and m tables, where each table can seat exactly k guests. You have a relationship matrix relationship[i][j] indicating how well guests i and j get along (higher values mean a better relationship). Design an algorithm to assign guests to tables that maximize the total relationship score, the sum of relationship values for all pairs of guests seated at the same table.

Example:

```
Input:

relationships = [
  [0, 3, 1, 8, 2],
  [3, 0, 5, 2, 7],
  [1, 5, 0, 4, 6],
  [8, 2, 4, 0, 1],
  [2, 7, 6, 1, 0]
]
tables = 2, seats_per_table = 3

Output: 32
```

Explanation: Placing guests [0,3,4] at table 1 and [1,2] at table 2 gives a relationship score of 8 (guests 0,3) + 2 (guests 0,4) + 1 (guests 3,4) + 5 (guests 1,2) = 16. The optimal arrangement is [0,1,4] in Table 1 and [2,3] in Table 2, giving a total score of 32.

Approach: This is an NP-hard graph partitioning problem. We'll use a greedy approach combined with local search. First, we'll place guests randomly, then iteratively swap guest assignments between tables to improve the total relationship score until no further improvements can be made.

67. Linked List: Boat Fleet Chain Inspection

Problem: You manage a fleet of boats stored in a linked list. Each boat node has properties id, maintenanceNeeded (boolean), and a pointer to the next boat. Implement an algorithm to reorder the fleet such that all boats needing maintenance appear at the beginning of the chain while preserving their relative order.

  Example:

```
Input: 1(false) → 2(true) → 3(false) → 4(true) → 5(false)

Output: 2(true) → 4(true) → 1(false) → 3(false) → 5(false)
```

Approach: We can use a two-pointer approach to partition the linked list. We'll maintain two chains: one for boats needing maintenance and one for boats that don't. We'll add each boat to the appropriate chain as we traverse the original list. Then, we'll connect the two chains to form the reordered list.

68. Linked List: Baseball Lineup Rotation

Problem: A baseball team's lineup is represented as a circular linked list, where each player node contains a name, battingAverage, and a pointer to the next player. Implement an algorithm to rotate the lineup by k positions (moving the first k players to the end) and find the player with the highest batting average in the new lineup window of size m.

  Example:

```
Input:
Lineup: A(0.275) → B(0.305) → C(0.330) → D(0.290) →
```

```
E(0.260) → A..., k=2, m=3

Output:
"C" (After rotating by 2, the lineup window of size 3 is
C(0.330) → D(0.290) → E(0.260), and C has the highest average)
```

Approach: We'll perform two key operations: first, rotate the circular linked list by k positions, and second, find the player with the highest batting average within the following m nodes. We'll advance to the kth node for rotation, make it the new head, and ensure the list remains circular.

69. Two Pointers: Coffee Bean Blend Matcher

Problem: You run a specialty coffee shop with n types of coffee beans, each with a unique acidity level stored in a sorted array of acidity. Customers request custom blends with a specific target acidity level. Design an algorithm that determines if there are exactly two different beans that can be combined in equal proportions to create a blend with the requested acidity level.

Example:

```
Input:
acidity = [3.2, 4.5, 5.0, 5.8, 6.3, 7.1], targetAcidity = 5.65

Output:
true
```

Explanation: Beans with acidity 3.2 and 5.8 can be combined to get an average acidity of (3.2 + 5.8) / 2 = 4.5. Beans with acidity of 4.5 and 5.0 can be combined to get (4.5 + 5.0) / 2 = 4.75. Beans with acidity 5.0 and 6.3 can be blended to reach the target of 5.65.

Approach: We'll use the Two Pointers technique to search for pairs efficiently. Since the array is sorted, we can place one pointer at the beginning and another at the end. We calculate the average acidity of these two beans, then adjust our pointers based on whether this blend is above or below our target acidity. If the blend's acidity is less than the target, we move the left pointer right (increasing the blend's acidity); if it's greater, we move the right pointer left (decreasing the blend's acidity).

70. Sliding Window: Holiday Card Joy Maximizer

Problem: You're organizing a holiday card display with n cards arranged in a row. Each card has a "joy rating" representing its festive appeal. You must select a contiguous sequence of cards that will fit your display frame, and can hold between minCards and maxCards inclusive. Find the maximum possible total joy rating you can achieve.

Example:

```
Input: joyRatings = [4, 2, 7, 5, 9, 8, 3, 1], minCards = 3,
maxCards = 5

Output: 24
```

Explanation: The optimal selection is cards [7, 5, 9, 8] with joy ratings summing to 29.

Approach: We'll use a sliding window approach to find the optimal sequence. First, we'll establish the minimum required window and calculate its sum. Then, we'll grow the window up to maxCards, tracking the maximum sum. For each valid window size, we'll slide it across all possible positions to find the maximum joy rating.

71. Stack: Fashion Display Stack Optimizer

Problem: You manage a trendy clothing store where clothing items are stacked on display tables. Each item has a type (e.g., "shirt", "pants") and a popularity rating. During busy periods, customers often remove items to examine them but don't always return them properly, creating disorganized stacks. Implement a system that efficiently handles the following operations: 1) add a new item to the top of the stack, 2) remove the top item, 3) find and remove the most popular item of a specific type, and 4) reorganize the stack to have the most popular items on top.

Example:

```
Operations:
addItem("shirt", 8)
addItem("pants", 6)
addItem("shirt", 4)
addItem("jacket", 9)
findAndRemoveType("shirt") // Should return the shirt with
popularity 8, not 4
```

Approach: We'll use a primary stack for the main display and a temporary stack for reordering operations. To find and remove items of a specific type, we'll move items to the temporary stack until we find the target, tracking the most popular match. We'll then restore the remaining items to maintain their original order.

72. Heap/Priority Queue: Restaurant Priority Seating System

Problem: You manage a popular restaurant with limited seating. Customers arrive throughout the day, each with a party size and priority value. Priority is determined by VIP status (1-5 stars), reservation status (yes/no), and waiting time. Implement a system that manages waitlists and seats customers when tables become available.

The priority score is calculated as: (VIP_stars * 10) + (reservation ? 20 : 0) + minutes_waiting

When a table becomes available, seat the customer with the highest priority score whose party size fits the available table.

Example:

```
Input:
Tables: [4, 6, 2, 8]  # Available table sizes

Events:
["ARRIVE", 0, "A", 3, 0, false]  # [event_type, time,
customer_id, party_size, VIP_stars, has_reservation]
["ARRIVE", 5, "B", 4, 2, true]
["ARRIVE", 10, "C", 2, 5, false]
["TABLE_READY", 15, 6]  # [event_type, time, table_size]
["ARRIVE", 16, "D", 5, 3, true]
["TABLE_READY", 20, 4]
["TABLE_READY", 25, 2]
["TABLE_READY", 30, 8]


Output:
["B", 15]  # [customer_id, time_seated]
["D", 20]
["C", 25]
["A", 30]
```

Approach: Use a max heap (priority queue) to track customers by priority score:

1. Maintain a max heap of waiting customers ordered by priority score.
2. Process events chronologically:
   - Calculate the initial priority score and add it to the waitlist for ARRIVE events.
   - For TABLE_READY events, find the highest-priority customer whose party fits the table
3. Update priority scores at each time step as waiting time increases.
4. When seating a customer, remove them from the waitlist and record the seating time

393

73. Backtracking: Optimal Race Day Strategy

Problem: You manage a stable with N horses, preparing for a prestigious racing tournament with M races on a single day. Each horse has a specific performance rating for each race (based on distance, track condition, and competition level). A horse can only compete in one race daily, and certain races have entry restrictions. You aim to assign horses to races to maximize the total expected points while respecting all constraints.

Constraints:

· Each horse can enter at most one race.
· Each race has a maximum participant limit.
· Some horses are ineligible for certain races.
· You must assign at least one horse to each race

Example:

```
Input:
N = 5 horses, M = 3 races
Performance ratings (horse, race) -> points:
[
  [80, 40, 60],  # Horse 0 ratings for races 0,1,2
  [20, 90, 30],  # Horse 1
  [45, 50, 70],  # Horse 2
  [60, 45, 30],  # Horse 3
  [50, 55, 55]   # Horse 4
]
Race capacity: [2, 2, 2]  # Each race can have 2 horses
Ineligibility: [(0, 1), (3, 2)]  # Horse 0 cannot race in race
1, Horse 3 cannot race in race 2

Output: 245 (Maximum possible points)
Assignments: Horse 0 → Race 0, Horse 1 → Race 1, Horse 2 →
Race 2, Horse 3 → Race 0, Horse 4 → Race 1
```

Approach: We'll use backtracking to explore all valid horse-to-race assignments.

1. Try to assign each horse to a valid race.
2. For each assignment, recursively assign the next horse.
3. Track the maximum total points found.
4. When all horses are assigned, calculate the total points and update the maximum if needed.
5. Use pruning to skip branches that cannot improve the current maximum.
6. Ensure every race has at least one horse assigned

74. Graphs: Detective Case Assignment Network

Problem: The Central Police Station has N detectives and M cases. Each detective has expertise in some instances, affecting the time they need to solve them. Detectives can collaborate, but communication between detectives takes time based on their working relationship. Your task is assigning detectives to cases to minimize the time needed to solve all cases.

Each case has a complexity value and a type, and each detective has an expertise level for each case type. The time a detective needs to solve a case is equal to (case complexity/detective expertise for that type). When detectives collaborate, add the communication overhead to the solution time.

Find the minimum possible time to solve all cases, assigning each case to exactly one detective or collaboration pair.

Example:

```
Input:
Detectives: 4
Cases: 3
Detective expertise (detective_id, type -> expertise):
{
```

```
0: {'homicide': 8, 'theft': 3, 'fraud': 2},
1: {'homicide': 5, 'theft': 7, 'fraud': 1},
2: {'homicide': 2, 'theft': 4, 'fraud': 9},
3: {'homicide': 6, 'theft': 3, 'fraud': 4}
}
Communication overhead (detective pairs -> hours):
{(0,1): 2, (0,2): 4, (0,3): 1, (1,2): 3, (1,3): 5, (2,3): 2}
Cases (case_id, type, complexity):
[(0, 'homicide', 40), (1, 'theft', 28), (2, 'fraud', 36)]

Output: 12.5
Explanation:
Case 0: Assigned to detective 0 (40/8 = 5 hours)
Case 1: Assigned to detective 1 (28/7 = 4 hours)
Case 2: Collaboration between detectives 2 and 3 (36/(9+4) + 2
= 3.5 hours)
Total time: max(5, 4, 3.5) = 5 hours (parallel work) + 7.5
hours (sequential work) = 12.5 hours
```

Approach: Model this as a graph problem where detectives are nodes, and collaboration possibilities are edges.

75. Dynamic Programming: Seasonal Orange Grove Harvest

Problem: You manage an orange grove represented as an n×m grid. Each cell (i,j) contains a number representing the quality of trees and groves. The grove experiences seasonal changes - each harvesting season lasts exactly T days, and the yield multiplier for oranges on day d is seasonalYield[d].

Starting from the top-left corner (0,0), you must plan a path to the bottom-right (n-1,m-1), moving only right or down each day. When you visit a cell on day d, you harvest (grove[i,j] × seasonalYield[d]) oranges.

Find the maximum possible orange harvest before the season ends.

Example:

```
Input:
grove = [
  [2, 3, 1],
  [1, 4, 2],
  [0, 5, 3]
]
seasonalYield = [1, 2, 3, 1, 0.5]
T = 5

Output: 33.5
```

Approach: Use 3D DP, where state (i,j,d) represents the max harvest at position (i,j) on day d. The recurrence relation considers moves from either left or above, applying the seasonal yield multiplier at each step.

8

Problem Solutions

1. Character Pattern Matching

Python Solution:

```python
def has_same_pattern(str1, str2):
    if len(str1) != len(str2):
        return False

    map1 = {}
    map2 = {}

    for c1, c2 in zip(str1, str2):
        if c1 in map1:
            if map1[c1] != c2:
                return False
        else:
            map1[c1] = c2

        if c2 in map2:
            if map2[c2] != c1:
                return False
        else:
```

```
    map2[c2] = c1

return True
```

2. Product Price Pairing

Python Solution:

```python
def find_price_pair(prices, budget):
  price_map = {}

  for i, price in enumerate(prices):
    complement = budget - price

    if complement in price_map:
        return [price_map[complement], i]

    price_map[price] = i

  return []
```

3. Vocabulary Pattern Clusters

Python Solution:

```python
def group_word_patterns(words):

    groups = {}

    for word in words:
        # Generate key by sorting characters
```

```
    key = ''.join(sorted(word))

    # Add word to its group
    if key not in groups:
        groups[key] = []
    groups[key].append(word)

    # Return lists of grouped words
    return list(groups.values())
```

4. Trending Hashtag Analysis

Python Solution:

```
import heapq

from collections import Counter

def top_k_trending_hashtags(hashtags, k):
    # Count frequencies
    counter = Counter(hashtags)

    # Use heap to find top k frequent hashtags
    return heapq.nlargest(k, counter.keys(),
                          key=counter.get)
```

5. Supply Network Resilience Calculator

Python Solution:

```
def calculate_resilience(production):

    n = len(production)
    resilience = [1] * n

    # Calculate products of all elements to the left
    left_product = 1
    for i in range(n):
        resilience[i] = left_product
        left_product *= production[i]

    # Calculate products of all elements to the right
    # and multiply with existing values
    right_product = 1
    for i in range(n-1, -1, -1):
        resilience[i] *= right_product
        right_product *= production[i]

    return resilience
```

6. Optimal Document Segment

Python Solution:

```
def optimal_document_segment(document, tokens):

    if not document or not tokens:
        return ""

    # Count frequencies of tokens
    token_count = {}
    for char in tokens:
        token_count[char] = token_count.get(char, 0) + 1

    # Initialize variables
```

```
window_count = {}
required_tokens = len(token_count)
formed = 0

# Result tracking
min_len = float('inf')
result_start = 0

# Window pointers
left, right = 0, 0

# Expand window
while right < len(document):
    # Add right character to window
    char = document[right]
    window_count[char] = window_count.get(char, 0) + 1

    # Check if this character satisfies a token requirement
    if (char in token_count and
        window_count[char] == token_count[char]):
        formed += 1

    # Try to contract window from left
    while left <= right and formed == required_tokens:
        char = document[left]

        # Update result if current window is smaller
        if right - left + 1 < min_len:
            min_len = right - left + 1
            result_start = left

        # Remove left character from window
        window_count[char] -= 1

        # Check if removing this character breaks a token
        # requirement
        if (char in token_count and
            window_count[char] < token_count[char]):
            formed -= 1
```

```
        left += 1

    right += 1

return ("" if min_len == float('inf') else
        document[result_start:result_start + min_len])
```

7. Sliding Window Extrema Product

Python Solution:

```python
from collections import deque

def sliding_window_extrema_product(prices, k):
    n = len(prices)
    result = []

    if n == 0 or k == 0 or k > n:
        return result

    max_deque = deque()
    min_deque = deque()

    # Process the first window
    for i in range(k):
        # Remove smaller elements from max_deque
        while max_deque and prices[i] >= prices[max_deque[-1]]:
            max_deque.pop()
        max_deque.append(i)

        # Remove larger elements from min_deque
        while min_deque and prices[i] <= prices[min_deque[-1]]:
            min_deque.pop()
        min_deque.append(i)

    # Calculate product for the first window
```

```
        result.append(prices[max_deque[0]] * prices[min_deque[0]])

        # Process the rest of the windows
        for i in range(k, n):
            # Remove elements outside the current window
            while max_deque and max_deque[0] <= i - k:
                max_deque.popleft()
            while min_deque and min_deque[0] <= i - k:
                min_deque.popleft()

            # Remove smaller elements from max_deque
            while max_deque and prices[i] >= prices[max_deque[-1]]:
                max_deque.pop()
            max_deque.append(i)

            # Remove larger elements from min_deque
            while min_deque and prices[i] <= prices[min_deque[-1]]:
                min_deque.pop()
            min_deque.append(i)

            # Calculate product for the current window
            result.append(prices[max_deque[0]] *
                      prices[min_deque[0]])

    return result
```

8. Longest Palindromic Substring

Python Solution:

```
def longest_palindrome(s: str) -> str:

    if not s:
        return ""

    start = 0
```

```
    max_length = 1

    # Helper function to expand around center
    def expand_around_center(left, right):
        nonlocal start, max_length
        while (left >= 0 and right < len(s) and
                s[left] == s[right]):
            current_length = right - left + 1
            if current_length > max_length:
                max_length = current_length
                start = left
            left -= 1
            right += 1

    # Check each position as potential center
    for i in range(len(s)):
        # Odd length palindromes (like "aba")
        expand_around_center(i, i)
        # Even length palindromes (like "abba")
        expand_around_center(i, i + 1)

    return s[start:start + max_length]

# Example usage
print(longest_palindrome("babad"))  # "bab" or "aba"
print(longest_palindrome("cbbd"))   # "bb"
```

9. Two Sum

Python Solution:

```
def two_sum(nums, target):

    num_map = {}  # value -> index

    for i, num in enumerate(nums):
```

```
        complement = target - num

        if complement in num_map:
            return [num_map[complement], i]

        num_map[num] = i

    return None  # No solution found

# Example usage
print(two_sum([2, 7, 11, 15], 9))  # [0, 1]
print(two_sum([3, 2, 4], 6))        # [1, 2]
```

10. Level Order Traversal

Python Solution:

```
from collections import deque


# Definition for a binary tree node
class TreeNode:
    def __init__(self, val=0, left=None, right=None):
        self.val = val
        self.left = left
        self.right = right

def level_order(root):
    if not root:
        return []

    result = []
    queue = deque([root])

    while queue:
        level_size = len(queue)
```

```
            current_level = []

        for _ in range(level_size):
            node = queue.popleft()
            current_level.append(node.val)

            if node.left:
                queue.append(node.left)
            if node.right:
                queue.append(node.right)

        result.append(current_level)

    return result

# Example usage
# Construct the tree [3,9,20,null,null,15,7]
root = TreeNode(3)
root.left = TreeNode(9)
root.right = TreeNode(20)
root.right.left = TreeNode(15)
root.right.right = TreeNode(7)

print(level_order(root))  # [[3],[9,20],[15,7]]
```

11. Fibonacci with Memoization

Python Solution:

```
# Recursive with memoization

def fibonacci_memo(n, memo={}):
    if n == 0:
        return 0
    if n == 1:
```

```
        return 1

    if n not in memo:
        memo[n] = (fibonacci_memo(n - 1, memo) +
                    fibonacci_memo(n - 2, memo))

    return memo[n]

# Iterative version (more efficient)
def fibonacci_iterative(n):
    if n == 0:
        return 0
    if n == 1:
        return 1

    prev, curr = 0, 1

    for _ in range(2, n + 1):
        next_val = prev + curr
        prev = curr
        curr = next_val

    return curr

# Example usage
print(fibonacci_memo(6))        # 8
print(fibonacci_memo(10))       # 55
print(fibonacci_iterative(6))   # 8
print(fibonacci_iterative(10))  # 55
```

12. Number of Islands

Python Solution:

```python
def num_islands(grid):

    if not grid or not grid[0]:
        return 0

    rows, cols = len(grid), len(grid[0])
    count = 0

    # Helper function to perform DFS from a land cell
    def dfs(r, c):
        # Check if out of bounds or if cell is water
        if (r < 0 or c < 0 or r >= rows or c >= cols or
            grid[r][c] == '0'):
            return

        # Mark as visited by changing to water
        grid[r][c] = '0'

        # Check all four directions
        dfs(r + 1, c)  # down
        dfs(r - 1, c)  # up
        dfs(r, c + 1)  # right
        dfs(r, c - 1)  # left

    # Iterate through each cell in the grid
    for r in range(rows):
        for c in range(cols):
            if grid[r][c] == '1':
                count += 1  # Found a new island
                dfs(r, c)   # Mark all connected land as visited

    return count

# Example usage
grid = [
    ["1","1","0","0","0"],
    ["1","1","0","1","0"],
    ["0","0","0","0","0"],
    ["0","0","0","1","1"]
]
```

```
print(num_islands(grid))   # 3
```

13. First Non-Repeating Character

Python Solution:

```python
def first_uniq_char(s):

    # Count the occurrences of each character
    char_count = {}
    for char in s:
        char_count[char] = char_count.get(char, 0) + 1

    # Find the first character with count 1
    for i, char in enumerate(s):
        if char_count[char] == 1:
            return i

    return -1  # No unique character found

# Example usage
print(first_uniq_char("apple"))        # 0
print(first_uniq_char("loveapples"))   # 1
print(first_uniq_char("aabb"))         # -1
```

14. Reverse a Linked List

Python Solution:

```python
# Definition for singly-linked list

class ListNode:
    def __init__(self, val=0, next=None):
```

```
        self.val = val
        self.next = next

def reverse_list(head):
    prev = None
    current = head

    while current:
        # Save the next node
        next_node = current.next

        # Reverse the pointer
        current.next = prev

        # Move pointers forward
        prev = current
        current = next_node

    # prev is the new head
    return prev

# Helper function to create a linked list from an array
def create_linked_list(arr):
    if not arr:
        return None

    head = ListNode(arr[0])
    current = head

    for i in range(1, len(arr)):
        current.next = ListNode(arr[i])
        current = current.next

    return head

# Helper function to convert linked list to array
def linked_list_to_array(head):
    result = []
    current = head
```

```
    while current:
        result.append(current.val)
        current = current.next

    return result

# Example usage
list_head = create_linked_list([1, 2, 3, 4, 5])
reversed_head = reverse_list(list_head)
print(linked_list_to_array(reversed_head))  # [5, 4, 3, 2, 1]
```

15. Balanced Network Traffic

Python Solution:

```
import heapq

from dataclasses import dataclass
from typing import List, Tuple

@dataclass
class Request:
    id: int
    size: int

@dataclass
class Server:
    id: int
    capacity: int
    current_load: int = 0
    last_active: int = 0

def assign_requests(requests: List[Request],
                servers: List[Server]) -> List[Tuple[int,
                int]]:
```

```
server_heap = [(0, 0, server.id) for server in servers]
heapq.heapify(server_heap)

server_map = {server.id: server for server in servers}

assignments = []
current_time = 0

for request in requests:
    current_time += 1

    if not server_heap:
        break

    load, last_active, server_id = heapq.heappop(
        server_heap)
    server = server_map[server_id]

    if server.current_load + request.size <= server.capacity:
        server.current_load += request.size
        server.last_active = current_time
        assignments.append((server_id, request.id))

        heapq.heappush(server_heap,
                        (server.current_load, -current_time,
                        server_id))

return assignments
```

16. Dependency Resolver

Python Solution:

```
from collections import defaultdict, deque
```

```
def resolve_dependencies(tasks):
    graph = defaultdict(list)
    in_degree = {task: 0 for task in tasks}

    for task, dependencies in tasks.items():
        for dep in dependencies:
            graph[dep].append(task)
            in_degree[task] += 1

    queue = deque([task for task, degree in in_degree.items()
                  if degree == 0])
    result = []

    while queue:
        current = queue.popleft()
        result.append(current)

        for dependent in graph[current]:
            in_degree[dependent] -= 1
            if in_degree[dependent] == 0:
                queue.append(dependent)

    if len(result) != len(tasks):
        return None

    return result
```

17. Intelligent Cache System

Python Solution:

```
import time

class CacheItem:
    def __init__(self, key, value):
        self.key = key
```

```python
        self.value = value
        self.frequency = 1
        self.last_access = time.time()

    def access(self):
        self.frequency += 1
        self.last_access = time.time()

    def get_score(self, current_time):
        """Calculate item's value based on frequency and
        recency."""
        # Higher frequency and recency = higher score
        recency_score = 1.0 / (1.0 + (current_time -
        self.last_access))
        return self.frequency * recency_score

class IntelligentCache:
    def __init__(self, capacity):
        self.capacity = capacity
        self.cache = {}  # key -> CacheItem

    def get(self, key):
        if key not in self.cache:
            return None

        # Update frequency and last access time
        self.cache[key].access()
        return self.cache[key].value

    def put(self, key, value):
        # If key already exists, update value and access info
        if key in self.cache:
            self.cache[key].value = value
            self.cache[key].access()
            return

        # If cache is full, evict least valuable item
        if len(self.cache) >= self.capacity:
            self._evict()
```

```
        # Add new item
        self.cache[key] = CacheItem(key, value)

    def _evict(self):
        """Evict the item with the lowest score."""
        if not self.cache:
            return

        current_time = time.time()
        min_score = float('inf')
        min_key = None

        for key, item in self.cache.items():
            score = item.get_score(current_time)
            if score < min_score:
                min_score = score
                min_key = key

        if min_key:
            del self.cache[min_key]
```

18. Text Editor Line Tracker

Python Solution:

```
class Node:
    def __init__(self, position):
        self.position = position
        self.left = None
        self.right = None
        self.height = 1

class TextEditor:
    def __init__(self):
        self.text = ""
        self.root = None
```

```python
def insert(self, position, text):
    if position < 0 or position > len(self.text):
        raise ValueError("Invalid position")

    self.text = self.text[:position] + text +
    self.text[position:]

    new_line_positions = [position + i for i, char in
                     enumerate(text) if char == '\n']
    text_length = len(text)

    self._update_positions(self.root, position, text_length)

    for line_pos in new_line_positions:
        self.root = self._insert_node(self.root, line_pos)

def delete(self, position, length):
    if position < 0 or position + length > len(self.text):
        raise ValueError("Invalid position or length")

    deleted_text = self.text[position:position + length]
    deleted_lines = [position + i for i, char in
                enumerate(deleted_text) if char == '\n']

    self.text = self.text[:position] + self.text[position +
    length:]

    for line_pos in deleted_lines:
        self.root = self._delete_node(self.root, line_pos)

    self._update_positions(self.root, position, -length)

def getLineNumber(self, position):
    if position < 0 or position > len(self.text):
        raise ValueError("Invalid position")

    return self._count_smaller(self.root, position)

def _get_height(self, node):
```

```python
    if not node:
        return 0
    return node.height

def _get_balance(self, node):
    if not node:
        return 0
    return self._get_height(node.left) -
    self._get_height(node.right)

def _right_rotate(self, y):
    x = y.left
    T2 = x.right

    x.right = y
    y.left = T2

    y.height = max(self._get_height(y.left),
                self._get_height(y.right)) + 1
    x.height = max(self._get_height(x.left),
                self._get_height(x.right)) + 1

    return x

def _left_rotate(self, x):
    y = x.right
    T2 = y.left

    y.left = x
    x.right = T2

    x.height = max(self._get_height(x.left),
                self._get_height(x.right)) + 1
    y.height = max(self._get_height(y.left),
                self._get_height(y.right)) + 1

    return y

def _insert_node(self, node, position):
    if not node:
```

```
        return Node(position)

    if position < node.position:
        node.left = self._insert_node(node.left, position)
    elif position > node.position:
        node.right = self._insert_node(node.right, position)
    else:
        return node

    node.height = max(self._get_height(node.left),
                      self._get_height(node.right)) + 1

    balance = self._get_balance(node)

    if balance > 1 and position < node.left.position:
        return self._right_rotate(node)

    if balance < -1 and position > node.right.position:
        return self._left_rotate(node)

    if balance > 1 and position > node.left.position:
        node.left = self._left_rotate(node.left)
        return self._right_rotate(node)

    if balance < -1 and position < node.right.position:
        node.right = self._right_rotate(node.right)
        return self._left_rotate(node)

    return node

def _delete_node(self, node, position):
    if not node:
        return node

    if position < node.position:
        node.left = self._delete_node(node.left, position)
    elif position > node.position:
        node.right = self._delete_node(node.right, position)
    else:
        if not node.left:
```

```
            return node.right
        elif not node.right:
            return node.left

        successor = self._get_min_value_node(node.right)
        node.position = successor.position
        node.right = self._delete_node(node.right,
                                    successor.position)

    if not node:
        return node

    node.height = max(self._get_height(node.left),
                    self._get_height(node.right)) + 1

    balance = self._get_balance(node)

    if balance > 1 and self._get_balance(node.left) >= 0:
        return self._right_rotate(node)

    if balance > 1 and self._get_balance(node.left) < 0:
        node.left = self._left_rotate(node.left)
        return self._right_rotate(node)

    if balance < -1 and self._get_balance(node.right) <= 0:
        return self._left_rotate(node)

    if balance < -1 and self._get_balance(node.right) > 0:
        node.right = self._right_rotate(node.right)
        return self._left_rotate(node)

    return node

def _get_min_value_node(self, node):
    current = node
    while current.left:
        current = current.left
    return current

def _update_positions(self, node, start_pos, shift):
```

```
    if not node:
        return

    if node.position >= start_pos:
        node.position += shift

    self._update_positions(node.right, start_pos, shift)

    if node.position >= start_pos:
        self._update_positions(node.left, start_pos, shift)

def _count_smaller(self, node, position):
    if not node:
        return 0

    if position < node.position:
        return self._count_smaller(node.left, position)
    else:
        return (1 + self._count_smaller(node.left, position) +
                self._count_smaller(node.right, position))
```

19. Message Rate Limiter

Python Solution:

```
from collections import defaultdict, deque

class RateLimiter:
    def __init__(self, message_limit, time_window):
        self.message_limit = message_limit
        self.time_window = time_window
        self.user_messages = defaultdict(deque)

    def can_send(self, user_id, timestamp):
        message_queue = self.user_messages[user_id]
        while (message_queue and
```

```
        message_queue[0] <= timestamp - self.time_window):
    message_queue.popleft()

if len(message_queue) < self.message_limit:
    message_queue.append(timestamp)
    return True


return False
```

20. Evidence Processing Queue

Python Solution:

```
import heapq

def process_evidence(evidence, hours_per_day):
    processing_order = []
    current_day = 0
    hours_left_today = hours_per_day

    # Priority queue as min heap with negative scores
    evidence_queue = []

    # Initial queue population
    for item in evidence:
        priority = (-(item["importance"] /
                item["processing_time"]) *
                (1 / item["days_until_expiration"]))
        heapq.heappush(evidence_queue,
                (priority, item["id"], item))

    while evidence_queue:
        # Get highest priority evidence
        _, item_id, item = heapq.heappop(evidence_queue)

        # Check if it's expired
```

```python
    if item["days_until_expiration"] <= current_day:
        continue

    # Process the evidence
    processing_order.append(item_id)

    # Update time tracking
    remaining_time = item["processing_time"]
    while remaining_time > 0:
        if hours_left_today >= remaining_time:
            hours_left_today -= remaining_time
            remaining_time = 0
        else:
            remaining_time -= hours_left_today
            current_day += 1
            hours_left_today = hours_per_day

            # Recalculate priorities for remaining evidence
            updated_queue = []
            while evidence_queue:
                _, id, ev = heapq.heappop(evidence_queue)
                if ev["days_until_expiration"] > current_day:
                    new_priority = (-(ev["importance"] /
                            ev["processing_time"]) *
                            (1 / (ev["days_until_expiration"] -
                            current_day)))
                    heapq.heappush(updated_queue,
                            (new_priority, id, ev))
            evidence_queue = updated_queue

return processing_order
```

21: Circular Array Rotation Sequence

Python Solution:

```python
def query_rotated_array(arr, queries):
    """
    Compute the result of queries on a circular array
    after rotations.

    Args:
        arr: List of integers representing the circular array
        queries: List of [rotation, index] pairs for each query

    Returns:
        List of integers representing the query results
    """
    n = len(arr)
    results = []

    for rotation, index in queries:
        # Calculate the effective rotation (in case rotation > n)
        effective_rotation = rotation % n

        # The element at position 'index' after rotating right by
        # 'effective_rotation' is originally at position
        # (index - effective_rotation) % n
        original_position = (index - effective_rotation) % n
        results.append(arr[original_position])

    return results

# Test with the example
arr = [3, 7, 1, 9, 5]
queries = [[2, 1], [4, 3], [0, 2]]
print(query_rotated_array(arr, queries))  # Output: [3, 3, 1]
```

22. Optimized Task Scheduler

Python Solution:

```
from collections import Counter

def min_time_to_finish_tasks(tasks, n):
    """

    Calculate the minimum time required to execute all tasks
    with cooldown.

    Args:
        tasks: List of characters, each representing a task
        n: Integer cooldown period

    Returns:
        Integer representing the minimum time required
    """
    if not tasks:
        return 0

    # Count frequency of each task
    task_counts = Counter(tasks)

    # Find maximum frequency
    max_freq = max(task_counts.values())

    # Count how many tasks have the maximum frequency
    max_freq_tasks = sum(1 for count in task_counts.values()
                        if count == max_freq)

    # Calculate the time using the formula:
    # (max_freq - 1) * (n + 1) + max_freq_tasks
    # This creates "frames" of size (n+1) with max frequency
    tasks
    # at start of each frame
    result = (max_freq - 1) * (n + 1) + max_freq_tasks

    # The result should be at least the total number of tasks
    # (in case we have many different tasks and don't need all
    # calculated idle slots)
    return max(result, len(tasks))

# Test with the example
```

```
tasks = ['A', 'A', 'B', 'C', 'A', 'B']
n = 2
print(min_time_to_finish_tasks(tasks, n))  # Output: 7

# Another test case
tasks2 = ['A', 'A', 'A', 'B', 'B', 'B']
n2 = 2
# Output: 8 (A->B->idle->A->B->idle->A->B)
print(min_time_to_finish_tasks(tasks2, n2))
```

23. Interval Coverage Optimization

Python Solution:

```
def min_team_members(intervals, K):
    # Sort intervals by start time
    intervals.sort(key=lambda x: x[0])

    # Keep track of covered intervals
    covered = [False] * len(intervals)
    team_count = 0

    while not all(covered):
        team_count += 1

        # Find the earliest uncovered interval
        earliest_uncovered = None
        for i in range(len(intervals)):
            if not covered[i]:
                earliest_uncovered = i
                break

        if earliest_uncovered is None:
            break
```

```
    # Start shift at the beginning of the earliest uncovered
    shift_start = intervals[earliest_uncovered][0]
    shift_end = shift_start + K

    # Cover all intervals that fit within this shift
    for i in range(len(intervals)):
        if (not covered[i] and
            intervals[i][0] >= shift_start and
            intervals[i][1] <= shift_end):
            covered[i] = True

    return team_count

# Test with example
intervals = [[1, 3], [2, 5], [6, 8], [8, 10], [11, 12]]
K = 5
print(min_team_members(intervals, K))  # Output: 2
```

24. Dynamic Maze Flood Fill

Python Solution:

```
from collections import deque

def flood_fill_time(maze, startX, startY, targetX, targetY):
    rows, cols = len(maze), len(maze[0])
    visited = [[False for _ in range(cols)] for _ in range(rows)]

    # BFS queue with (x, y, time)
    queue = deque([(startX, startY, 0)])
    visited[startX][startY] = True

    directions = [(1, 0), (-1, 0), (0, 1), (0, -1)]

    while queue:
        x, y, time = queue.popleft()
```

```
        # If water reaches target
        if x == targetX and y == targetY:
            return time

        for dx, dy in directions:
            nx, ny = x + dx, y + dy

            # Check if new position is valid
            if (0 <= nx < rows and 0 <= ny < cols and
                not visited[nx][ny] and maze[nx][ny] == 0):
                visited[nx][ny] = True
                queue.append((nx, ny, time + 1))

    return -1

# Test example
maze = [
    [0, 0, 0, 0],
    [1, 1, 0, 1],
    [0, 2, 0, 0],
    [0, 1, 1, 0]
]
print(flood_fill_time(maze, 2, 1, 0, 0))  # Output: 3
```

25. Adaptive Resource Scheduler

Python Solution:

```
def schedule_tasks(tasks):
    # Sort tasks by priority (descending) and then by deadline
    sorted_tasks = sorted(tasks,
                          key=lambda x: (-x['priority'],
                          x['deadline']))
```

```
    # Result list to store tasks in execution order
    result = []

    # Timeline to track when resources are allocated
    timeline = {}  # time -> resources being used
    current_time = 0

    for task in sorted_tasks:
        task_id = task['id']
        resources = task['resource_needs']
        deadline = task['deadline']

        # Find earliest time slot where task can be executed
        execution_time = current_time

        # Simple implementation: schedule tasks one after another
        result.append(task_id)
        current_time += resources

    return result

# Test with example
tasks = [
    {"id": "T1", "priority": 3, "resource_needs": 5,
     "deadline": 10},
    {"id": "T2", "priority": 5, "resource_needs": 3,
     "deadline": 5},
    {"id": "T3", "priority": 2, "resource_needs": 2,
     "deadline": 7},
    {"id": "T4", "priority": 5, "resource_needs": 1,
     "deadline": 3}
]

print(schedule_tasks(tasks))  # Output: ["T4", "T2", "T1", "T3"]
```

26. Distributed Cache Consistency

Python Solution:

```python
import heapq

def final_cache_state(n, operations, delays):
    # Initialize caches for each node
    caches = [{} for _ in range(n)]

    # Priority queue to simulate events with timestamps
    event_queue = []

    # Add initial operations to queue
    for node_id, key, value, timestamp in operations:
        # Process operation at source node immediately
        heapq.heappush(event_queue,
                    (timestamp, node_id, node_id, key,
                        value, timestamp))

        # Schedule propagation to other nodes
        for target_node in range(n):
            if target_node != node_id:
                arrival_time = timestamp +
                delays[node_id][target_node]
                heapq.heappush(event_queue,
                            (arrival_time, target_node, node_id,
                            key,
                                value, timestamp))

    # Process all events
    while event_queue:
        arrival_time, target_node, source_node, key, value,
        op_timestamp = heapq.heappop(event_queue)

        # Apply the operation if it's newer than what we have
        if (key not in caches[target_node] or
            caches[target_node].get(key + "_timestamp", 0) <
            op_timestamp):
            caches[target_node][key] = value
            caches[target_node][key + "_timestamp"] = op_timestamp
```

```
    # Clean up internal timestamp tracking
    for cache in caches:
        for key in list(cache.keys()):
            if key.endswith("_timestamp"):
                del cache[key]

    return caches

# Test with example
nodes = 3
operations = [
    (0, "x", 10, 1),    # Node 0 sets x=10 at time 1
    (1, "y", 20, 2),    # Node 1 sets y=20 at time 2
    (2, "x", 30, 3),    # Node 2 sets x=30 at time 3
    (0, "y", 40, 4)     # Node 0 sets y=40 at time 4
]
delays = [
    [0, 2, 3],    # Delays from node 0 to others
    [2, 0, 1],    # Delays from node 1 to others
    [3, 1, 0]     # Delays from node 2 to others
]

print(final_cache_state(nodes, operations, delays))
```

27. Maximum Subarray With Target Sum

Python Solution:

```
def max_subarray_with_target_sum(nums, target):
    # Map to store the first occurrence of each cumulative sum
    sum_index_map = {0: -1}  # Initialize with 0 sum at index -1

    max_length = 0
    current_sum = 0
```

431

```
    for i, num in enumerate(nums):
        current_sum += num

        # Check if we can form a subarray with sum = target
        if current_sum - target in sum_index_map:
            subarray_start = sum_index_map[current_sum - target] +
            1
            current_length = i - subarray_start + 1
            max_length = max(max_length, current_length)

        # Only store the first occurrence of each sum
        if current_sum not in sum_index_map:
            sum_index_map[current_sum] = i

    return max_length

# Test with example
nums = [1, -1, 5, -2, 3, 0, 2, -4, 1]
target = 3
print(max_subarray_with_target_sum(nums, target))  # Output: 4
```

28. K-Nearest Neighbors in Sliding Window

Python Solution:

```
import heapq
from collections import deque

class KNearestInWindow:
    def __init__(self, window_size, k):
        self.window_size = window_size
        self.k = k
        self.window = deque()
        # Max heap containing (distance, point) pairs
        self.heap = []
```

```
def distance(self, point):
    # Euclidean distance to origin
    return point[0]**2 + point[1]**2

def add_point(self, point):
    dist = self.distance(point)

    # Add point to window
    self.window.append((dist, point))

    # Remove oldest point if window is too large
    if len(self.window) > self.window_size:
        oldest_dist, oldest_point = self.window.popleft()

        # Check if oldest point was in heap
        in_heap = False
        for i, (d, p) in enumerate(self.heap):
            if p == oldest_point:
                in_heap = True
                break

        # If oldest point was in heap, rebuild the heap
        if in_heap:
            self.rebuild_heap()

    # Add new point to heap if closer than farthest
    # or if heap isn't full yet
    if len(self.heap) < self.k:
        heapq.heappush(self.heap, (-dist, point))
    elif -dist > self.heap[0][0]:
        heapq.heappushpop(self.heap, (-dist, point))

def rebuild_heap(self):
    # Get all points in current window
    points_in_window = [p for _, p in self.window]

    # Clear heap and rebuild
    self.heap = []
    for point in points_in_window:
```

```
            dist = self.distance(point)
            if len(self.heap) < self.k:
                heapq.heappush(self.heap, (-dist, point))
            elif -dist > self.heap[0][0]:
                heapq.heappushpop(self.heap, (-dist, point))

    def get_k_nearest(self):
        # Return the k nearest points
        return [point for _, point in sorted(
            self.heap, key=lambda x: -x[0])]

# Test with example
points = [(1, 2), (3, 4), (0, 1), (5, 2),
          (2, 0), (1, 5), (3, 1)]
window_size = 5
k = 3

knn = KNearestInWindow(window_size, k)
for point in points:
    knn.add_point(point)

print(knn.get_k_nearest())  # [(2, 0), (0, 1), (3, 1)]
```

29: Matrix Circuit

Python Solution:

```
def can_complete_circuit(matrix, start_row, start_col):
    if matrix[start_row][start_col] == 1:
        return False  # Invalid starting position

    rows, cols = len(matrix), len(matrix[0])
    directions = [(0, 1), (1, 0), (0, -1), (-1, 0)]  # r,d,l,u
    visited = set()

    def dfs(row, col, path_length):
```

```
    # If we've returned to start after visiting 3+ cells
    if ((row, col) == (start_row, start_col) and
        path_length >= 3):
      return True

    visited.add((row, col))

    for dr, dc in directions:
      new_row, new_col = row + dr, col + dc

      # Check if new position is valid and not visited
      if ((0 <= new_row < rows and
          0 <= new_col < cols and
          matrix[new_row][new_col] == 0 and
          (new_row, new_col) not in visited) or
          ((new_row, new_col) == (start_row, start_col) and
          path_length >= 3)):

        if dfs(new_row, new_col, path_length + 1):
            return True

    # Backtrack
    visited.remove((row, col))
    return False

  return dfs(start_row, start_col, 0)

# Test case
matrix = [
  [0, 1, 0, 0],
  [0, 0, 0, 1],
  [1, 1, 0, 0],
  [0, 0, 0, 0]
]
print(can_complete_circuit(matrix, 0, 0))  # Should return True
```

30. Artwork Gallery Heist

Python Solution:

```python
def max_artwork_value(values):

    n = len(values)
    if n == 0:
        return 0
    if n == 1:
        return values[0]

    # Initialize previous two values
    prev2 = values[0]
    prev1 = max(values[0], values[1])

    # Compute max value
    for i in range(2, n):
        current = max(prev1, prev2 + values[i])
        prev2 = prev1
        prev1 = current

    return prev1
```

31. Range Duplicate Finder

Python Solution:

```python
def has_nearby_duplicates(nums, k):

    window = set()

    for i, num in enumerate(nums):
        # Remove element outside window
        if i >= k:
            window.remove(nums[i - k])
```

```
        # Check if current element is in window
        if num in window:
            return True

        window.add(num)

    return False
```

32. Temperature Forecast Analysis

Python Solution:

```python
def days_until_warmer(temperatures):

    n = len(temperatures)
    result = [0] * n
    stack = []

    for i in range(n):
        while stack and temperatures[i] >
        temperatures[stack[-1]]:
            prev_idx = stack.pop()
            result[prev_idx] = i - prev_idx

        stack.append(i)

    return result
```

33. Scenic Skyline Viewpoints

Python Solution:

```
def max_viewing_area(heights):

    left, right = 0, len(heights) - 1
    max_area = 0

    while left < right:
        width = right - left
        height = min(heights[left], heights[right])
        max_area = max(max_area, width * height)

        if heights[left] < heights[right]:
            left += 1
        else:
            right -= 1

    return max_area
```

34. Mountain Valley Rainwater Collection

Python Solution:

```
def trap_rainwater(heights):

    if not heights or len(heights) < 3:
        return 0

    left, right = 0, len(heights) - 1
    left_max, right_max = heights[left], heights[right]
    total_water = 0

    while left < right:
        if heights[left] < heights[right]:
            left += 1
            if heights[left] < left_max:
                total_water += left_max - heights[left]
            else:
```

```
                    left_max = heights[left]
        else:
            right -= 1
            if heights[right] < right_max:
                total_water += right_max - heights[right]
            else:
                right_max = heights[right]

    return total_water
```

35. Maximum Property Value Appreciation

Python Solution:

```python
def max_property_profit(prices):

    if not prices or len(prices) < 2:
        return 0

    min_price = float('inf')
    max_profit = 0

    for price in prices:
        if price < min_price:
            min_price = price
        else:
            current_profit = price - min_price
            max_profit = max(max_profit, current_profit)

    return max_profit
```

36. Frequency Threshold Detection

Python Solution:

```python
def has_frequency_threshold(nums, k):

    counter = {}

    for num in nums:
        counter[num] = counter.get(num, 0) + 1
        if counter[num] >= k:
            return True

    return False
```

37. X-Sudoku Validator

Python Solution:

```python
def is_valid_x_sudoku(board):

    rows = [set() for _ in range(9)]
    cols = [set() for _ in range(9)]
    boxes = [set() for _ in range(9)]
    main_diag = set()
    anti_diag = set()

    for i in range(9):
        for j in range(9):
            num = board[i][j]
            if num == 0:
                continue

            # Check row
            if num in rows[i]:
                return False
            rows[i].add(num)
```

```
# Check column
if num in cols[j]:
    return False
cols[j].add(num)

# Check 3x3 box
box_idx = (i // 3) * 3 + j // 3
if num in boxes[box_idx]:
    return False
boxes[box_idx].add(num)

# Check main diagonal
if i == j:
    if num in main_diag:
        return False
    main_diag.add(num)

# Check anti-diagonal
if i + j == 8:
    if num in anti_diag:
        return False
    anti_diag.add(num)

    return True
```

38. Vehicle Convoy Formation

Python Solution:

```
def count_convoys(target, positions, speeds):

    # Pair positions with speeds and sort by position
    # in descending order
    cars = sorted(zip(positions, speeds), reverse=True)
```

CRUSHING THE TECHNICAL INTERVIEW: DATA STRUCTURES AND ALGORITHMS

```
convoys = 0
prev_time = -1

for position, speed in cars:
    # Calculate time to reach target
    time = (target - position) / speed

    # If this vehicle takes longer to reach target,
    # it forms a new convoy
    if time > prev_time:
        convoys += 1
        prev_time = time

return convoys
```

39. Maximum Productivity Zone

Python Solution:

```
def max_productivity_zone(capacities):

    stack = []
    max_area = 0
    n = len(capacities)

    for i in range(n):
        # Process stations with higher capacity than current
        while stack and capacities[stack[-1]] > capacities[i]:
            height = capacities[stack.pop()]
            width = i if not stack else i - stack[-1] - 1
            max_area = max(max_area, height * width)

        stack.append(i)

    # Process remaining stations in stack
```

```
while stack:
    height = capacities[stack.pop()]
    width = n if not stack else n - stack[-1] - 1
    max_area = max(max_area, height * width)

return max_area
```

40. Layered Security Clearance Search

Python Solution:

```
def find_clearance_code(matrix, target):

    if not matrix or not matrix[0]:
        return False

    rows, cols = len(matrix), len(matrix[0])
    left, right = 0, rows * cols - 1

    while left <= right:
        mid = (left + right) // 2
        row, col = mid // cols, mid % cols

        if matrix[row][col] == target:
            return True
        elif matrix[row][col] < target:
            left = mid + 1
        else:
            right = mid - 1

    return False
```

41. Document Processing Throughput

Python Solution:

```python
def min_processing_speed(batches, h):

    def can_complete(speed):
        hours = 0
        for batch in batches:
            # Ceiling division to calculate hours needed
            hours += (batch + speed - 1) // speed
        return hours <= h

    left, right = 1, max(batches)

    while left < right:
        mid = left + (right - left) // 2
        if can_complete(mid):
            right = mid
        else:
            left = mid + 1

    return left
```

42. Encrypted Circular Buffer Search

Python Solution:

```python
def find_minimum(nums):

    left, right = 0, len(nums) - 1

    # Already sorted case
    if nums[left] <= nums[right]:
        return nums[left]

    while left < right:
```

```
        mid = left + (right - left) // 2

        # If mid is greater than right, minimum is in right half
        if nums[mid] > nums[right]:
            left = mid + 1
        # If mid is less than right, minimum is in left half
        # (including mid)
        else:
            right = mid

    return nums[left]
```

43. Parallel Matrix Diagonal Sum

Python Solution:

```
def max_diagonal_sum(matrix):

    if not matrix or not matrix[0]:
        return 0

    n = len(matrix)
    max_sum = float('-inf')

    # Check diagonals starting from top row
    for col in range(n):
        diagonal_sum = 0
        r, c = 0, col

        while r < n and c < n:
            diagonal_sum += matrix[r][c]
            r += 1
            c += 1

        max_sum = max(max_sum, diagonal_sum)
```

```
# Check diagonals starting from leftmost column
# Start from 1 to avoid recounting (0,0)
for row in range(1, n):
    diagonal_sum = 0
    r, c = row, 0

    while r < n and c < n:
        diagonal_sum += matrix[r][c]
        r += 1
        c += 1

    max_sum = max(max_sum, diagonal_sum)

return max_sum
```

44. Version-Based Configuration Store

Python Solution:

```python
from collections import defaultdict

import bisect

class ConfigStore:
    def __init__(self):
        self.store = defaultdict(list)

    def set(self, feature, version, value):
        versions = self.store[feature]
        i = bisect.bisect_left([v for v, _ in versions],
        version)

        if i < len(versions) and versions[i][0] == version:
            versions[i] = (version, value)
        else:
```

```
            versions.insert(i, (version, value))

    def get(self, feature, version):
        if feature not in self.store:
            return ""

        versions = self.store[feature]
        i = bisect.bisect_right([v for v, _ in versions],
        version)

        if i == 0:
            return ""

        return versions[i-1][1]
```

45. Minimum Processing Power

Python Solution:

```
def min_processing_power(tasks, max_seconds):
    def can_complete(power):
        total_time = 0
        for task in tasks:
            # Ceiling division
            total_time += (task + power - 1) // power
        return total_time <= max_seconds

    left, right = 1, max(tasks)

    while left < right:
        mid = (left + right) // 2
        if can_complete(mid):
            right = mid
        else:
            left = mid + 1
```

```
    return left
```

46. Clone Binary Tree with Connection Pointers

Python Solution:

```python
class TreeNode:
  def __init__(self, val=0, left=None, right=None,
               connection=None):
    self.val = val
    self.left = left
    self.right = right
    self.connection = connection

def cloneTree(root):
  if not root:
    return None

  # Phase 1: Clone tree structure and create mapping
  node_map = {}

  def cloneStructure(node):
    if not node:
      return None

    if node in node_map:
      return node_map[node]

    new_node = TreeNode(node.val)
    node_map[node] = new_node

    new_node.left = cloneStructure(node.left)
    new_node.right = cloneStructure(node.right)

    return new_node
```

```
    new_root = cloneStructure(root)

    # Phase 2: Set connection pointers
    def setConnections(node):
        if not node:
            return

        if node.connection:
            node_map[node].connection = node_map[node.connection]

        setConnections(node.left)
        setConnections(node.right)

    setConnections(root)

    return new_root
```

47. Rotate Linked List Around Pivot

Python Solution:

```
class ListNode:

    def __init__(self, val=0, next=None):
        self.val = val
        self.next = next

def partition_list(head, pivot):
    if not head:
        return None

    # Create dummy heads for both partitions
    less_head = ListNode(0)
    greater_head = ListNode(0)
```

```
    less = less_head
    greater = greater_head

    # Traverse the original list
    current = head
    while current:
        if current.val < pivot:
            less.next = current
            less = less.next
        else:
            greater.next = current
            greater = greater.next

        current = current.next

    # Connect the two lists
    greater.next = None
    less.next = greater_head.next

    return less_head.next
```

48. Interleave K Linked Lists

Python Solution:

```
class ListNode:

    def __init__(self, val=0, next=None):
        self.val = val
        self.next = next

def interleave_lists(lists):
    if not lists:
        return None

    # Remove any empty lists
```

```
lists = [lst for lst in lists if lst]
if not lists:
    return None

dummy = ListNode(0)
tail = dummy

while lists:
    # Process one node from each list in round-robin fashion
    for i in range(len(lists)):
        # Append current node to result
        tail.next = lists[i]
        tail = tail.next

        # Move to next node in current list
        lists[i] = lists[i].next

    # Remove any lists that became empty
    lists = [lst for lst in lists if lst]

return dummy.next
```

49. Path Matching Binary Tree

Python Solution:

```
class TreeNode:

    def __init__(self, val=0, left=None, right=None):
        self.val = val
        self.left = left
        self.right = right

def matching_path(root1, root2):
    # Collect all paths in the first tree
    paths1 = []
```

```
    collect_paths(root1, [], paths1)

    # Collect all paths in the second tree
    paths2 = []
    collect_paths(root2, [], paths2)

    # Check for matching paths
    for path1 in paths1:
        if path1 in paths2:
            return True

    return False

def collect_paths(node, current_path, all_paths):
    if not node:
        return

    # Add current node to the path
    current_path.append(node.val)

    # If leaf node, add the path to all_paths
    if not node.left and not node.right:
        all_paths.append(current_path.copy())
    else:
        # Continue DFS
        collect_paths(node.left, current_path, all_paths)
        collect_paths(node.right, current_path, all_paths)

    # Backtrack
    current_path.pop()
```

50. Symmetric Tree Transformation

Python Solution:

```python
class TreeNode:

    def __init__(self, val=0, left=None, right=None):
        self.val = val
        self.left = left
        self.right = right

def symmetrize_tree(root):
    if not root:
        return None

    # Transform left and right subtrees first
    root.left = symmetrize_tree(root.left)
    root.right = symmetrize_tree(root.right)

    # Check if subtrees are symmetric
    if not is_symmetric(root.left, root.right):
        # Not symmetric, make them symmetric
        if root.left and not root.right:
            # Only left child exists, mirror it
            root.right = mirror_tree(root.left)
        elif root.right and not root.left:
            # Only right child exists, mirror it
            root.left = mirror_tree(root.right)
        else:
            # Both children exist but not symmetric
            # Choose left subtree as reference and mirror it
            root.right = mirror_tree(root.left)

    return root

def is_symmetric(left, right):
    if not left and not right:
        return True
    if not left or not right:
        return False
    if left.val != right.val:
        return False

    return (is_symmetric(left.left, right.right) and
```

```
                    is_symmetric(left.right, right.left))

def mirror_tree(node):
    if not node:
        return None

    # Create a new mirrored node
    mirrored = TreeNode(node.val)
    mirrored.left = mirror_tree(node.right)
    mirrored.right = mirror_tree(node.left)

    return mirrored
```

51. Expression Tree Execution

Python Solution:

```
def evaluate_expression(expr):

    def evaluate(index):
        char = expr[index]

        # Check if it's an operand (letter)
        if 'a' <= char <= 'z':
            return ord(char) - ord('a') + 1, index + 1

        # It's an operator, evaluate the two operands
        left_val, next_index = evaluate(index + 1)
        right_val, next_index = evaluate(next_index)

        # Apply the operator
        if char == '+':
            return left_val + right_val, next_index
        elif char == '-':
            return left_val - right_val, next_index
        elif char == '*':
```

```
            return left_val * right_val, next_index
        elif char == '/':
            return left_val // right_val, next_index
        elif char == '$':
            return max(left_val, right_val), next_index
        elif char == '&':
            return min(left_val, right_val), next_index

    result, _ = evaluate(0)
    return result
```

52. Balanced Bracket Sequence Generator

Python Solution:

```
def generate_bracket_expressions(expr):

    result = set()
    brackets = ["()", "[]", "{}"]

    # Check if we can insert a bracket pair at each position
    for i in range(len(expr) + 1):
        for bracket in brackets:
            new_expr = expr[:i] + bracket[0] + expr[i:]

            # Try all positions for the closing bracket
            for j in range(i + 1, len(new_expr) + 1):
                candidate = new_expr[:j] + bracket[1] +
                new_expr[j:]
                if is_valid(candidate):
                    result.add(candidate)

    # Add each type of bracket pair around the entire expression
    for bracket in brackets:
        result.add(bracket[0] + expr + bracket[1])
```

```
        return list(result)

def is_valid(expr):
    stack = []
    bracket_map = {")": "(", "]": "[", "}": "{"}

    for char in expr:
        if char in "([{":
            stack.append(char)
        elif char in ")]}":
            if not stack or stack.pop() != bracket_map[char]:
                return False

    return len(stack) == 0
```

53. Balanced Tree Reconstruction

Python Solution:

```
class TreeNode:

    def __init__(self, val=0, left=None, right=None):
        self.val = val
        self.left = left
        self.right = right

def balance_bst(root):
    # Step 1: Collect nodes in sorted order via in-order
    traversal
    def in_order_traversal(node, nodes):
        if not node:
            return
        in_order_traversal(node.left, nodes)
        nodes.append(node.val)
        in_order_traversal(node.right, nodes)
```

```
    nodes = []
    in_order_traversal(root, nodes)

    # Step 2: Reconstruct balanced BST
    def build_balanced_bst(values, start, end):
        if start > end:
            return None

        mid = (start + end) // 2
        node = TreeNode(values[mid])

        # Recursively build left and right subtrees
        node.left = build_balanced_bst(values, start, mid - 1)
        node.right = build_balanced_bst(values, mid + 1, end)

        return node

    return build_balanced_bst(nodes, 0, len(nodes) - 1)
```

54. Optimal Node Removal for Minimum Height

Python Solution:

```
class TreeNode:

    def __init__(self, val=0, left=None, right=None):
        self.val = val
        self.left = left
        self.right = right

def min_height_after_removal(root, k):
    memo = {}  # Memoization to avoid recalculating

    def dfs(node, remaining_removals):
```

```
    if not node:
        return 0

    # Check memoization
    key = (id(node), remaining_removals)
    if key in memo:
        return memo[key]

    # Option 1: Remove this node (and its subtree)
    height_if_removed = 0  # Height is 0 if node is removed

    # Option 2: Keep this node
    left_height = dfs(node.left, remaining_removals)
    right_height = dfs(node.right, remaining_removals)
    height_if_kept = 1 + max(left_height, right_height)

    min_height = height_if_kept

    # Try removing the node if we have removals left
    if remaining_removals > 0:
        min_height = min(min_height, height_if_removed)

    # Try removing left or right subtrees
    if remaining_removals > 0:
        for remove_left in range(remaining_removals + 1):
            remove_right = remaining_removals - remove_left
            height_remove_subtrees = 1 + max(
                dfs(node.left, remove_left),
                dfs(node.right, remove_right)
            )
            min_height = min(min_height,
            height_remove_subtrees)

    memo[key] = min_height
    return min_height

return dfs(root, k)
```

55. Context-Sensitive Search Suggestion System

Python Solution:

```python
class TrieNode:
    def __init__(self):
        self.children = {}
        self.is_end_of_word = False
        self.last_searched = -1  # Timestamp for history

class SearchSuggestionSystem:
    def __init__(self, dictionary=None):
        self.dictionary_trie = TrieNode()
        self.history_trie = TrieNode()
        self.search_count = 0  # Acts as timestamp for recency

        # Initialize with dictionary words if provided
        if dictionary:
            for word in dictionary:
                self.add_to_dictionary(word)

    def add_to_dictionary(self, word):
        node = self.dictionary_trie
        for char in word:
            if char not in node.children:
                node.children[char] = TrieNode()
            node = node.children[char]
        node.is_end_of_word = True

    def add_to_history(self, words):
        for word in words:
            self.search_count += 1
            node = self.history_trie
            for char in word:
                if char not in node.children:
                    node.children[char] = TrieNode()
                node = node.children[char]
            node.is_end_of_word = True
```

```
            node.last_searched = self.search_count   # Update
            timestamp

            # Also ensure it's in the dictionary
            self.add_to_dictionary(word)

    def suggest(self, prefix):
        results = []

        # First, get all matching words from history
        history_matches = []
        self._collect_suggestions(
            self.history_trie, prefix, "", history_matches, True
        )

        # Then get all matching words from dictionary
        dict_matches = []
        self._collect_suggestions(
            self.dictionary_trie, prefix, "", dict_matches, False
        )

        # Combine results (history first, then dictionary,
        # without duplicates)
        seen = set()
        # Sort by recency (descending)
        for word, _ in sorted(
                history_matches, key=lambda x: -x[1]
        ):
            if word not in seen:
                results.append(word)
                seen.add(word)

        for word in sorted(dict_matches):  # Sort alphabetically
            if word not in seen:
                results.append(word)
                seen.add(word)

        return results

    def _collect_suggestions(
```

```
        self, root, prefix, current_word, results, is_history
):
    node = root

    # Navigate to the node corresponding to the prefix
    for char in prefix:
        if char not in node.children:
            return  # Prefix not found
        node = node.children[char]
        current_word += char

    # DFS to collect all words with this prefix
    self._dfs_collect(node, current_word, results, is_history)

def _dfs_collect(
        self, node, current_word, results, is_history
):
    if node.is_end_of_word:
        if is_history:
            results.append((current_word, node.last_searched))
        else:
            results.append(current_word)

    # Sort alphabetically
    for char, child_node in sorted(node.children.items()):
        self._dfs_collect(
            child_node, current_word + char, results, is_history
        )
```

56. Fuzzy Word Finder

Python Solution:

```
class TrieNode:
```

```python
    def __init__(self):
        self.children = {}
        self.is_end_of_word = False

class FuzzyWordFinder:
    def __init__(self, dictionary):
        self.root = TrieNode()

        # Build the trie from the dictionary
        for word in dictionary:
            self.insert(word)

    def insert(self, word):
        node = self.root
        for char in word:
            if char not in node.children:
                node.children[char] = TrieNode()
            node = node.children[char]
        node.is_end_of_word = True

    def search(self, query, k):
        # Store results as (word, substitutions) pairs
        results = []

        def dfs(node, index, current_word, substitutions):
            # Base case: reached the end of the query
            if index == len(query):
                if node.is_end_of_word:
                    results.append((current_word,
                    substitutions))
                return

            # Process current character
            current_char = query[index]

            # Try all possible paths in the trie
            for next_char, next_node in node.children.items():
                # Exact match - no substitution needed
                if next_char == current_char:
                    dfs(
```

```
                    next_node,
                    index + 1,
                    current_word + next_char,
                    substitutions
                )
            # Substitution needed
            elif substitutions < k:
                dfs(
                    next_node,
                    index + 1,
                    current_word + next_char,
                    substitutions + 1
                )

    dfs(self.root, 0, "", 0)

    # Sort by substitutions, then alphabetically
    results.sort(key=lambda x: (x[1], x[0]))
    return [word for word, _ in results]
```

57. Minimum Allocation Threshold for Equal Array Groups

Python Solution:

```
def min_max_group_sum(nums, k):

    def can_split(threshold):
        groups = 1
        current_sum = 0

        for num in nums:
            # If a single element exceeds threshold,
            # splitting is impossible
            if num > threshold:
```

```
            return False

        # Try adding the current number to the current group
        if current_sum + num <= threshold:
            current_sum += num
        else:
            # Start a new group
            groups += 1
            current_sum = num

            # If we need more than k groups, return False
            if groups > k:
                return False

    return True

# Binary search on the possible threshold values
left = max(nums)
right = sum(nums)

while left < right:
    mid = (left + right) // 2
    if can_split(mid):
        right = mid
    else:
        left = mid + 1

return left
```

58. Kth Ancestral Element in Sorted Arrays

Python Solution:

```
def kth_ancestral_element(arrays, k):
    # Define boundaries for binary search
```

```
    left = min(array[0] for array in arrays if array)
    right = max(array[-1] for array in arrays if array)

    while left < right:
        mid = (left + right) // 2

        # Count ancestral elements less than or equal to mid
        count = 0
        for array in arrays:
            # Binary search to find position of first element > mid
            pos = binary_search(array, mid)
            count += pos

        if count < k:
            left = mid + 1
        else:
            right = mid

    return left

def binary_search(array, target):
    left, right = 0, len(array)

    while left < right:
        mid = (left + right) // 2
        if array[mid] <= target:
            left = mid + 1
        else:
            right = mid

    return left  # Returns count of elements <= target
```

59. Key Collection Sequence

Python Solution:

```
from collections import deque

def minimum_steps_to_collect_keys(maze):
    # Find the starting position and count keys
    rows, cols = len(maze), len(maze[0])
    start_row, start_col = 0, 0
    keys = []

    for r in range(rows):
        for c in range(cols):
            if maze[r][c] == 'S':
                start_row, start_col = r, c
            elif 'a' <= maze[r][c] <= 'z':
                keys.append(maze[r][c])

    # Sort keys to ensure alphabetical order
    keys.sort()

    # Directions for movement: up, right, down, left
    directions = [(-1, 0), (0, 1), (1, 0), (0, -1)]

    # Current position
    curr_row, curr_col = start_row, start_col
    total_steps = 0
    collected_keys = set()

    # Collect each key in alphabetical order
    for key in keys:
        # BFS to find shortest path to current key
        queue = deque([(curr_row, curr_col, 0)])  # (row, col,
        steps)
        visited = set([(curr_row, curr_col)])
        found = False

        while queue and not found:
            r, c, steps = queue.popleft()

            # Check if we found the key
            if maze[r][c] == key:
                total_steps += steps
```

```
            curr_row, curr_col = r, c
            collected_keys.add(key)
            found = True
            break

    # Try all four directions
    for dr, dc in directions:
        nr, nc = r + dr, c + dc

        # Check if the new position is valid
        if (0 <= nr < rows and 0 <= nc < cols and
            maze[nr][nc] != '#' and
            (nr, nc) not in visited):

            # Check if it's a door and we have the key
            if 'A' <= maze[nr][nc] <= 'Z':
                key_needed = maze[nr][nc].lower()
                if key_needed not in collected_keys:
                    continue

            queue.append((nr, nc, steps + 1))
            visited.add((nr, nc))

    # If we couldn't find the key, return -1
    if not found:
        return -1

return total_steps
```

60. Group Anagrams By Frequency

Python Solution:

```
def groupAnagramsByFrequency(strs):
```

```
    groups = {}
    result = []

    for s in strs:
        # Create frequency counter for each string
        freq = [0] * 26
        for char in s:
            freq[ord(char) - ord('a')] += 1

        # Convert frequency array to tuple to use as dictionary
        key
        freq_tuple = tuple(freq)

        if freq_tuple in groups:
            groups[freq_tuple].append(s)
        else:
            groups[freq_tuple] = [s]
            # Track order of appearance
            result.append(groups[freq_tuple])

    return result
```

61. Maximum Product Path

Python Solution:

```
def maxProductPath(grid):

    if not grid or not grid[0]:
        return 0

    rows, cols = len(grid), len(grid[0])
    max_dp = [[0 for _ in range(cols)] for _ in range(rows)]
    min_dp = [[0 for _ in range(cols)] for _ in range(rows)]

    # Initialize the first cell
```

```
max_dp[0][0] = min_dp[0][0] = grid[0][0]

# Initialize first row
for j in range(1, cols):
    max_dp[0][j] = max_dp[0][j-1] * grid[0][j]
    min_dp[0][j] = min_dp[0][j-1] * grid[0][j]

# Initialize first column
for i in range(1, rows):
    max_dp[i][0] = max_dp[i-1][0] * grid[i][0]
    min_dp[i][0] = min_dp[i-1][0] * grid[i][0]

# Fill the dp arrays
for i in range(1, rows):
    for j in range(1, cols):
        if grid[i][j] >= 0:
            max_dp[i][j] = max(
                max_dp[i-1][j], max_dp[i][j-1]
            ) * grid[i][j]
            min_dp[i][j] = min(
                min_dp[i-1][j], min_dp[i][j-1]
            ) * grid[i][j]
        else:
            max_dp[i][j] = min(
                min_dp[i-1][j], min_dp[i][j-1]
            ) * grid[i][j]
            min_dp[i][j] = max(
                max_dp[i-1][j], max_dp[i][j-1]
            ) * grid[i][j]

return max_dp[rows-1][cols-1]
```

62. Island Count with Restrictions

Python Solution:

```python
def numIslands(grid):

    if not grid or not grid[0]:
        return 0

    rows, cols = len(grid), len(grid[0])
    count = 0

    def dfs(i, j):
        if (i < 0 or i >= rows or j < 0 or j >= cols or
            grid[i][j] == '0' or grid[i][j] == '2'):
            return

        # Mark as visited
        grid[i][j] = '0'

        # Explore all four directions
        dfs(i+1, j)
        dfs(i-1, j)
        dfs(i, j+1)
        dfs(i, j-1)

    for i in range(rows):
        for j in range(cols):
            if grid[i][j] == '1':
                count += 1
                dfs(i, j)

    return count
```

63. Find Kth Element in Two Sorted Arrays

Python Solution:

```python
def findKthElement(nums1, nums2, k):

    # Ensure nums1 is the smaller array for simpler binary
    search
    if len(nums1) > len(nums2):
        return findKthElement(nums2, nums1, k)

    m, n = len(nums1), len(nums2)
    left, right = max(0, k - n), min(k, m)

    while left <= right:
        mid1 = (left + right) // 2
        mid2 = k - mid1

        l1 = float('-inf') if mid1 == 0 else nums1[mid1 - 1]
        r1 = float('inf') if mid1 == m else nums1[mid1]
        l2 = float('-inf') if mid2 == 0 else nums2[mid2 - 1]
        r2 = float('inf') if mid2 == n else nums2[mid2]

        if l1 <= r2 and l2 <= r1:
            return max(l1, l2)
        elif l1 > r2:
            right = mid1 - 1
        else:
            left = mid1 + 1

    return -1  # Should not reach here if arrays are sorted
```

64. Evaluate Reverse Polish Notation with Custom Operations

Python Solution:

```python
def evalRPN(tokens):
```

```
    stack = []

    for token in tokens:
        if token in ["+", "-", "*", "/", "^"]:
            b = stack.pop()
            a = stack.pop()

            if token == "+":
                stack.append(a + b)
            elif token == "-":
                stack.append(a - b)
            elif token == "*":
                stack.append(a * b)
            elif token == "/":
                # Integer division that truncates towards zero
                stack.append(int(a / b))
            elif token == "^":
                stack.append(a ** b)
        else:
            stack.append(int(token))

    return stack[0]
```

65. Optimal Kennel Assignment

Python Solution:

```
def maxKennelCompatibility(compatibility):

    n = len(compatibility)
    grid_size = int(n**0.5)
    if grid_size * grid_size != n:
        return -1  # Can't form a perfect square grid

    # Define adjacent positions in the grid
    def get_adjacent(i, j):
```

```
    directions = [(0, 1), (1, 0), (0, -1), (-1, 0)]
    adjacent = []
    for di, dj in directions:
        ni, nj = i + di, j + dj
        if 0 <= ni < grid_size and 0 <= nj < grid_size:
            adjacent.append((ni, nj))
    return adjacent

# Convert grid position to dog index
def pos_to_idx(i, j):
    return i * grid_size + j

# Calculate compatibility between two grid positions
def get_compatibility(pos1, pos2, assignment):
    dog1 = assignment[pos1[0]][pos1[1]]
    dog2 = assignment[pos2[0]][pos2[1]]
    if dog1 == -1 or dog2 == -1:
        return 0
    return compatibility[dog1][dog2]

# Backtracking function
def backtrack(assignment, row, col, used, current_score,
            best_score):
    # If we've filled the entire grid, return the score
    if row == grid_size:
        return max(current_score, best_score)

    # Calculate next position
    next_row, next_col = row, col + 1
    if next_col == grid_size:
        next_row, next_col = row + 1, 0

    # Try placing each dog at the current position
    for dog in range(n):
        if not used[dog]:
            used[dog] = True
            assignment[row][col] = dog

            # Calculate additional compatibility
            # from this placement
```

```
            additional_score = 0
            for adj_row, adj_col in get_adjacent(row, col):
                if assignment[adj_row][adj_col] != -1:
                    additional_score += compatibility[dog][
                        assignment[adj_row][adj_col]
                    ]

            # Recursive call
            best_score = backtrack(
                assignment, next_row, next_col, used,
                current_score + additional_score, best_score
            )

            # Backtrack
            assignment[row][col] = -1
            used[dog] = False

    return best_score

    # Initialize grid with -1 (no dog assigned)
    assignment = [[-1 for _ in range(grid_size)]
                  for _ in range(grid_size)]
    used = [False] * n

    return backtrack(assignment, 0, 0, used, 0, 0)
```

66. Wedding Seating Arrangement

Python Solution:

```
import random

def maxWeddingHappiness(relationships, tables,
                        seats_per_table):
    n = len(relationships)
    if n > tables * seats_per_table:
```

```
    return -1  # Not enough seats for all guests

# Calculate relationship score for table arrangement
def table_score(table_guests):
    score = 0
    for i in range(len(table_guests)):
        for j in range(i+1, len(table_guests)):
            score += 
            relationships[table_guests[i]][table_guests[j]]
    return score

# Calculate total relationship score for all tables
def total_score(seating):
    score = 0
    for table in seating:
        score += table_score(table)
    return score

# Initialize with random seating
guests = list(range(n))
random.shuffle(guests)

# Distribute guests among tables
seating = []
for t in range(tables):
    start_idx = t * seats_per_table
    end_idx = min(start_idx + seats_per_table, n)
    if start_idx < n:
        seating.append(guests[start_idx:end_idx])
    else:
        seating.append([])

# Local search optimization
improved = True
while improved:
    improved = False
    best_swap_gain = 0
    best_swap = None

    # Try all possible guest swaps between tables
```

```
for t1 in range(tables):
    for t2 in range(tables):
        if t1 == t2:
            continue

        for i, guest1 in enumerate(seating[t1]):
            for j, guest2 in enumerate(seating[t2]):
                # Skip if table 1 is already full
                if len(seating[t2]) >= seats_per_table:
                    continue

                # Calculate score before swap
                old_score = (table_score(seating[t1]) +
                            table_score(seating[t2]))

                # Perform swap
                new_t1 = seating[t1].copy()
                new_t2 = seating[t2].copy()
                new_t1.remove(guest1)
                new_t2.remove(guest2)
                new_t1.append(guest2)
                new_t2.append(guest1)

                # Calculate score after swap
                new_score = table_score(new_t1) +
                            table_score(new_t2)
                gain = new_score - old_score

                if gain > best_swap_gain:
                    best_swap_gain = gain
                    best_swap = (t1, i, t2, j)

# Apply the best swap if it improves the score
if best_swap_gain > 0:
    t1, i, t2, j = best_swap
    guest1 = seating[t1][i]
    guest2 = seating[t2][j]
    seating[t1].remove(guest1)
    seating[t2].remove(guest2)
    seating[t1].append(guest2)
```

```
        seating[t2].append(guest1)
        improved = True


    return total_score(seating)
```

67. Boat Fleet Chain Inspection

Python Solution:

```
class BoatNode:

    def __init__(self, id, maintenanceNeeded, next=None):
        self.id = id
        self.maintenanceNeeded = maintenanceNeeded
        self.next = next

def reorderFleet(head):
    if not head or not head.next:
        return head

    # Create dummy heads for our two chains
    maintenance_dummy = BoatNode(0, False)
    no_maintenance_dummy = BoatNode(0, False)

    # Pointers to track the end of each chain
    maintenance_tail = maintenance_dummy
    no_maintenance_tail = no_maintenance_dummy

    # Traverse the original list
    current = head
    while current:
        next_boat = current.next
        current.next = None  # Detach the node

        if current.maintenanceNeeded:
```

```
                maintenance_tail.next = current
                maintenance_tail = current
            else:
                no_maintenance_tail.next = current
                no_maintenance_tail = current

            current = next_boat

        # Connect the two chains
        maintenance_tail.next = no_maintenance_dummy.next

        # Return the head of the merged chain
        return maintenance_dummy.next
```

68. Baseball Lineup Rotation

Python Solution:

```
class PlayerNode:

    def __init__(self, name, battingAverage, next=None):
        self.name = name
        self.battingAverage = battingAverage
        self.next = next

def rotateLineupAndFindBest(head, k, m):
    if not head or head.next == head or k == 0:
        return findBestBatter(head, m)

    # Find the kth node and the last node
    current = head
    for _ in range(k - 1):
        current = current.next

    # The kth node will be our new head
    new_head = current.next
```

```
    # Traverse to find the last node (pointing back to original
    head)
    last = new_head
    while last.next != head:
        last = last.next

    # Adjust pointers to rotate
    current.next = head   # Connect kth node to head
    last.next = new_head  # Update circular reference

    # Find the best batter in the window
    return findBestBatter(new_head, m)

def findBestBatter(head, m):
    if not head:
        return None

    best_player = head
    current = head

    # Check the first m players
    for _ in range(m - 1):
        current = current.next
        if current.battingAverage > best_player.battingAverage:
            best_player = current

        # Handle circular list boundary
        if current == head:
            break

    return best_player.name
```

69. Coffee Bean Blend Matcher

Python Solution:

```
def canCreateBlend(acidity, targetAcidity):

    left, right = 0, len(acidity) - 1

    while left < right:
        blend_acidity = (acidity[left] + acidity[right]) / 2

        # Account for floating-point precision
        if abs(blend_acidity - targetAcidity) < 0.001:
            return True
        elif blend_acidity < targetAcidity:
            left += 1
        else:
            right -= 1

    return False
```

70. Holiday Card Joy Maximizer

Python Solution:

```
def maxHolidayJoy(joyRatings, minCards, maxCards):
    n = len(joyRatings)
    if n < minCards:
        return 0

    # Calculate sum of initial minimum window
    current_sum = sum(joyRatings[:minCards])
    max_joy = current_sum

    # Try each valid window size from minCards to maxCards
    for window_size in range(minCards, min(maxCards + 1, n + 1)):
        # If increasing window size from previous iteration
        if window_size > minCards:
            current_sum += joyRatings[window_size - 1]
```

```
    # Initial window of current size
    temp_max = current_sum

    # Slide the window across the array
    for i in range(window_size, n):
        current_sum += joyRatings[i] - joyRatings[i -
        window_size]
        temp_max = max(temp_max, current_sum)

    max_joy = max(max_joy, temp_max)

    # Reset current_sum for next window size
    current_sum = sum(joyRatings[:window_size])

    return max_joy
```

71. Fashion Display Stack Optimizer

Python Solution:

```
class ClothingItem:
    def __init__(self, type, popularity):
        self.type = type
        self.popularity = popularity

class FashionStack:
    def __init__(self):
        self.mainStack = []
        self.tempStack = []

    def addItem(self, type, popularity):
        self.mainStack.append(ClothingItem(type, popularity))

    def removeTopItem(self):
        if not self.mainStack:
            return None
```

```python
        return self.mainStack.pop()

    def findAndRemoveType(self, targetType):
        if not self.mainStack:
            return None

        mostPopular = None
        mostPopularIndex = -1

        # Find most popular item of the target type
        for i in range(len(self.mainStack) - 1, -1, -1):
            if self.mainStack[i].type == targetType:
                if (mostPopular is None or
                    self.mainStack[i].popularity >
                        mostPopular.popularity):
                    mostPopular = self.mainStack[i]
                    mostPopularIndex = i

        if mostPopularIndex == -1:
            return None

        # Move items to temp stack until reaching target item
        for _ in range(len(self.mainStack) - mostPopularIndex - 1):
            self.tempStack.append(self.mainStack.pop())

        # Remove the target item
        result = self.mainStack.pop()

        # Restore items from temp stack
        while self.tempStack:
            self.mainStack.append(self.tempStack.pop())

        return result

    def reorganizeByPopularity(self):
        if not self.mainStack:
            return

        # Move all items to temp stack
        while self.mainStack:
```

```
        self.tempStack.append(self.mainStack.pop())

    # Sort items by popularity and restore to main stack
    sortedItems = sorted(
        self.tempStack,
        key=lambda x: x.popularity,
        reverse=True
    )
    self.tempStack = []

    for item in sortedItems:
        self.mainStack.append(item)
```

72. Restaurant Priority Seating System

Python Solution:

```
import heapq

def restaurant_priority_seating(tables, events):
    # Max heap in Python (implemented as min heap with negatives)
    waitlist = []  # (-priority_score, customer_id, party_size,
                   #  arrival_time, vip_stars, has_reservation)
    results = []

    # Process events in chronological order
    for event in events:
        event_type = event[0]
        current_time = event[1]

        # Update all customers' priorities based on waiting time
        updated_waitlist = []
        while waitlist:
            neg_priority, customer_id, party_size, arrival_time, \
            vip_stars, has_reservation = heapq.heappop(waitlist)
            waiting_time = current_time - arrival_time
```

```python
        new_priority = (vip_stars * 10) + \
                       (20 if has_reservation else 0) +
                       waiting_time
        heapq.heappush(updated_waitlist, (
            -new_priority, customer_id, party_size,
            arrival_time, vip_stars, has_reservation
        ))
    waitlist = updated_waitlist

if event_type == "ARRIVE":
    customer_id = event[2]
    party_size = event[3]
    vip_stars = event[4]
    has_reservation = event[5]

    # Calculate initial priority
    initial_priority = (vip_stars * 10) + \
                       (20 if has_reservation else 0)

    # Add to waitlist
    heapq.heappush(waitlist, (
        -initial_priority, customer_id, party_size,
        current_time, vip_stars, has_reservation
    ))

elif event_type == "TABLE_READY":
    table_size = event[2]

    # Find highest priority customer that fits at this
    table
    temp_waitlist = []
    seated = False

    while waitlist and not seated:
        neg_priority, customer_id, party_size,
        arrival_time, \
        vip_stars, has_reservation = heapq.heappop(waitlist)

        if party_size <= table_size:
            # Seat this customer
```

```
            results.append([customer_id, current_time])
            seated = True
        else:
            # Put back in temporary waitlist
            heapq.heappush(temp_waitlist, (
                neg_priority, customer_id, party_size,
                arrival_time, vip_stars, has_reservation
            ))

    # Restore any customers we examined but didn't seat
    while temp_waitlist:
        heapq.heappush(waitlist,
        heapq.heappop(temp_waitlist))

    return results
```

73. Optimal Race Day Strategy

Python Solution:

```
def optimize_race_day(performance_ratings, race_capacity,
                  ineligibility):
    n_horses = len(performance_ratings)
    n_races = len(race_capacity)

    # Convert ineligibility to a more usable format
    ineligible = set((h, r) for h, r in ineligibility)

    # Track race assignments and points
    best_assignment = [None] * n_horses
    best_points = 0

    # Recursive backtracking function
    def backtrack(horse_idx, assignments, race_counts,
                total_points):
        nonlocal best_points, best_assignment
```

```python
    # Base case: all horses assigned
    if horse_idx == n_horses:
        # Ensure all races have at least one horse
        if all(count > 0 for count in race_counts):
            if total_points > best_points:
                best_points = total_points
                best_assignment = assignments.copy()
        return

    # Try assigning the current horse to each race
    for race in range(n_races):
        # Skip if ineligible or race is at capacity
        if ((horse_idx, race) in ineligible or
            race_counts[race] >= race_capacity[race]):
            continue

        # Try this assignment
        assignments[horse_idx] = race
        race_counts[race] += 1

        backtrack(
            horse_idx + 1,
            assignments,
            race_counts,
            total_points + performance_ratings[horse_idx][race]
        )

        # Undo the assignment for the next iteration
        race_counts[race] -= 1
        assignments[horse_idx] = None

# Start backtracking with horse 0
backtrack(0, [None] * n_horses, [0] * n_races, 0)

return best_points, best_assignment
```

74. Detective Case Assignment Network

Python Solution:

```python
from collections import defaultdict

import heapq

def solve_cases(detectives, cases, expertise,
            communication_overhead):
    n_detectives = detectives
    n_cases = cases

    # Calculate all possible solving times
    solving_times = []

    # Individual detective times
    for case_id, (case_type, complexity) in enumerate(cases):
        for detective_id in range(n_detectives):
            if case_type in expertise[detective_id]:
                time = (complexity /
                        expertise[detective_id][case_type])
                solving_times.append(
                    (time, case_id, [detective_id])
                )

    # Collaborative detective times
    for (det1, det2), overhead in communication_overhead.items():
        for case_id, (case_type, complexity) in enumerate(cases):
            if (case_type in expertise[det1] and
                case_type in expertise[det2]):
                combined_expertise = (
                    expertise[det1][case_type] +
                    expertise[det2][case_type]
                )
                time = complexity / combined_expertise + overhead
                solving_times.append(
                    (time, case_id, [det1, det2])
```

```
    )

# Sort by time (ascending)
solving_times.sort()

# Greedy assignment with detective availability constraints
assigned_cases = set()
busy_detectives = set()
parallel_time = 0
sequential_time = 0

while len(assigned_cases) < n_cases:
    for time, case_id, detective_ids in solving_times:
        if case_id in assigned_cases:
            continue

        # Check if all detectives are available
        if not any(d in busy_detectives for d in
        detective_ids):
            assigned_cases.add(case_id)
            busy_detectives.update(detective_ids)

            # Update times
            if parallel_time < time:
                sequential_time += time - parallel_time
                parallel_time = time
            break
    else:
        # No more assignments possible, reset busy detectives
        sequential_time += parallel_time
        parallel_time = 0
        busy_detectives.clear()

return sequential_time + parallel_time
```

75. Seasonal Orange Grove Harvest

Python Solution:

```python
from collections import defaultdict
import heapq

def solve_cases(detectives, cases, expertise,
                communication_overhead):
    n_detectives = detectives
    n_cases = cases

    # Calculate all possible solving times
    solving_times = []

    # Individual detective times
    for case_id, (case_type, complexity) in enumerate(cases):
        for detective_id in range(n_detectives):
            if case_type in expertise[detective_id]:
                time = complexity / \
                    expertise[detective_id][case_type]
                solving_times.append((time, case_id,
                    [detective_id]))

    # Collaborative detective times
    for (det1, det2), overhead in communication_overhead.items():
        for case_id, (case_type, complexity) in enumerate(cases):
            if (case_type in expertise[det1] and
                case_type in expertise[det2]):
                combined_expertise = (expertise[det1][case_type] +
                                      expertise[det2][case_type])
                time = complexity / combined_expertise + overhead
                solving_times.append((time, case_id, [det1, det2]))

    # Sort by time (ascending)
    solving_times.sort()

    # Greedy assignment with detective availability constraints
    assigned_cases = set()
    busy_detectives = set()
    parallel_time = 0
```

```python
    sequential_time = 0

    while len(assigned_cases) < n_cases:
        for time, case_id, detective_ids in solving_times:
            if case_id in assigned_cases:
                continue

            # Check if all detectives are available
            if not any(d in busy_detectives for d in
            detective_ids):
                assigned_cases.add(case_id)
                busy_detectives.update(detective_ids)

                # Update times
                if parallel_time < time:
                    sequential_time += time - parallel_time
                    parallel_time = time
                break
        else:
            # No more assignments possible, reset busy detectives
            sequential_time += parallel_time
            parallel_time = 0
            busy_detectives.clear()

    return sequential_time + parallel_time
```

9

Tips for Hiring Managers & Interviewers

Take-Home Coding Project Challenges

Let me share something that has been on my mind lately: the growing trend of take-home coding assignments in tech interviews. As someone who's been through countless interview processes, I've noticed a concerning pattern worth discussing.

If, as a developer, you're given a lengthy coding assignment during hiring, consider it a major red flag. Developers should be extra cautious when interviewing with these companies.

Companies that request extensive unpaid coding projects during interviews often reveal concerning patterns. You likely already have a robust GitHub portfolio showcasing real-world projects, architectural decisions, and problem-solving skills developed over years - not hours. A thoughtful hiring manager could explore your existing work, discuss your architectural choices, and understand your engineering philosophy through meaningful conversation. I typically ask people to share a link to their favorite project they have done.

Take this recent example: "Build a full-stack application with authentication, real-time updates, and optimal performance." If you're a strong candidate, you've already built systems like this in production environments, but that code is proprietary to the company you work for, and you can't share it. However, your real-world experience demonstrates the following

- Handling complex state management
- Implementing secure authentication flows
- Optimizing performance at scale
- Writing maintainable, well-tested code

A better option is to sit down and discuss those decisions and implementations with the candidate: How are they handling state management? What does their authentication flow look like? Why was that chosen over other options?

When a company insists on lengthy unpaid assignments, it is sending the signal that it doesn't value your time and experience. This often reflects deeper cultural issues, such as a limited investment in engineer growth, a preference for quick fixes over sustainable solutions, and an absence of respect for work-life balance.

These challenges are also highly discriminatory in practice. Look at the circumstance of the developer who has kids with an away baseball game on that weekend, the developer who is also a part-time caregiver to their aging parent, or the developer who has commitments to their church or community. None of these people will be able to dedicate the same amount of time or attention to the coding challenge. No matter the intent, these take-home coding projects are set up to prioritize young, single, childless developers who are comfortable giving up their weekends and nights for the sake of their employer.

You will also find that the companies that rely heavily on take-homes often have high turnover and burned-out engineers.

Instead, signal that your company will:

- Review existing work thoughtfully.
- Have reasonable technical discussions.

- Use focused, time-boxed coding exercises if needed.
- Compensate for any substantial project work.

Why Top Tech Companies Don't Use Take-Home Tests

Here's an interesting observation: FAANG companies (Facebook, Amazon, Apple, Netflix, Google) and other industry leaders don't rely on take-home assignments. Instead, their process typically looks like this:

1. 30-minute HR screening
2. 45-60 minute technical interview, or several of them with multiple levels of the technical organization
3. On-site interviews (with travel expenses covered)
4. Hiring committee - reads the interviewer's report and, depending on the outcomes, they will make an offer.

The total initial time investment before On-site is about 1.5 hours. Compare that to spending 4+ hours on a take-home project without a guarantee of progress.

A Better Hiring Funnel

Let me share what I've learned works better:

1. Filter candidates more aggressively upfront.
2. Keep initial screenings short and focused.
3. Conduct longer remote interviews to ask questions that probe how deeply and broadly candidates know a subject. I ask more complex questions until the candidate can no longer answer (or I run out of knowledge) so I can gauge the limits of their mastery of concepts.
4. If you must use a take-home project:

- Limit it to 2 hours maximum.

493

- Provide precise, unambiguous requirements.
- Have your own junior and mid-level engineers validate the time estimate.
- Offer compensation for larger projects.
- Provide feedback to all candidates who submit

For Candidates

Your time is valuable. Top companies know this, so they invest in flying candidates out for interviews rather than asking for extensive unpaid work.

Final Thoughts

While it's fun to experiment with the latest libraries and frameworks, understanding fundamental computer science principles is more valuable in the long term. These are the building blocks that stand the test of time.

For companies still relying on extensive take-home projects, consider whether you're missing out on top talent who choose to invest their time elsewhere. And for fellow developers, it's okay to be selective about where you invest your time during the job search process.

A company's interview process often reflects its overall culture and how it values its employees' time. Choose wisely.

10

Resources

Top Leetcode Problems

I don't like grinding endlessly to prepare for an interview, but I also recognize that it is a requirement for some companies. With that in mind, here are the most commonly used/useful technical interview problems. This list is often referred to as the Leetcode 75

Array

- Two Sum - https://leetcode.com/problems/two-sum/
- Best Time to Buy and Sell Stock - https://leetcode.com/problems/best-time-to-buy-and-sell-stock/
- Contains Duplicate - https://leetcode.com/problems/contains-duplicate/
- Product of Array Except Self - https://leetcode.com/problems/product-of-array-except-self/
- Maximum Subarray - https://leetcode.com/problems/maximum-subarray/
- Maximum Product Subarray - https://leetcode.com/problems/maximum-product-subarray/

- Find Minimum in Rotated Sorted Array - https://leetcode.com/problems/find-minimum-in-rotated-sorted-array/
- Search in Rotated Sorted Array - https://leetcode.com/problems/search-in-rotated-sorted-array/
- 3Sum - https://leetcode.com/problems/3sum/
- Container With Most Water - https://leetcode.com/problems/container-with-most-water/

Binary

- Sum of Two Integers - https://leetcode.com/problems/sum-of-two-integers/
- Number of 1 Bits - https://leetcode.com/problems/number-of-1-bits/
- Counting Bits - https://leetcode.com/problems/counting-bits/
- Missing Number - https://leetcode.com/problems/missing-number/
- Reverse Bits - https://leetcode.com/problems/reverse-bits/

Dynamic Programming

- Climbing Stairs - https://leetcode.com/problems/climbing-stairs/
- Coin Change - https://leetcode.com/problems/coin-change/
- Longest Increasing Subsequence - https://leetcode.com/problems/longest-increasing-subsequence/
- Longest Common Subsequence -
- Word Break Problem - https://leetcode.com/problems/word-break/
- Combination Sum - https://leetcode.com/problems/combination-sum-iv/
- House Robber - https://leetcode.com/problems/house-robber/
- House Robber II - https://leetcode.com/problems/house-robber-ii/
- Decode Ways - https://leetcode.com/problems/decode-ways/
- Unique Paths - https://leetcode.com/problems/unique-paths/
- Jump Game - https://leetcode.com/problems/jump-game/

Graph

- Clone Graph - https://leetcode.com/problems/clone-graph/
- Course Schedule - https://leetcode.com/problems/course-schedule/
- Pacific Atlantic Water Flow - https://leetcode.com/problems/pacific-atlantic-water-flow/
- Number of Islands - https://leetcode.com/problems/number-of-islands/
- Longest Consecutive Sequence - https://leetcode.com/problems/longest-consecutive-sequence/
- Alien Dictionary - https://leetcode.com/problems/alien-dictionary/
- Graph Valid Tree - https://leetcode.com/problems/graph-valid-tree/
- Number of Connected Components in an Undirected Graph - https://leetcode.com/problems/number-of-connected-components-in-an-undirected-graph/

Interval

- Insert Interval - https://leetcode.com/problems/insert-interval/
- Merge Intervals - https://leetcode.com/problems/merge-intervals/
- Non-overlapping Intervals - https://leetcode.com/problems/non-overlapping-intervals/
- Meeting Rooms - https://leetcode.com/problems/meeting-rooms/
- Meeting Rooms II - https://leetcode.com/problems/meeting-rooms-ii/

Linked List

- Reverse a Linked List - https://leetcode.com/problems/reverse-linked-list/
- Detect Cycle in a Linked List - https://leetcode.com/problems/linked-list-cycle/
- Merge Two Sorted Lists - https://leetcode.com/problems/merge-two-

sorted-lists/
- Merge K Sorted Lists - https://leetcode.com/problems/merge-k-sorted-lists/
- Remove Nth Node From End Of List - https://leetcode.com/problems/remove-nth-node-from-end-of-list/
- Reorder List - https://leetcode.com/problems/reorder-list/

Matrix

- Set Matrix Zeroes - https://leetcode.com/problems/set-matrix-zeroes/
- Spiral Matrix - https://leetcode.com/problems/spiral-matrix/
- Rotate Image - https://leetcode.com/problems/rotate-image/
- Word Search - https://leetcode.com/problems/word-search/

String

- Longest Substring Without Repeating Characters - https://leetcode.com/problems/longest-substring-without-repeating-characters/
- Longest Repeating Character Replacement - https://leetcode.com/problems/longest-repeating-character-replacement/
- Minimum Window Substring - https://leetcode.com/problems/minimum-window-substring/
- Valid Anagram - https://leetcode.com/problems/valid-anagram/
- Group Anagrams - https://leetcode.com/problems/group-anagrams/
- Valid Parentheses - https://leetcode.com/problems/valid-parentheses/
- Valid Palindrome - https://leetcode.com/problems/valid-palindrome/
- Longest Palindromic Substring - https://leetcode.com/problems/longest-palindromic-substring/
- Palindromic Substrings - https://leetcode.com/problems/palindromic-substrings/

- Encode and Decode Strings - https://leetcode.com/problems/encode-and-decode-strings/

Tree

- Maximum Depth of Binary Tree - https://leetcode.com/problems/maximum-depth-of-binary-tree/
- Same Tree - https://leetcode.com/problems/same-tree/
- Invert/Flip Binary Tree - https://leetcode.com/problems/invert-binary-tree/
- Binary Tree Maximum Path Sum - https://leetcode.com/problems/binary-tree-maximum-path-sum/
- Binary Tree Level Order Traversal - https://leetcode.com/problems/binary-tree-level-order-traversal/
- Serialize and Deserialize Binary Tree - https://leetcode.com/problems/serialize-and-deserialize-binary-tree/
- Subtree of Another Tree - https://leetcode.com/problems/subtree-of-another-tree/
- Construct Binary Tree from Preorder and Inorder Traversal - https://leetcode.com/problems/construct-binary-tree-from-preorder-and-inorder-traversal/
- Validate Binary Search Tree - https://leetcode.com/problems/validate-binary-search-tree/
- Kth Smallest Element in a BST - https://leetcode.com/problems/kth-smallest-element-in-a-bst/
- Lowest Common Ancestor of BST - https://leetcode.com/problems/lowest-common-ancestor-of-a-binary-search-tree/
- Implement Trie (Prefix Tree) - https://leetcode.com/problems/implement-trie-prefix-tree/
- Add and Search Word - https://leetcode.com/problems/add-and-search-word-data-structure-design/
- Word Search II - https://leetcode.com/problems/word-search-ii/

Heap

- Merge K Sorted Lists - https://leetcode.com/problems/merge-k-sorted-lists/
- Top K Frequent Elements - https://leetcode.com/problems/top-k-frequent-elements/
- Find Median from Data Stream - https://leetcode.com/problems/find-median-from-data-stream/

[**Source**] https://www.teamblind.com/post/New-Year-Gift—-Curated-List-of-Top-75-LeetCode-Questions-to-Save-Your-Time-OaM1orEU
Curated List of Top 75 LeetCode Questions to Save Your Time

Recommended Books

Here are the other books I can recommend to get you ready for your interview:

Algorithms and Data Structures

- McDowell, Gayle Laakmann. *Cracking the Coding Interview*. 6th ed., CareerCup, 2015.
- Cormen, Thomas H., et al. *Introduction to Algorithms*. 4th ed., MIT Press, 2022.

Software Design

- Gamma, Erich, et al. *Design Patterns: Elements of Reusable Object-Oriented Software*. Addison-Wesley Professional, 1994.
- Martin, Robert C. *Clean Code: A Handbook of Agile Software Craftsmanship*. Prentice Hall, 2008.
- Hunt, Andy, and Dave Thomas. *The Pragmatic Programmer: Your Journey to Mastery*. 20th Anniversary Edition, Addison-Wesley Profes-

sional, 2019.

System Design

- Kleppmann, Martin. *Designing Data-Intensive Applications: The Big Ideas Behind Reliable, Scalable, and Maintainable Systems.* 1st ed., O'Reilly Media, 2017.
- Xu, Alex. *System Design Interview – An Insider's Guide.* Independently published, 2020.
- Xu, Alex. *System Design Interview – An Insider's Guide: Volume 2.* Independently published, 2022.
- Beyer, Betsy, et al. *Site Reliability Engineering: How Google Runs Production Systems.* O'Reilly Media, 2016.

Behavioral Interview Preparation

- Lin, Lewis C. *Decode and Conquer: Answers to Product Management Interviews.* 3rd ed., Impact Interview, 2016.
- Dumas, Michelle. *The STAR Interview Method: How to Excel at Job Interviews.* Independently published, 2021.

11

Appendix: Take Home Code Project

In-Memory Cache For Online Advertising Agency

This exercise consists of two parts: design and implementation. It is designed to take a few hours, but there is no hard time limit – please do not feel rushed. Also, questions are welcome, so feel free to ask.

Design

Provide a class design for an N-way, set-associative cache.

Design requirements:

- The cache itself is entirely in memory (i.e., it does not communicate with a backing store or use any I/O)
- The client interface should be type-safe for keys and values and allow for both the keys and values to be of an arbitrary type (e.g., strings, integers, classes, etc.). For a given instance of a cache, all keys and values will be the same type.
- Design the interface as a library to be distributed by clients. Assume that the client doesn't have source code for your library and that internal data structures aren't exposed to the client.

- The design should allow the client to implement any replacement algorithm. Please include the LRU and MRU algorithms in your solution.
- Example use case: Data associated with user ID is stored as an in-memory cache on an application server to avoid a database dip for every request.

Submit the design as a PDF.

Implementation

Implement the above design. Java is preferred, but if you are unfamiliar with Java, C# or Python may be used.

Implementation requirements:

1. Prioritize correctness, robustness, and extensibility over extra features and optimizations.
2. Write your code using the quality bar you would use for production code.

Submit your response as a .zip of your entire solution. Include with the .zip of your sources a readme on how to compile and run.

About the Author

Keith Henning has been in the software industry for more than 30 years. In his career, he has worked for the largest computer hardware and retail companies in the world as a software engineer and architect, such as Dell and Walmart, leading teams and driving innovation. Currently, he is the Director of Enterprise Architecture and a Chief Architect for Merchandising and Supply Chain for Dollar General. He holds a MS in Computer Science from The Georgia Institute of Technology and Technology and a Juris Doctor from the University of Arkansas, William H. Bowen School of Law. He and his wife, Kathryn, live in Fayetteville, AR with their three cats.

You can connect with me on:

🌐 http://technical-interviews.com